# EXPERIENCING INFERTILITY

# EXPERIENCING INFERTILITY

## Revised Edition

*Stories to Inform and Inspire*

Ellen Sarasohn Glazer

Jossey-Bass Publishers
San Francisco

Jossey-Bass books and products are available through most
bookstores. To contact Jossey-Bass directly, call (888)
378-2537, fax to (800) 605-2665, or visit our website at
www.josseybass.com.

Substantial discounts on bulk quantities of Jossey-Bass books
are available to corporations, professional associations, and
other organizations. For details and discount information,
contact the special sales department at Jossey-Bass.

 Manufactured in the United States of America on Lyons Falls
Turin Book. This paper is acid-free and 100 percent totally
chlorine-free.

Library of Congress Cataloging-in-Publication Data

Experiencing infertility : stories to inform and inspire / [edited by]
    Ellen Sarasohn Glazer. — Rev. ed.
        p.    cm.
    Earlier published under the title: Without child.
    ISBN 0-7879-4383-5
    1. Infertility—Popular works.   2. Infertility—Psychological
aspects.   I. Glazer, Ellen Sarasohn.   II. Without child.
    RC889.W575  1998
    616.6′92—dc21                                              98-40392

REVISED EDITION

PB Printing   10 9 8 7 6 5 4 3 2 1

# CONTENTS

*This book is dedicated to its contributors, whose courage and generosity made it possible. It is dedicated also to Susan Lewis Cooper, whose guidance, advice, and indomitable spirit echo throughout its pages.*

# EXPERIENCING INFERTILITY

# INTRODUCTION

AS MOST OF US LEARN someplace along the way, life is a series of unexpected journeys. Few journeys are more complicated and challenging than the ones that couples take—hopefully together—through infertility. Theirs are journeys that may be short or long, relatively smooth or terribly bumpy, fairly straightforward or filled with unexpected twists and turns and even detours along the way. Despite travails en route, most travelers through infertility do end their journey with children whom they cherish, while others find successful resolution by choosing to live without children.

The journey through infertility can be a lonely one in a world that expects couples to have children with ease. In a world that celebrates fertility, there are few places for the involuntarily childless couple. Whether it be at holiday gatherings or in religious settings or even in the workplace, the infertile couple is left out as others rejoice over new pregnancies and celebrate the arrival of newborns.

One of the ways in which infertile travelers cope with their loneliness and isolation is to find others on similar journeys. RESOLVE—a national organization that offers support, information, and advocacy for infertile couples—has been a great resource in this regard. Countless women and men have been helped by the companionship that they have found at RESOLVE meetings, and many lifelong friendships have been formed through RESOLVE. My friendship with Susan Cooper is among them.

By the mid-1980s Susan and I were both "graduates" of infertility. Our families were complete and our careers were in place. We decided to devote much of our time to working with infertile individuals and couples. Because we had learned about the power of shared experience, we decided to write a book about infertility—a book that would include our personal and professional ideas but that would primarily be a compilation of other people's voices. We felt—and continue to feel—that one of the best ways to cope with the challenges of infertility and to heal from its trauma is by knowing that you are not alone.

*Without Child,* our first book—and this book's ancestor—is a collection of poems and essays about people's journeys through infertility. Although some of the entries are timeless and are reprinted in this book, others became dated soon after the book was published. What has not changed, however, is the power and poignancy of shared expression.

Earlier this year, Susan and I learned that we had the opportunity to do a new version of *Without Child.* The opportunity was inviting, but the timing was not—especially for Susan. Although she made significant contributions to the content of the chapter introductions and is responsible for some of the best essays in this book, she was ultimately unable to be a coauthor. This was a loss for me, as my adventures coauthoring three books with her were among the most satisfying experiences of my life. Readers should know that although Susan's name is not on the cover of this book, her ideas and her voice helped shape it. I could not have pulled it together without her.

*Experiencing Infertility,* like its predecessor, *Without Child,* is not a comprehensive, detailed discussion of infertility, nor is it a book about the emotional and ethical aspects of current reproductive technology (for that I refer readers to Susan's and my book, *Choosing Assisted Reproduction: Social, Emotional and Ethical Considerations,* published in 1998 by Perspectives Press in Indianapolis). Rather, this book attempts to address several aspects of the infertility experience and to do so primarily through a diverse chorus of voices.

Perhaps the most satisfying part of the preparation of this book was the assembling of its "chorus." Unlike *Without Child,* for which we placed notices in RESOLVE newsletters requesting essays and poetry from people we had never met, *Experiencing Infertility* is composed primarily of the voices of people whom Susan and I know, with whom we have worked. To assemble this book, we contacted our former infertility patients, adoption clients, colleagues, and friends and asked them to consider contributing their stories. Their responses were incredibly moving; most were eager to participate in the project and appreciated the opportunity to share their experiences with others. When asked, one woman who had just suffered a devastating loss said, "Thank you. I think that this will help me heal." Another stated, "It would feel so good to help someone else. When I was struggling with infertility, it meant so much when others told me what they had been through." Still another, newly pregnant after in vitro fertilization, said, "If what I write can help just one person, I will feel great about it."

First in talking with contributors and later in reading what they had written, it was gratifying to see where they, too, had traveled. Although some of the essays in this book reflect continuing struggles with infertility, most voices here speak from the perspective of resolution. Having known many contributors when they were in the throes of crisis, it was a great pleasure to talk with them at this point. It was especially gratifying to hear children in the background.

In addition to new contributors, I welcome back some of the contributors to *Without Child*. In some instances I have simply reprinted the original essay or poem. In other instances, an update from the author is included. Some authors have chosen to update their stories; others, their feelings. I found both to be of great interest and assume that others will as well.

Some people whom we asked to contribute did not participate in this book. Their reasons for not participating seem as important to this project as others' reasons for actively being part of it. One woman wanted very much to tell her story—the story of twin ectopics (in the same tube)—but realized that it would be too painful for her to tell it. She experienced her story as something very delicate and vulnerable and feared that it—and she—would be somehow damaged in the retelling. Another woman wanted very much to share her experience of surviving breast cancer and then adopting, but her writing was tragically interrupted by her father's diagnosis with cancer. And finally there were potential contributors who simply found that life was too busy with children and careers and commitments to take on one more project. In short, life goes on after infertility.

Some topics related to infertility are covered at length, with many essays; others receive little space. The reason for this is not a bias for one topic over another, but rather my desire to include well-written essays and poems that tell interesting stories. For example, several lovely pieces on adoption came in, but very few on gestational care or resolving without children. Readers should know that these inequities do not reflect an editorial judgment of the relative importance of the topics.

Readers should also know that there are a few essays in this book that are "ghostwritten." Some contributors told me their stories and asked me to compose their essays. In some instances, these essays are published under the contributor's name. In other instances, pseudonyms are used.

When Susan and I sat down to write *Without Child*, we had little children at home. Now we are preparing for empty nests. Our long-sought and much cherished children, Elizabeth and Mollie Glazer, Seth and Amanda Cooper, were our inspiration then and remain so. They have taught us again and again—in ways funny, poignant, kind, and tormenting—that motherhood is the most rewarding—and most impossible—job that either of us will ever do. I thank Susan, her children, my children, and each contributor for making this book happen.

# I

# DISCOVERING AND
# ASSESSING THE PROBLEM

THE JOURNEY that individuals and couples take through—and beyond—infertility begins in different ways. For some, it begins as an individual problem, something a person learns about as a teenager or young adult. An infection, an illness, or a congenital abnormality is identified and infertility is predicted. For most, however, the discovery of infertility comes unexpectedly, in the context of marriage and in the expectation of parenthood.

Living in an age of birth control, most couples believe that they can plan conception. They decide when the time is right and assume that within the next few months, they will be happily, blissfully with child. Although some may be apprehensive—because they are older or the woman has had some gynecological problems or because they have seen several friends go through infertility—most approach "baby making" with a sense of excitement and anticipation.

Couples react to initial failures to conceive in different ways (and partners within a couple may have different reactions). Some people assume a wait-and-see attitude, feeling that it will just take time. Others panic quickly, deciding—even after a month or two—that there is an insurmountable problem. However, for most people, infertility is something they become aware of over time. As months go by and as efforts at conception become more intentional and more precisely timed, there is the dawning realization that a problem exists. The question then becomes how to address it.

Depending on where they live, the medical and financial resources available, and their age and individual temperaments, couples approach the assessment of infertility in a variety of ways. Many begin with the woman's gynecologist, assuming that it is a female problem. Some start with a semen analysis, either because they have reason to suspect a male factor or because they recognize that a semen analysis is one of the simplest tools for assessing infertility. Other couples go directly to an infertility specialist. In this latter group are those who are familiar with infertility, either through their work or their friends, as well as those who are especially anxious and eager to move ahead quickly with diagnosis and with treatment. Couples in which the woman is in her late thirties or, certainly, her early forties often try only a short time before consulting an infertility specialist.

Regardless of how a couple approaches the diagnostic phase of their infertility journey, many troublesome feelings arise. Women, in particular, approach infertility with feelings of guilt and self-blame. They rapidly conclude that it is most likely their fault and fear that their husbands will want to leave them if they are unable to have children. Often they have a personal explanation for why the infertility has occurred, focusing, perhaps, on a history of multiple sexual partners or on an abortion. Although these tend to be the most common self-explanations for infertility, women worry about an assortment of past transgressions, including being too career-minded, marrying outside the faith, and inadequate prayer and service to God. Because this self-blame is so tormenting, many women vow to move forward in their quest for a child with a commitment to avoid further regret. For some the avoidance of regret becomes almost as much a driving force as the desire for a child.

Although men are often less vocal about their feelings, they too may approach infertility with trepidation, worrying that they will be identified as having the problem (and worrying, too, about how they will feel if their wife is unable to bear children). Perhaps equating fertility and virility, potency and masculinity, men whose sperm parameters are off in any dimension—motility, count, morphology—may suffer from a sense of shame and lowered self-esteem. Some discover that although they may not have given it a lot of thought prior to infertility, parenthood is a central life goal for them. The prospect of possibly not achieving this goal is devastating.

In addition to the feelings of fear and self-blame, there are other emotional challenges that couples face as they enter the world of infertility diagnosis. A significant one involves the loss of privacy: couples quickly realize that although their decision to have a child was a very private one—and their initial efforts were continued in that privacy—they are now about to take this very personal area of their lives public. One of the first questions that their physician asks them is about the frequency of their sexual intercourse. These questions are followed by ones that become ever more specific and intrusive: "Do you get a discharge from your nipples?" "Do you get a discharge from your penis?"

At the same time that they are experiencing a loss of privacy, couples must begin to consider the ways in which they can maintain some privacy. They begin to face decisions about whom they will tell that there is a problem and what they will tell them. If their infertility journey proves to be a long and complicated one, these are questions that they will revisit many times along the way.

The diagnosis of infertility is a physical as well as an emotional intrusion. Women must undergo a series of tests, some of which are uncomfortable, others painful. These tests take a fair amount of time, and some of them must be precisely timed, thereby intruding on women's sense of control over their lives and their schedules. The process is one that often leaves a woman with questions about her body, with feelings of sadness and a loss of self-esteem, and with anger and resentment for what she must go through, especially if her friends are conceiving with apparent ease.

Women are used to being poked and prodded; that is the nature of the gynecological exam, and most women have had several exams before ever encountering infertility. Familiarity, however, does not mean complacency. Some of the embarrassment of being naked with one's feet in stirrups diminishes with time, but a sense of helplessness and vulnerability persists throughout the diagnostic process and continues in treatment.

Although many aspects of the assessment of a woman's fertility are unpleasant, most involve few, if any, physical risks. However, as diagnosis proceeds, some women are advised to consider minor surgical procedures, including laparoscopy and hysteroscopy, some of which involve anesthesia and bring with them the risks associated with surgery. Deciding whether to have these procedures is difficult for women who wonder if they are making a mistake taking their healthy bodies into surgery. "Am I asking for trouble?" "Would we be better off leaving well enough alone?" These questions are ones that they may ask themselves repeatedly as they make their way into—and through—infertility treatment. They are questions that become most profound when people consider assisted reproductive technology.

For men the diagnosis of infertility is difficult in different ways. Although some men undergo a testicular biopsy, which can be painful and is certainly intrusive, the extent of testing for most men is the semen analysis. This seemingly simple procedure, which involves "only" masturbation and ejaculation into a container, is embarrassing—even humiliating—for many men. They say that they feel exposed when they are ushered into the "collection room" and offered an assortment of sexually provocative magazines.

Although women doubt and question their bodies as they go through infertility diagnosis, it is men, as we noted earlier, who feel measured by the process. The semen analysis, with its range of scores, feels like a very threatening aptitude or achievement test. For this reason, it is not at all uncommon for women to complain that they went through a series of difficult tests promptly and without hesitation, yet their husbands, who are going to have "only a simple, painless lab test," seem to invite unnecessary delays.

Assessment of a couple's infertility can reveal a range of problems. At one end of the spectrum are those couples who are burdened with the non-diagnosis of "unexplained infertility." Once called "normal infertiles," these are the people for whom no problem can be found. Many of them respond very well to treatment, but they leave the diagnostic phase of their journey with many more questions than answers. Some fear that they have not had an adequate assessment. Others are plagued with fears that it is their fault—that the problem is "in their head" or the result of stress. Worse still are those who feel that unexplained infertility may be an indictment of their relationship. Perhaps either one would be fertile with another partner?

At the other extreme of the diagnostic spectrum are those couples who receive truly bad news. These are people who enter the diagnostic process assuming that a treatable problem will be found and who leave it with the knowledge that nothing can be done to help them achieve a pregnancy. Included in this group are *some* men with azoospermia (others with azoospermia can be treated) and women with complete ovarian failure. Couples whose problem necessitates in vitro fertilization (due to the woman's blocked fallopian tubes, for example) but who cannot afford this therapy are also in this group. For these couples there is shock, loss, grief, and, eventually, decision making. Sadly, some are offered sperm or egg donation before they have a chance to absorb and grieve the loss that has occurred.

Fortunately, most couples leave the diagnostic process with information and some degree of hope. Most have some information about why they are not conceiving and some introduction to treatment approaches. The next step along their journey through infertility involves education: they will need to learn about their problem, about the treatment options available, about the skills of local—and distant—physicians, and about the costs they face in terms of time, energy, and finances.

We hear now from three veterans of infertility diagnosis. First, Larry Cooper captures the embarrassments and indignities of testing in "The Sperm Sample." In a similar vein, Ellen Jean Tepper's "PK" chronicles some of the "pleasures" of that particular test. Then, on a much more serious note, Jane Frankel addresses the pain and confusion that follow a diagnosis of premature ovarian failure.

○

## THE SPERM SAMPLE
### *Larry Cooper*

A strong desire to become a father got me through my male infertility workup. Beforehand, I had no idea how awkward and embarrassing a medical procedure can be. Looking back now, as the father of two, I can laugh, but at the time I found very little humor in it all.

I approached the office with trepidation, focusing on my genitals, figuring they would be the only part of me in which the doctor was interested. Sure enough, his exam began with a scrotal feel (probably not the technical name) and moved on to questions about frequency and position of intercourse. I tried to act calm and cool as I answered him. Then he told me to make an appointment for a semen analysis.

As the day of reckoning approached, I wondered what the procedure would be like. Would there be a dimly lit room showing stag films? A soft couch with a supply of *Playboy* magazines? A nice-looking, well-endowed nurse to help me out if I needed it? No such luck!

My initial worry was that there would be a crowded elevator and that everyone on it would know where I was going and what I was going to do. The lab, however, was located in a remote research building, part of the Harvard teaching hospital where our specialist worked. There was no one on the elevator, and as I approached the lab, the corridor was clear. I began to wonder if this was an unusual event. I imagined that the staff would be talking about me for days.

The lab itself was reminiscent of my high school chemistry classroom. There were tables filled with test tubes, beakers, and petri dishes. I wondered whether these vessels were full of billions of unrequited sperm, and I wondered how mine would fare among them. Would they be good swimmers? Would they move forward like they are supposed to or just move around in circles? And was there anything I could do to cheer them on?

I cleared my throat so that one of the lab technicians would know that I had arrived. In fact she had been expecting me. I could not decide whether this was evidence for the unusual or the ordinary theory. I was handed a jar and told to go down the hall to the men's room and deposit a sample in the jar. As I walked to the lavatory, I wondered how this would work. Would the men's room be a fantasy environment filled with *Playboy* and other "inspirational" tools, or was this two-inch-deep glass jar to be my only companion?

Again I was taken back in time, to junior high school; the men's room reminded me of the boys' room in that seventy-year-old institution. The only fixtures were a sink with a mirror above it, a urinal, and a single enclosed toilet stall. I looked around and laughed—far from a pleasure palace, it was the least likely place to inspire X-rated fantasies! I decided to be mature about the situation. I looked at the jar and said to myself, "Let's get this over with." Since the men's room door did not lock, I decided that the enclosed toilet stall was the only possible place for this rendezvous with myself. I wondered how many men had masturbated here before me. Had those with poor aim somehow left their mark? Fortunately, the stall did lock, but I worried that someone might decide to use the urinal while I was trying to fill the jar. I feared I would be distracted in my mission.

Since it was winter, I removed my overcoat, but there was no place to hang it. I draped it over the stall wall, doing the same with my sport jacket. But what if someone came in and recognized my clothing? Just as I was thinking that I should have come in disguise, I noticed the worst. The toilet had no cover. I would either have to sit on the open toilet seat as though I were using it for its intended purpose, or I would have to stand up. After trying both, I decided that standing up would give me a better shot at hitting the target.

Fortunately, my fears of being impotent with a glass jar proved unfounded. As I took aim and fired, I remembered what it felt like to be an awkward adolescent, masturbating quietly on the other side of my parents' bedroom wall, praying that I would not be discovered. I did hit the target, and returned triumphantly to the lab. As I held the jar up proudly, I felt the earth cave in under my feet as the lab attendant exclaimed, "Oh, back so soon!"

○

## PK

*Ellen Jean Tepper*

Of PK tests, I have known many: poor ones, worse ones, invalid ones, and, at long last, the mediocre.

I came upon my first PK test rather innocently. For a year or so I had been treated for ovulatory problems with Clomid, but no pregnancy had resulted, and my doctor, Dr. P, and I had both begun to wonder whether there were other factors affecting my fertility. He'd suggested another series of tests, including the PK. Otherwise known as the Sims-Hühner or postcoital test, the PK test evaluates how a man's sperm fares in his partner's cervical mucus.

Dr. P's instructions were simple enough. Dave and I were to "abstain" for two days prior to the test. Then, between seven and eight A.M. on the appointed morning, we were to "have relations." I was to go directly to Dr. P's office.

"Are you sure that you had relations this morning?" Dr. P looked puzzled when he returned from the microscope.

Needless to say, I was sure. At least I was sure that that morning we had done what we had been doing together for thirteen years. I worried, for a moment, that we had been doing it wrong all this time. Then I wondered more seriously about the brisk walk that I'd taken when I'd found I had a few minutes to spare.

"Dr. P, do you think that they fell out on my way over? Maybe I shouldn't have gone for a walk after having sex?" (I hoped he wouldn't mind my using the word *sex*.) He assured me that sperm don't simply fall out of vaginas, but added that he had no explanation for where they were. Even if there was a problem, he explained, we'd see lots of dead sperm. The fact that there were none was truly a mystery. I could tell that he was still wondering whether we'd really had sex.

Dr. P recommended that we give the sperm forty-eight hours to regroup and try again.

"You move too fast. You must have dropped them out on the way over." That was Dave's response. I was careful not to tell him about the walk. "Just move slowly next time, and things will be fine."

I approached my second PK test cautiously. I drove slowly, kept my legs pressed together, and waddled into the office. I avoided urinating, fearful that the sperm would land in Dr. P's toilet. This time I had done it right.

Dr. P returned from the microscope. He looked somber. "There are sperm there, but this time they are all dead."

My third and fourth PK tests occurred one month later. Dr. P had suggested that we plan two tests, spaced forty-eight hours apart. The first would repeat what we had done, hopefully with different results. "Maybe it was just a bad month?" Dr. P posited. "Sometimes sperm production is compromised by an infection or a virus." But he went on to suggest that we try artificial insemination with Dave's sperm if there was another bad test.

PK test no. 3 was a repeat of the first. No walk. No peeing. Still no sperm, living or dead. Test no. 4 was to fall on Rosh Hashanah, the Jewish New Year.

"You mean that we're going to have to leave temple early to have a quickie and then rush off to your doctor's office?" Dave was hardly enchanted with the idea.

The Rosh Hashanah service is a celebration of fertility. The Torah portion talks about Sarah, so long barren, who finally gave birth. I was lost in some thoughts about her fertility and that of her "sisters," Leah and Rachel, when Dave commented, "I guess Mary was the only one in the Bible without a fertility problem." It was time to go.

So Dr. P celebrated his New Year and we celebrated ours standing over the microscope, looking for live sperm. There were none.

"Well, I guess there is something seriously wrong with the sperm. They look normal but they self-destruct."

"They self-destruct or they're being destroyed by the mucus?" I wondered why Dr. P was blaming it on the sperm? While I kind of liked the idea that I was not the only one with a problem, I couldn't follow his reasoning. Dave's sperm had passed several laboratory evaluations with flying colors. My fertility, by contrast, had little to recommend it. "Dr. P, why don't you inseminate me with donor sperm and see how they do?"

"But you could become pregnant!"

I was willing to take my chances on that one.

PK test no. 5. This time I wasn't sure how I wanted things to turn out. If it was bad, it would confirm my fear that there was something inexplicably wrong with my mucus. I didn't like that idea, but there was some advantage to having only one patient in the family. If the donor sperm fared well, then Dave too was implicated. We would have two specialists, possibly two treatment regimes. We might find ourselves in the unexpected and difficult position of having to consider donor insemination seriously.

"Well, I was right," pronounced Dr. P. "The problem is with the sperm. This PK test with donor sperm is fine."

"Really?" I was stunned. "Are there lots of live sperm? And can they really swim?"

"No, I found two, and they are both moving."

"But I thought that anything less than five was a very poor test."

"One is all it takes," Dr. P declared. "Dave, I think it's time for you to see a specialist."

Dave agreed to this recommendation. I left the office that day convinced that two out of three people were crazy and that I wasn't one of them.

What followed was a negative workup by Dr. K, the urologist whom Dr. P had recommended. Dr. K's findings supported the results of all the earlier semen analyses. Dave's sperm were plentiful, of good quality, with excellent motility. He confirmed what I'd known all along.

"I'm afraid that Dr. K is missing something. Those sperm are simply not normal."

"But Dr. P," I tried to reason, "the donor sperm died too. You are placing a lot of faith in those two little buggers that managed to survive my attack mucus. I'd rather put my faith in Dr. K's lab."

We were clearly at a stalemate.

I was preparing to seek a second opinion when my mother-in-law's latest mailing on infertility arrived. These dispatches had been coming about once a month for the past four years. I knew that she meant well but had tired of hearing about the doctor in Bangor, Maine, who had cured her cousin's best friend's niece, or the recipe for warm rum and milk that was sure to relax the uterus at bedtime.

"Arm and Hammer Is the Latest Fertility Drug." The headline caught my eye, and I read on: "Women whose cervical mucus is too acidic can establish a more hospitable environment by douching with baking soda and warm water one-half hour before intercourse." The clipping was from *Parade* magazine. What the heck—I was willing to give it a try.

"You can believe in black magic if you want," Dr. P told me, "but the truth is that your husband has a serious fertility problem. The two of you cannot have a child together."

At this point, I figured that I had two choices. I could go out and find another infertility specialist, wait a few months for an appointment, and then wait another week or so for a PK test. Or I could figure out a way to get someone else in Dr. P's office to do the test.

"Hello, I need to make an appointment for my husband and me to talk with Dr. P. I'll need to confirm a time with Dave, but I wanted to find out which days Dr. P is available."

"He's in the office every day but Wednesday and Friday mornings, when he's in the operating room. Also, he'll be out of town for two weeks beginning on the sixteenth."

There I had it. My mucus would be optimal for a few days during Dr. P's vacation.

My sixth PK test was done by Dr. M, a young man who must have been doing a fellowship with Dr. P. He came upon me innocently, unaware that he was soon to bring Dave's sperm back from death row. "I hear that you've come for a PK test."

"Yes," I interrupted, not wanting him to have a chance to say that I didn't need another. "Yes, I haven't done too well on them in the past, but I want to give it one last try. And today I'm prepared to pay five dollars for every live sperm you can find." Dr. M laughed. Then he took the specimen and headed for the microscope. Moments later I heard him calling.

"Come quick! Look! You owe me a lot of money." And there they were. Not an army, but about five or six live sperm. "They look great. They're swimming freely!" Dr. M was ready to take out the champagne.

When Dr. P heard the news, he said that Dr. M was seeing things. I was tempted to argue, to prove my point with another PK. Instead, I got a refill of my Clomid and invested in another large box of baking soda.

As it turned out, two tablespoons was all I needed—my daughter is now nearly fifteen.

○

## TOO SOON
### *Jane Frankel*

Having conceived and carried my now three-year-old daughter, Anna, without difficulty, I never expected to have a problem the second time around. My husband, Jim, and I assumed that we could plan our second child as we had our first and that all would go smoothly. Now, several months—and a devastating diagnosis—later, we are still adjusting to the surprises we have encountered. Because I am the one with the diagnosis, it seems that I am the one who is feeling the infertility most intensely.

I have known other people who have had difficulty conceiving, so I didn't panic or become particularly upset when we did not conceive a second child easily. I'd read about fertility treatments in the popular press and figured that there was now a high-tech solution for every problem. We live in an area with many fine fertility clinics, so I optimistically—and naively—made an appointment.

Our first meeting with a specialist confirmed what we had hoped: a little Pergonal and some well-timed intercourse and I'd be pregnant soon. Both Jim and I are used to hard work, so this formula sounded fine to us, rosy in fact. What we didn't know until a few weeks later was that all the hard work in the world couldn't predictably fix the problem that I have. Three days after my thirty-first birthday we received a call from my doctor telling us that routine blood work had revealed that I have premature ovarian failure. In her words, my FSH (follicle-stimulating hormone) was "shockingly high."

There was no way that I could have been prepared for this diagnosis and the information that was to follow. As I said, we had assumed that there was, at worst, a treatable infertility problem. To learn that I was "peri-menopausal" and that my ovaries were shutting down was startling and overwhelming. It was as though I was being hit over the head with two boulders at once: one said that I wouldn't bear any more children, and the other said that I was entering menopause about twenty years earlier than I'd anticipated. When I hung up the phone, all I could do was reach for my daughter for comfort and cry.

As the news began to settle in, I realized that it was the prediction of an early menopause that was most upsetting. Somehow I could accept infertility, since we have a wonderful daughter and since both Jim and I are comfortable with adoption. What devastated me was the idea that I was a thirty-year-old trapped in the body of a fifty-year-old. That was what I felt like—a freak. I didn't know how I could ever tell my friends and family this news. They would understand infertility, but who could ever understand what was happening to me?

Certainly I could not understand. I am youthful and energetic; I eat right and take care of myself. I didn't wait until I was older to have children and I left a promising career in law to enter a field (teaching) that would give me more time with my children. There was no way that something like this was supposed to be happening to me, and as I said, I could not begin to understand it.

In the weeks following the diagnosis I worked hard to come to grips with the situation—that's my style. Though devastated, I tried to take charge of the situation and learn as much as I could about my options. Although I'd been told that there was very little chance that I could conceive again, I was also told that it was a possibility—that there was sometimes a spontaneous cure and that treatment could sometimes help. So we consulted another specialist and began planning a course of treatment. To our great surprise, our new specialist called us at home on a Sunday evening and excitedly told us that I was pregnant! He had been running some hormonal tests, spotted something odd, and did a pregnancy test. He was calling to tell us that we had one of the rare spontaneous pregnancies that occur in women with premature ovarian failure.

Jim and I were elated, but I was also very nervous. I knew that this was my last shot at pregnancy. If anything happened, could I beat the odds again? I feared not, and the first ten weeks crept by slowly. We finally allowed ourselves to be encouraged when an ultrasound at eleven weeks revealed a healthy, normally developing fetus. Unfortunately, I miscarried two weeks later. That was seven months ago.

Over the past several months Jim and I have taken several steps toward adoption, and they have felt good. Our doctors suggested donor eggs, but that is an option that never felt right to us. But adoption does feel right, and we find ourselves increasingly excited about welcoming a child into our family in this way. So the infertility piece of my diagnosis has become easier and, surprisingly, the menopause piece has as well.

Although I am still baffled by what has happened—and is happening— to my body, I am doing somewhat better. I still find myself looking for signs of menopause, fearing them, imagining they are there and wondering why they are not, if this is my diagnosis. However, this vigilance is diminishing, and I find that I am slowly regaining some confidence in my body. As someone who never used to worry about my health and who then became terribly fearful, I am gradually returning to a sense of well-being. I still worry about an early death, but much less than I did months ago.

Despite lingering feelings, the intense sadness has passed and my bruised self-image is healing.

## 2

# NAVIGATING
# THROUGH TREATMENT

ENTERING INFERTILITY TREATMENT is a complicated process for most couples, one that involves complex decision making and is accompanied by an array of unsettling feelings. Although most couples find that the process feels less daunting as their path through treatment becomes more familiar, it takes time for them to feel comfortable with the invasive and technological aspects of treatment. In the meantime, most are anxious, fearful, and confused.

Decisions regarding treatment begin with decisions about where and when to seek it. For some couples, options are few and decisions are easy. Due to geographic limitations or insurance restrictions, there is only one treatment facility available to some. Similarly, those limited by finances or by the specifics of their diagnosis may have few treatment options. By contrast, there are couples living near major metropolitan areas who have insurance coverage for assisted reproductive technology, thereby giving them many choices in infertility care. Though fortunate to have these choices, they can also feel confused by them.

How do people choose physicians and treatment centers when they have several options? Some go on the recommendations of friends, colleagues, or advisers at the local RESOLVE chapter. Others study statistics, trying to make some determination about which treatment center is best. As they begin to understand statistics, most find that it is very difficult to assess a treatment center on that basis because different programs have different criteria for accepting patients. Furthermore, some clinics specialize in certain treatments or in working with a particular group of patients. Thus, a particular diagnosis may point a couple toward a specific physician or center.

Decisions about which assisted reproductive technologies to pursue and how long to pursue them are especially complex. Again, these decisions are sometimes governed by insurance carriers or by the availability of treatment in a particular geographical area, but the couple's feelings about infertility and assisted conception, as well as their religious beliefs, also play critical roles in their decision making. Some couples know from the start of their infertility experience that they will do anything to have a baby. Others begin with considerable doubt about how far they will go. Still others feel that they must set certain firm boundaries on their treatment efforts. Governed by religious or moral principles regarding natural versus technological conception, or by fears of the risks associated with treatment, some couples know that they will never pursue assisted reproductive technology; others know that they will pursue high-tech treatment but only with their own gametes.

Those couples who do decide to pursue assisted reproductive technology face decisions within that decision. Those undergoing in vitro fertilization must decide how many embryos to have transferred, a decision that involves carefully balancing their chances for pregnancy (which increase with the number of embryos transferred) against the risk of multiple births (which also increase with the number of embryos transferred). This decision is especially challenging for couples who feel barren and who cannot believe that *one* embryo, let alone two or three or more, could take. This is a particularly difficult decision for couples who would honor religious or personal proscriptions against multifetal reduction (the process of reducing a high-risk multiple pregnancy to a safer singleton or twin pregnancy) or who oppose discarding or freezing of embryos.

All infertile couples discover that their lives are organized into twenty-eight-day cycles. Couples entering high-tech treatment come to realize that their lives are further governed by treatment cycles. Although these treatment cycles sometimes coincide with menstrual cycles, they may be shaped more by medications and procedures. Before making a commitment at work or in their personal lives, couples must first consult their treatment calendar to determine their ability to travel.

Couples who undergo assisted reproductive technology face new challenges as they begin these procedures. In addition to the complex decision making about what to do, where to do it, and for how long, they face the daunting task of taking on an involved treatment protocol. Daily injections, frequent blood tests and ultrasound monitoring, and precisely timed procedures now take hold of their schedules. For women who are afraid of needles or who fear the potential side effects of medication, treatment cycles bring additional burdens.

Infertility is frequently described as a roller-coaster ride, a description which certainly applies to many high-tech treatment cycles. Cycles usually begin with an upswing of energy: the start of a cycle is busy and very time consuming. When a couple is going through a treatment for the first time, tremendous energy is spent in simply remembering the details of the treatment regimen, and tremendous hope is invested in the outcome. Then, as the cycle progresses toward an intrauterine insemination or an egg retrieval and embryo transfer, the energy intensifies.

The second half of a high-tech treatment cycle can feel more like the plateau in a roller-coaster ride. The energy of the experience has diminished; the process has become one of waiting and wondering. The couple knows that a startling crash is probably up ahead, but they are hoping for good news.

What comes as a surprise to many couples is that the end of a treatment cycle is not as they anticipated. Those who have a negative pregnancy test will "crash," but often they will also be surprised at how soon they feel ready to try again. Perhaps even more surprised are those who have a positive test and discover that pregnancy after infertility, especially after assisted reproduction, is yet another roller-coaster ride. These delighted but tentative parents-to-be cautiously make their way from one blood test to another and from one ultrasound to the next.

For all infertile couples, the journey through treatment has an end point. Each couple hopes that this end point will come early in the form of a successful pregnancy. However, many couples do travel a much longer and more arduous path through treatment before reaching resolution. Inevitably, there are many couples who never achieve pregnancy through treatment—or who lose the pregnancies that do occur. They come to a place where they know that they must end the journey they are on and begin another one. Many take a much-needed break before moving on to an alternative path to parenthood or to resolution without children.

In the pages that follow, Taika Brand-Matthews offers three poems that speak to some of the rigors of infertility treatment. "Motionless" is about the upsetting aftermath of a difficult intrauterine insemination. Both "Fat Infertility" and "Rituals" capture the hold that infertility has on her daily life. Then we turn to Karen Propp's essay, "On Losing One's Virginity Again," a fascinating and powerful look at assisted conception.

○

## MOTIONLESS

### *Taika Brand-Matthews*

Her hips are propped up
on the cold examining table.
Her back hurts. She holds
a tiny, clay figure of a woman
in her hand until it becomes warm.
There is motion inside of her.

Later, she is driving through
the center of town when pain rips
her abdomen open.
The sky before her empties,
turns bright. Then everything vanishes—
her friend's car ahead of her, the road,
her hands on the steering wheel.
"I'm dying," she says.

Her eyes are closed to the men
that surround her. Each cautious word
they ask is met with silence.
They lift her from the road onto the stretcher.
She can feel the prickle of twigs, dirt, dry grass
caught in her dress—trapped in the white sheet
they've wrapped her in.

Doors swing toward her.
In the tomb of the ambulance all is still.
The oxygen signs, pushes its breath
into her mouth, her nose,
down into her lungs.
She looks out the tiny windows
into the ashen sky.
"You're gray. Your face is totally gray,"
she remembers her friend telling her.

They shift her body onto the hospital bed.
Debris crackles beneath her like paper.
One shot and the pain drains away
like the colors of the world
only moments before.

The hours are long with doctors and silence.
"Tell me a story with a happy ending,"
she asks of the empty room.

The long, bony arms of the bed hold her.
She searches the corridor for her husband's face—
wishes the tall man, dark-eyed baby
she sees were hers,
here to take her home.

○

## FAT INFERTILITY

### *Taika Brand-Matthews*

Fat infertility sits
with his big behind
on the see-saw.

He is sitting on the ground
looking up at the rest of my life
hanging above him,
spilling off of the seat,
dangling by threads in the air.

There I am,
in the sky,
holding
on to the handle
for my dear life.

○

# RITUALS

## *Taika Brand-Matthews*

### I. NIGHT RITUAL

It begins again:
she arches her back,
lifts her behind up
like an infant, tucks the red
hair-towel under her body.
She will fold it up
between her legs like a diaper
when he leaves.

Her prayer,
that in fourteen days the color that
will run out from between her legs
will not be the scarlet there now.

### II. MORNING RITUAL

It begins:
the clanging alarm clock,
the digital thermometer
beeping eighteen times in her
mouth;
her temperature, 97 degrees;
the closet light,
the click of the dogs' toenails going
down the stairs;
the red towel draped over the chair,
the weatherman on Channel 4 as
she pees.

### III. AFTERNOON RITUAL

It begins:
coffee with a friend on the way
home;
pepper shaken onto the steamed
milk—

the surprise of it
like her mother's gray roots when
her dyed, red hair grows out,
The rush of adrenaline in her
mouth.
The fire,
the bitter reminder of age.

○

## ON LOSING ONE'S VIRGINITY AGAIN
### *Karen Propp*

On Tuesday, I underwent minor surgery that retrieved my eggs from my ovaries. Then my husband and I waited a couple of days to learn if his sperm had successfully fertilized my eggs in a petri dish, and finally, on Friday, after learning that the long-tailed critters had triumphed and the eggs had divided into multiple cells, I returned to the hospital for an embryo transfer. What a strange, two-part, out-of-the-body conception! I feel as if I've lost my virginity again. Like the first time, I have lost innocence but gained knowledge and a new sense of self. The world has shifted on its axis.

How can I articulate this surreal experience of losing my virginity for a second time, to the high ceremonies of assisted reproductive technology, at the age of nearly forty? The first time, I giggled about it with friends at slumber parties. I pawed through *The Heart Is a Lonely Hunter* and *Lady Chatterley's Lover,* seeking words for what I felt. But now I cannot draw from any wellspring of literature or history. I have few associations or comparisons to describe this new rite of passage that an increasing number of women are experiencing.

Nor do I have access to a vast store of women's tales like those available for pregnancy and childbirth. "We think back through our mothers if we are women," as Virginia Woolf reminds us. Tell your mother, aunt, cousin, or hairdresser that you are pregnant and she will invariably recall an incident from her own childbearing. But there were no petri dishes in what Alice Walker calls our mothers' gardens, those fertile beds of artistic and biological creativity from which we contemporary women grew. During our efforts to create new life with the new technologies, not one of our mothers can tell us, "I learned to shift my weight so the injections didn't hurt," or "The medications didn't bother me as much as the uncertainty."

Some of our sisters and some of our friends may say this, but none of our mothers. We will have to be those mothers.

I imagine us many years hence, hovering over scrapbooks of ultrasound photos, recounting how many cycles it took to get pregnant and what clinic assisted the process. Will we recognize each other at nursery school by twins in the family? Will we know each other at college weekends because we are older than the majority of parents? Will there forever remain a catch in the throat when speaking about our children? A catch that says, I, too, have experienced a miracle? And what will we tell our grown techno-offspring? That you were one of three embryos? That for the first forty-eight hours of life you were in a petri dish? One thing is for sure: we can date conception with absolute certainty. In the end, barring any long-term medical complications, does it matter how a person began? It matters to the mother at the beginning of a pregnancy, I think, and maybe to the child during adolescence, trying to forge an identity. To a woman trying to conceive through in vitro fertilization, it is all that matters. Here, then, are my particulars.

Tuesday morning, Samuel and I drive our thirty-minute route to the hospital. The ground is frozen and covered with a thin layer of frost, the traffic heavy, the radio tuned to a BBC news hour whose headlines I am too preoccupied to hear. You'd think my thoughts might turn profound or wise at this significant moment, but instead I think about last night, when I gave myself an enema in preparation for today's procedure. I knelt on the bathroom floor, face to the tile, ass in the air. In this humbling position I twisted my right arm to squeeze a bottle of clear fluid into my anus. Erotic ritual? Fertility prayer? Torture? Before these infertility treatments began I never knew there were so many ways to poke and penetrate the body.

At the hospital, in a private room, I hang my clothes in the closet, then slip into a cotton johnny so threadbare that as soon as I put it on I start to shiver, whether from an actual chill or from fear I do not know. Nothing could be further in elegance from the black evening dress about which Samuel and I used to fantasize, back before any of these treatments began. We imagined that I would wear that slinky dress to become impregnated with his banked sperm! In this pitiful gown and under the bright fluorescent lights that wash out my skin, I feel myself becoming weak and vulnerable—a patient. As a patient I lie down on the white gurney and cover myself with blankets. As a patient I offer my bare arm to the technician who bustles into the room, deftly inserts an IV tube into a vein in my hand, and leaves a bag of fluids to slowly drip into my blood.

Samuel and I have exchanged few words this morning. Even so, I am glad he is here, a familiar figure with wavy black hair, glasses, and a beard sitting on a tan vinyl chair, yellow notepad balanced on one leg. He reminds me that there is a life we share outside this hospital room. I turn on the Walkman I have brought and listen to one of my relaxation tapes. We could almost be at home, each of us engaged in our own activities but feeling the other nearby.

At home, for the past two weeks, morning and evening, I have injected myself with Fertinex, the newest FDA-approved ovum-stimulating drug, and as a result I have grown five mature eggs. There is about a 5 percent chance of impregnation per embryo, so the more embryos that are transferred, the better the odds for overall success. I have heard about the fifteen or twenty eggs other women produce, and when I compare myself to them I feel a bit like I did in junior high school when I envied Dawn Weaver's svelte figure and flawless skin. But I remind myself that five eggs is a good number for *me,* since the previous cycle I produced only two. Indeed, I feel proud of my five egg follicles, which I have seen as tiny dots on the ultrasound screen.

An aide comes into the room where Samuel and I are waiting and dutifully wheels me into the elevator that will take me upstairs to the pre-op room. She is young, with teased and treated hair and long fingernails painted platinum blue. The bright elevator buttons light up: 2, 3. Samuel is quiet; I am quiet. The young woman's gum chewing and spunky demeanor make me feel that were she not working these dour corridors, she would be in a place lively with music and conversation—a disco where I could wear my black dress. "Ready for your procedure?" she says rather brightly to me, as if asking whether I like the band.

Other, more cooperative women might not take issue, but I have developed an aversion to the word *procedure.* The egg retrieval is yet another procedure. In my experience, *procedure* is an all-purpose euphemism covering events that usually involve speculums, catheters, needles. They take place in antiseptic rooms with bright lights, involve few words and many steady breaths. I've looked it up. The dictionary defines *procedure* as "an act composed of steps," and *procedure* originates from the word *proceed,* which means "to go forward."

A medical term, *procedure* does nothing to help us women invent vocabulary for our newly scripted lives or tell the truth about our bodies. Everything in my infertility career has led up to these oh-so-postmodern rites of female passage: egg retrieval and the later embryo transfer. If I am to carry new life, these will be the determining moments. The word *procedure* and the accompanying hospital instructions about where to report and when I can or cannot eat are not sufficiently heroic for the great journey on which I and Samuel have embarked. For me at least, the steps the doctor will perform in a certain order—and make no mistake, they must be performed precisely—are our signal for an end-of-the-century metaphysical breakthrough.

The aide pushes me, or should I say the gurney, into another brightly lit room. Again, Samuel and I have to wait. This room is a holding area, a passageway to the operating room. Out of the corner of my doped-up eye, I see a man with black wiry hair hurrying in our direction. From a distance he resembles someone I once met on a blind date. The only topic we could find to talk about was downhill skiing, which at that time I hadn't done in fifteen years, and at the end of the drink or dinner, I forget which, I was terribly relieved to go home to my cat, attic room, and book-lined walls.

Mr. Blind Date saunters up to the bed on which I lie and looks into my face. I see by a momentary dip in his winning smile that he doesn't find me to be his type either. "We can't be sure of retrieving all five egg follicles . . . ," he says, voicing his disappointment. "Yes, we usually get 70 percent. . . . We'll do our best."

Can't be sure of retrieving all five! Wherever that was written, it must have been in a fine print I missed. Already, my five eggs seem less golden. *Egg harvesting*, it's sometimes called, as if a woman were a ripe field. I feel rocky and dry.

A tremendous set of doors opens, and I wave good-bye to Samuel as I am wheeled into the operating room. Here is the landscape I know only from the sets of TV shows—*Chicago Hope* or *ER*. Scattered around me are little tables, metal instruments, objects covered in aqua plastic bags. A blond woman appears at my side and puts her hand on my shoulder. "I'm Stephanie. I'm your embryologist today."

My eggs will soon be her responsibility. It will be Stephanie who looks through the microscope at the semen sample and chooses for each egg a single sperm, a sperm that came from my husband's body. Stephanie will cut off its tail and, by manipulating the robotic arms of the micropipettes, inject that sperm into my egg.

"You'll be careful to use the right sperm?" I ask tentatively.

"We match everything very carefully. Everything has your and your husband's names on it." I'm wearing a plastic bracelet with my name and address, and I realize now why the admitting nurse, the IV tube technician, the anesthesiologist, and the doctor all turned my wrist to check it this morning. Stephanie tips my wrist as well. Apparently, I am still who I am supposed to be.

The bearded anesthesiologist, who glides about silent as gas, appears at my side. "We're giving you something to make you comfortable," he tells me.

As if I could ever be comfortable amid all this strangeness. With the gas man's drugs, I will fall into a deeper sleep than Sleeping Beauty knew. My blind date doctor will use his special needle to puncture my vaginal walls. Up, up he will go, to get what he wants. With his sharp needle and ultrasound guidance, he will penetrate farther than any other lover. Who has ever seen my anatomy with such intimacy? Who has ever known me like this?

I take a deep breath and feel my legs pulled open, and then I know I must surrender my eggs to this new conception.

I wake woozy and a little sore. A nurse slips next to the bed and checks my pulse.

"Any pain? We have something if you do."

I query my belly and legs. Nothing stabs or pierces. I shake my head.

"You may spot a little."

I check the sheet and the pad between my legs for blood, wanting some visible sign that I have, indeed, lost my virginity this second time, but there is none.

By the clock on the wall I see that I have lost forty minutes of consciousness. Where did I go? Sweet nothings were surely whispered while I dozed and slipped dreamlessly to some mythic place where babies begin.

The wiry-haired doctor appears again at my side. "We retrieved four eggs, four good ones." And then he is off, with the bemused but harried air of a man who is used to leaving one woman's bed for the next.

Another bed is wheeled and placed next to mine. I turn my head and see a woman I recognize from the clinic's waiting room all those early mornings when I sat until my name was called for my blood to be drawn. This woman sat in a corner, her head bent, wearing a blue pea coat. Now her long-lashed eyes open and she turns her head groggily from side to side. I want to call out, *They did you too?* Against the hospital sheets, her copper-colored arms look incongruously healthy. Earlier, in pre-op, I'd glimpsed another young woman being wheeled out, her cheeks flushed pink, her hair lustrous. In a hospital setting, we infertility patients are instantly recognizable as neither ill nor injured.

*How are you feeling?* I want to ask the woman in the bed beside mine. *Isn't this strange?* Are we egg retrieval companions? Synchronous ovulators? Above us both, neon green lines on a monitor rise and fall to chart vital signs. No words rise from my muffled, medicinal rest. A nurse pulls a striped curtain around my bed and checks the round rubber pieces taped to my chest. It is December and over her scrubs she wears a smock covered with pictures of a jolly Santa Claus. My eggs have been taken, and soon I will be sent home.

At home, I sleep off the anesthesia and wake feeling that I've been punched in the gut. This, I've been told, is a normal reaction following the emptying of my ovaries. I call a few friends. I call my sister. I call my mother.

"There were four eggs," I tell my mother, "and now they must fertilize." The words sound stiff in my mouth. Am I reporting on an operation or announcing news concerning her future grandchild?

There is a silence on the other end of the line. I can feel her searching out what say. She settles on "How are you feeling?"

"Everything went well," I try. But that sounds vague and insufficient. I am tired, apprehensive, and relieved. I tell her this, but my words have no history and cannot resonate off of anyone else's experience. Who ever talks about eggs fertilizing in a glass dish? It sounds like an exhibit for a science fair.

I could aim to be a scientist at that fair and say, "The injection pipette pushed through the zona pellucida into the ooplasm."

I could draw associations. *In vitro* is Latin for 'in glass,'" I could say. Remember Duchamp's art piece, his large glass, *Bride Stripped Bare by Her Bachelors, Even*. I was a bride and you could call me stripped bare. Remember his mounted bicycle wheel and his urinal as sculpture? Maybe it's a matter of stripping away preconceptions in order to say: *This is a new female experience.*

The truth is, during the following next two days, I become sentimental. I think often and fondly about my eggs. Eggs in a laboratory twenty miles away; eggs joining to my husband's sperm as I shop for groceries or read a book. The entire chromosomal structure for a new human being could be coming into play while we eat dinner or pay the bills. These possibilities will never cease to amaze me.

Late Thursday afternoon, the call comes. Four eggs were successfully injected with sperm; four eggs fertilized; there are four possible embryos.

I walk around the pond near my house to breathe in the wintry air and admire the season's starkest trees, bare now of buds, arching against a silver gray sky. A runner in a yellow sweatshirt speeds around the bend. A shaggy dog lopes by, his red tongue lolling. A stout woman in a parka huffs along. Every one of these living creatures began, it suddenly occurs to me, as an embryo. The globed streetlights come on. Four embryos, I say to myself, and the words finally begin to sound familiar. Hallelujah. Four possible embryos.

It is mid-December in New England; the days shorten and then shorten more, until darkness falls by 4:15. Soon it will be the winter solstice, the darkest day of the year. I think about how the winter dark makes one travel inward, and I feel that is a good thing, for I want now to keep my energy quiet and introverted, near where the embryo might grow. By traveling inward, I find a new self to replace the one I shed when I lay down on the operating table in a drugged oblivion and allowed my vaginal walls to be punctured. The old self was nulligravid, fearful of pain, and wedded to the idea of a man and a woman alone in a bed where passion reigned. The new self was born from the daily discipline of measuring medicine into the syringe, and from the sixty-five injections administered into the fleshiest parts of thigh, buttocks, arm. The new self was born from the urgent air of the operating room, and from her name on the hospital identification bracelet. The new self does what is necessary without complaint. The new self believes in the seasonal dark and is ready for the best odds science can give.

That dark winter evening, as we have done every evening between the oocyte retrieval and the embryo transfer, my husband and I stand before the Hanukkah candles. Thursday night, the night before the embryo transfer, the last night of the holiday, we set eight candles in a row. Samuel lights a match and then hands it to me. "You say the blessing tonight."

I light the center candle and hold it up. "Baruch ata Adonai, we recognize the many miracles you have done for our people in history, but please, God, grant us one miracle in this house."

Samuel shakes his head. "You have to be more specific for what you ask. We don't want an ectopic pregnancy." He takes the candle from me and begins to light another tall red one. "We want the eggs to attach to the uterine wall and then we want one to grow into—"

"A child. A baby. We ask for the miracle of a baby growing inside me."

He hands me the candle and I ignite the remaining wicks. We stand there awhile with our backs to the dark window. I feel strangely calm. Whatever happens next, the eight small flames flickering in their brass menorah have drawn me into their light.

Morning. Hospital. Operating room. I am lying on a white bed with a white sheet draped over my raised knees. Surrounding me, dressed in blue scrubs, are Samuel, a cheery nurse, a stone-faced technician, and a tall, gangly doctor. The silence in the room is like that on a mountain peak. Miles and miles of thin air, clear sky, and a silence that fills you up and creates secret pockets, reservoirs of calm.

The doctor on duty today has the geeky look of someone who spent his adolescence at science fairs. Clipboard in hand, he leans into the bed, his bony elbow resting on my side. He shows Samuel and me a chart rating our embryos. One is five cells but with fragmentation, one is four cells with no fragmentation, one is three cells. Fragmentation, which the doctor explains is not a good thing, can occur when the cells divide. My fourth egg, although fertilized by the embryologist, never went on to divide. "That's the best one," the doctor says, pointing to the middle line where he's listed the four cell, no fragmentation embryo. "The other two, well . . . " he shrugs his shoulder. "We'll transfer them anyway."

I am disappointed and disheartened. The embryos are described as "fair" (rather than "good" or "poor") as in a school report card. "But people do get pregnant with three embryos, right?" I ask. My voice sounds more desperate than I'd intended.

The doctor purses his thin lips. I want him to say, "Yes, absolutely, you never know." But he knows his business. He sees the aggregate picture, the statistical probabilities, the plethora of pregnancy tests that turn up negative.

"At your age," he begins, and at that phrase, which I have heard too often of late, I cringe. Do the bright lights show up every wrinkle around my eyes, every graying hair on my head? "At your age, you have around a fifteen percent chance."

He must see my face fall. "OK, maybe eighteen."

The technician slips a sonogram wand onto my belly, and the monitor beside me lights up. We are back on the mountaintop, and I am taking in great drafts of the giddy air and letting my knees flop open against the bed railings. The doctor takes his seat on a stool and proffers a long catheter, which he will use to deposit the embryos into my uterus.

My uterus! It is up on the monitor screen for everyone to see, and it is a cavernous terrain with peaks and valleys. To think there was a time, back when I was still a virgin, when I never looked into my interior space. To think that I was ever alone with my body. To think . . .

But there is no thinking in this room; there is only breath and light. We are wrapped again in miles of billowy silence while Samuel, I, the nurse, the technician, and the doctor train our gaze. Samuel takes my hand. We are staring, staring. . . . I am tempted to say we are staring at the future, but in fact we are staring at the thin white line on the screen that is the catheter coming through with our three fair embryos.

Did my mother sense this white light in the room the morning my father reached for her and she forgot to put in her diaphragm and I began? Where she had passion, I have precision. Where she had desire, I have a terribly conscious intent. I will proceed. My pelvis is tipped and my breath is steady. My eyes are open. The ceiling is white and so are the walls.

## 3

# THE PATIENT-CAREGIVER RELATIONSHIP IN INFERTILITY

INFERTILITY TREATMENT is a collaborative endeavor, not only between husbands and wives, but also between infertile couples and their caregivers. From the first diagnostic tests through the rigors of in vitro fertilization (IVF), patients participate actively in their own care, care that requires frequent contact and interactions with physicians, nurses, and laboratory personnel. Although some of these interactions are difficult—since infertility involves frustration, disappointment, and loss—people often do remarkably well. In fact, close relationships develop between staff and patients, relationships that become very important to all participants, especially at times of defeat and disappointment.

What works? What is it that enables people to work effectively together, even in difficult circumstances? The following are some of the key ingredients in effective patient-caregiver collaboration. I encourage patients to expect each of these from their physician and his or her practice.

*A welcoming office setting where privacy is respected.* Most couples find it very difficult to leave the care of their regular gynecologist and to enter an infertility practice. Many associate infertility with sterility and fear that seeing a specialist means that they suffer from a problem that cannot be resolved. They arrive at their infertility doctor's office feeling cautious, vulnerable, and perhaps ashamed.

The importance of the front desk staff in an infertility practice cannot be overstated. As the first introduction to a physician and his or her practice, it is the people at the desk who set the tone of the office. If they are smiling, if they are courteous, if they extend themselves toward the new patients, arrival goes smoothly. Conversely, if they are disrespectful, curt, or cool, new patients will feel the loss of their other doctor and the stress of this referral all the more.

Because people have to sacrifice so much privacy in order to enter infertility treatment, it is essential that all efforts be made to maintain privacy in the infertility practice. This effort must begin with the front desk staff, who must be cautious in addressing new patients in a public setting. It is critical, too, that patient records, registration forms, and scheduling sheets be kept away from the public area of the practice.

A front desk staff that lets patients know if a physician is running late helps maintain collaborative relationships. Although it is never pleasant to be kept waiting, a delay is always easier to accept when you are notified and can adjust your expectations accordingly. Staff members who apologize, offer a cup of coffee, and make other efforts to be sure that you are comfortable while you wait provide an important service.

Finally, it is the role of the front desk staff to make sure that the waiting room is a comfortable setting. In addition to making sure that magazines are current and suitable (no parenting magazines, some magazines for men, and so on), that coffee and juice are available, and that the setting remains neat and clean, the front desk staff should keep an eye on interactions. Although many infertility patients welcome the opportunity to talk with others in the office, some people need quiet and privacy. Occasionally, a loud, overly talkative patient may disturb others who are waiting. A front desk staff that can come up with a creative intervention, such as a distraction for the bothersome patient, will be appreciated by the others who are waiting.

*A physician who is usually punctual.* Physicians can run late, especially when they spend extra time with patients as needed. However, there is a difference between an occasional, explained delay and consistent overbooking. Patients understand if a doctor runs a few minutes late, acknowledges the inconvenience, and then meets with them in a focused and leisurely way. What hurts is when a physician runs late and then is rushed, unfocused, and seemingly otherwise occupied.

*A physician who knows his or her patients.* Infertility patients take their efforts to conceive very seriously and need to know that their physician is invested in their care. Most understand that no physician can remember every detail of a case, but the physician should remember who people are and review patients' charts before meeting with them in consultation. There is nothing more unsettling than to be sitting in a physician's office while he or she thumbs quickly through your chart.

Patients should also be able to assume that their physician will try to avoid all interruptions during a consultation. Although there are times when interruptions are unavoidable, a physician who routinely takes phone calls while seeing patients is simply being rude. Similarly, a physician who is clearly running from one exam room to another leaves each patient with the sense that they are not taken seriously.

*Physicians and nurses who give careful thought to what they say and how they say it.* Infertility is a very stressful and often painful experience. Physicians and other caregivers must be able to accept patients' fears and pain and must always avoid the temptation of predicting success. Everyone feels good for a short time when such a prediction is made, but if it is wrong, the patients are devastated. Caregivers can express optimism without leaving their patients feeling set up, misled, or betrayed later on.

Caregivers' efforts to convey concern, support, and understanding are greatly appreciated by patients. Although it is a real gift to be able to find the right words, simply making an effort to find suitable words means a great deal. It is not difficult to see when a nurse or doctor is trying hard to find words, especially at such difficult times as a negative pregnancy test or a pregnancy loss. Simple phrases such as "I'm sorry" or "I wish it were otherwise" go a long way.

It sometimes helps when caregivers talk briefly about themselves and their own experiences. Although personal information is often inappropriate, infertility patients appreciate knowing something about the personal experiences of their caregivers. After all, when you are forced to give up so much of your own privacy—and reveal so much about yourself to a stranger—it is nice to know more about the person you are dealing with. Patients have found it especially helpful to hear from caregivers who have themselves endured infertility, pregnancy loss, or other relevant experiences.

*Physicians and caregivers who know when and how to bring up adoption and other alternative paths to parenthood.* One of the biggest dilemmas for infertility caregivers is determining when and how to suggest to patients that they consider other options. Perhaps more than in any other area of their practice, caregivers walk a very fine line. On the one hand, it is essential that they let patients know that they are losing hope for a successful pregnancy. However, since it is devastating for a patient to feel that his or her doctor is giving up, this subject must be approached with great delicacy.

Physicians face several tasks at once. Not only must they figure out when to raise the subject of alternatives with a patient, but they also must find a way to present options in a positive yet neutral way. In other words, most people want to know that their doctor has positive feelings about adoption and third party alternatives, but most also prefer that one option not be promoted above others. All too often, it seems that physicians will offer gamete (ovum or sperm) donation as another form of treatment and refer to adoption as a second-choice path to parenthood. Although some patients may initially want to believe that gamete donation is a treatment for infertility, they soon recognize that they are simply trying to fool themselves, and they often end up feeling extremely betrayed when a physician or nurse also pretends.

Often the most effective way to introduce positive sentiments about adoption is to do so in an indirect way. Baby pictures on the wall with a sign reading "Our Births and Adoptions" or a comment about some recent "good news" about an adoption lets patients know that their physician supports adoption and views it as a successful resolution to infertility. Similarly, the physician can present gamete donation as a fine alternative path to parenthood without misrepresenting it as treatment.

Unfortunately, some patient-caregiver relationships are problematic. Doctors and nurses are often stressed, especially in these hard times of managed care; hence, they cannot always be as available and as responsive as they would like. Similarly, there are times when patients are so troubled by their infertility that nothing anyone can do or say will feel right. Still, there is a difference between bad moments and poor care.

Patients should have—and hold to—certain expectations of and standards for their caregivers. If you are consistently disappointed, trust that feeling and consider moving on. This decision is never easy and may be especially difficult if you are living in an area with limited infertility services.

It is also important to remember that caregivers may not be aware of certain problems within their offices and that you may need to make them aware. For example, if phone calls are not returned in a timely way, it may mean that the physician is unresponsive, but it may also mean that he or she is not getting the messages (or not in a timely way). Hence, it is always a good idea to raise issues and concerns before simply assuming that the physician is at fault and that the situation cannot be remedied.

Ironically, many infertility patients discover that it is difficult to leave their infertility practitioner. It was difficult to enter infertility treatment, but it is also difficult to say good-bye to people who have come to play an important part in their daily lives. Certainly those patients who leave because of pregnancy feel a different pull than those who leave because they have reached an end point in treatment. Nonetheless, the loss of the caring relationships is real and quite poignant for all former infertility patients. Many practices ease this loss by holding annual baby parties, reunions for former patients who have had or adopted children. Unfortunately, there is no readily apparent format for maintaining connections with those patients who decide to resolve without children or who are still in the process of adopting.

In the pages that follow, we hear first from Donna Tetreault, an IVF nurse coordinator who writes about her experience on the caregiving side of infertility in "From the Other Side: A Nurse's Perspective." Then we turn to Dr. L. Daniel Gottsegen, who, soon after deciding to specialize in infertility, discovered that he would be struggling with infertility issues in his personal life. Now, many years later, he reflects on his experiences in "On Becoming and Being an Infertility Specialist."

<hr>

## FROM THE OTHER SIDE: A NURSE'S PERSPECTIVE
### *Donna Tetreault*

I did not seek reproductive medicine, either as a patient (my own children came years ago and easily) or initially as a nurse. So I had no way of knowing, on the day that I was asked to assist in the development of an infertility program, how much it would mean to me, nor did I have any idea how it would change my life. Today, after eleven years of working in infertility, I look back over my many experiences and focus on those that touched me most deeply. Certain patients stand out—either for their courage, their perseverance, or the difficulties they encountered or the spirit with which they encountered them. Some patients stand out for all of these reasons.

For whatever reason, one patient who comes immediately to mind is Esther. In some ways, she represents every patient to me. Perhaps that is because she taught me so much about working with and caring for infertile women. When we met we were both new to infertility—she as a patient and I as a nurse—and we had so much to learn together.

Esther had recently moved from another state, but prior to moving she had learned that she had an ovulatory problem and had been prescribed clomiphene citrate. Her previous physician had approached the problem with optimism, predicting that once her cycles became regular, she would conceive. Because she was reassured by this prediction and felt otherwise comfortable with her former physician, Esther did not make the transition to our practice easily. Instead she came in giving me a very clear message: trust is to be earned, not assumed. It was a message that I needed to hear and one that would serve me well in my work with countless other infertility patients.

So Esther and I embarked on a path together. Her goal was, of course, to become pregnant. My goal was more complicated: to help her become pregnant but, more important, to help her accept whatever treatment outcome she encountered. Both of our goals were challenged by the fact that Esther found working with a nurse unfamiliar and initially gave me a strong sense that I needed to earn her respect as well as her trust.

Among the most vivid memories I have of my work with Esther were the phone calls—the difficult, inevitable, end-of-the-cycle phone calls. I remember dreading those calls, finding it so hard to face the question that followed each negative pregnancy test: Why? Over and over again I would search for an answer, knowing that there was nothing that would help me offer a reasonable explanation. After all, the cycles were controlled by medication, monitored by blood tests and ultrasounds, and everything was seemingly so perfect. Then why did it all fail? I did not know, yet still I searched.

Although there were many extraordinarily difficult conversations, my relationship with Esther grew more comfortable over time. I no longer had to think about where I stood with her; she had truly entrusted us with her care. We earned that continued trust by continually inviting her participation in decision making, as well as that of her husband, Steve.

There came a point in our work with Esther and Steve when the treatment team realized that pregnancy was unlikely. After discussing this at length with the physician, I asked to be the one to approach Esther and Steve regarding other options. I knew that it would not be an easy meeting for any of us but felt that it was a natural extension of the work we had done thus far.

I rehearsed a lot. Before we met I went over my words again and again, trying to choose them as carefully as possible and to envision how the conversation would progress. I reminded myself of Esther's realistic, educated approach to decisions and of the fact that she was always open to suggestions. I hoped that I would be able to help her see that there are successful outcomes to infertility treatment other than pregnancy. I hoped that we would all leave the conversation feeling good about what had transpired.

We did. I can't say that it was easy, but I do feel that my advance preparation paid off. Although it was difficult to feel so anxious about a conversation with patients, I believe that my anxiety helped me stay tuned in and careful to listen to and watch for their reactions. I left the meeting with profound respect for Esther and Steve both as individuals and as a couple able to make extraordinarily difficult decisions together.

Although Esther and Steve represent every couple, they are not every couple. There have been so many, many more. Each taught me more about working with people struggling with infertility, and most recon-firmed the lessons that I learned early in my work with Esther and Steve and some of my other early infertility patients. When I look back, these are some of the most important lessons I have learned. I carry them with me to work each day and use them constantly.

First, I have learned to take advice from patients. They know what helps and what does not, and I listen carefully to what they have to say. Early in my infertility work, a patient named Dale gave me some impor-tant feedback about the way we were approaching patients. In a gentle but clear way, she point out things about our office procedures that made treatment unnecessarily uncomfortable for patients. For example, although we thought we were maintaining strict confidentiality, there were many times when a patient's full name was called out for all to hear.

Second, I have learned to greet the anxious, expectant faces that I see in the waiting room with a smile, eye contact, and a strong hello. I greet the men as well as the women. It took a few previously "invisible" men to teach me that the men are a vital part of infertile couples and that their presence—and their role—needs to be acknowledged.

Third, I have learned that the hardest part of infertility treatment is often the "letting go." It is very difficult to say good-bye, especially to a couple that has not had a successful pregnancy. We have worried, laughed, cried, and been elated together, so parting holds a sweet sorrow. I always say, "come back," whether that be to show us a big belly or ultrasounds or a new baby. Or it can just be to say hello.

I am grateful to each and every person I have met on my own journey through reproductive medicine. I have grown through their openness and willingness to share the most intimate part of their life with me. I hope that I have been able to return at least a portion of the gift that I have received.

○

# ON BECOMING AND BEING
# AN INFERTILITY SPECIALIST
## Daniel L. Gottsegen

When I first entered medical school I had not decided what field I wanted to specialize in, but I knew which fields did not interest me. Among them were obstetrics and gynecology. However, by my third year of medical school, many fields that once seemed attractive no longer interested me. To my surprise, I found that I was drawn to the "happy" aspects of OB-Gyn.

I began my fourth year of medical school with an elective in infertility. That four-week experience helping couples to conceive convinced me that this was what I wanted to do. For me, no area of medicine could be more satisfying than helping couples become parents.

When I made the decision to specialize in infertility, I had no idea that the problem would touch me in my personal life as well. But soon after I began my residency, my wife and I decided that we were ready to begin a family of our own. Despite my awareness of infertility, we assumed that she would conceive promptly. After all, we were young and healthy, with no history of problems known to cause infertility. To our surprise and frustration, a pregnancy did not occur. Soon, I was in the ironic position of learning to be an infertility specialist and a patient at the same time.

For two years, Susan and I endured the frustrations and anguish of infertility. In retrospect, I realize that it was often easier for me to counsel and sympathize with my patients than it was to respond to my wife in the midst of this crisis. It was one thing to learn to perform an endometrial biopsy or a PK test and quite another to watch my wife undergo painful or embarrassing procedures. Helping others conceive was exciting and gratifying, but those long, lonely mornings of awakening to our own temperature charts were exhausting and disappointing.

Fortunately, our efforts and patience paid off, and our story had a happy ending—two, in fact: Amy and Adam, now fourteen and twelve. I think that Susan and I have cherished our children all the more because we tried so long to have them. Since then, when the going has been rough, we've been able to draw on our years of struggle.

My professional life has also been enriched by infertility. While my practice is not limited exclusively to reproductive medicine, much of my work is in this field. Each day I have the opportunity and the challenge of helping couples conceive. I celebrate with those who are successful and suffer with those whose best efforts (as well as my own) do not work out.

The recent and rapid advances in the field of infertility have made my work particularly exciting. This past year, three colleagues and I started an in vitro fertilization program, which had had a long and cautious gestation. I waited until I thought that our patients would have a reasonable chance of success and was pleased when all of the women in the first group had successful egg retrieval and fertilization. I was jubilant when one woman became pregnant!

Each positive pregnancy test—whether it is the result of minimal intervention or prolonged treatment—brings a big smile to my face. Still, I remain sobered by all the failures. For all the good news, there remain daily messages saying, "Mrs. X called to say her period started—what next?" or "Mrs. Y (pregnant after four miscarriages) is now bleeding heavily."

With a busy practice, I worry that I am not always there for my patients when they need me most. I try hard to respond to them, particularly when they are most stressed, and to take the time to talk with them. We need to talk together about their feelings as well as about their treatment options. Time and again, I have found that these talks help to lessen the frustrations.

And so, when I think back on my first year of medical school, I am relieved that I had an open mind. I feel fortunate to have found a specialty that is both professionally challenging and personally rewarding. My patients, and the very special work that we do together, enrich my life.

## Update

As I reflect back on twenty-five years of practicing obstetrics and gynecology, I have shared many successes with patients in a variety of women's health care problems. Although I have received much satisfaction from treating patients with different disorders, all seem to pale in comparison to helping a couple achieve a pregnancy.

It is obvious from the patients I see year after year that my role in helping them with their infertility seems to leave a more lasting impression on them than is true of the patients I helped through more dramatic, life-threatening emergencies. I certainly can say without hesitation that infertility has and continues to be the most satisfying part of my practice.

# 4

# INFERTILITY AND MARRIAGE

---

*First comes love, then comes marriage, then comes*
*Sally with a baby carriage.*

THAT'S HOW THE OLD JINGLE GOES. It alludes to an easy, natural sequence of events, in which children are planned as joyously as an engagement party and as predictably as a wedding. Surely the jingle says nothing about scheduled sex or ovulation predictor kits; intrauterine insemination and frozen embryo transfers do not fit into the rhyme, nor do they fit into the picture.

The picture of an easy and natural sequence of events is joltingly disrupted for those couples who experience infertility, especially when it is prolonged and involves many complicated procedures. Instead of being able to move forward in their family life, setting a goal for themselves and working toward it, infertile couples find that their lives are on hold. What does this do to two people who have planned and anticipated a bright future together? How do they begin to readjust their expectations for the near—and possibly distant—future? How does a couple find ways to cope with what must feel like a multi-pronged assault on their partnership—an attack on their sexual relationship, their plans, their dreams, their time, and their finances?

Although there are some marriages that suffer severe and even irreparable damage as a result of infertility, this is unusual. Far more often couples pull together in the face of infertility and discover that they have remarkable resources for coping with this problem. Many emerge from the experience with increased respect for themselves, their partners, and their marital unit. Nonetheless, infertility is extraordinarily challenging, and for most couples there are times when they wonder if they will survive it.

40

The first question that many couples ask is whether their sexual relationship will ever recover from the assault of infertility. Gone are the spontaneity, the lovemaking, the passion. All have been replaced by sex that is timed, scheduled, and conducted in a task-like manner. Many couples say that it becomes difficult to even remember how it felt to enjoy making love: the marital bed has become a place where they feel they must try their hardest to make something happen.

Couples may discover renewed sexual pleasure when they stop timing intercourse and move on to assisted reproduction. Inseminations and in vitro fertilization both serve to separate sex from procreation, making it at least possible for the sexual act to again bring pleasure. Sadly, however, many couples report that by the time they get to assisted reproduction, they are exhausted. Sex has become associated with work, with disappointment and failure, and it is extremely difficult to alter or dismiss these associations.

Although saddened, most couples are able to accept the loss of sexual pleasure and to maintain the belief that this loss is temporary. They anticipate years together after infertility and time then to restore and renew the pleasures that came from their physical relationship. And—to the extent that they have the inclination and energy—some try to find other ways of giving and receiving physical pleasure.

One of the most formidable challenges to a marriage comes with the diagnosis of a specific infertility problem. Although couples are strongly encouraged to regard any problem as a shared problem, this is often easier said than done. If one partner is identified as having a problem and the other is presumed fertile, feelings of guilt and self-blame inevitably arise. People's reactions vary, but it is not uncommon for the infertile partner to assume that his or her spouse will want to leave the marriage and find a fertile partner. This is almost never the case, but the infertile partner may behave in a disturbing and provocative way in an attempt to cause the fertile partner to want to leave. It is this behavior, not the infertility itself, that can cause serious marital problems.

Male infertility in particular challenges couples. For one thing, men feel a good deal of shame about their infertility, seeing it as evidence of impaired masculinity. In addition, the most effective treatment of male infertility requires that the woman undergo extensive procedures. Hence, many men find themselves in the very difficult—even humiliating—situation of having their wife poked and prodded in order to bypass deficiencies in their semen.

Most couples work hard to find ways to share their problem. However, this is difficult, even in situations in which both partners are diagnosed as having a problem or in which the infertility is unexplained. The difficulty comes from the fact that two people are patients, but only one of them can ever become pregnant. Inevitably, the woman, as the candidate for pregnancy, becomes identified as the patient. It is not uncommon for men to say that they feel like helpless bystanders in the process. Some also complain that staff in infertility treatment programs inadvertently contribute to this feeling by always addressing the woman.

Although most try to share the problem, couples also complain about the difficulties that they have talking with each other. Invariably, one partner (usually the woman) laments the fact that the other partner (usually the man) does not talk about feelings. Conversely, men frequently complain that all their wives do is talk about the problem, so much that they become tired of hearing about it. It becomes a central task for couples undergoing infertility treatment to find ways to keep communication open without one person feeling bombarded with talk about "the Problem" and the other feeling cut off.

Some couples try to establish a format for talking about infertility. For example, they may designate a time each day or each week when they will discuss their treatment efforts. Or they may set a time limit: they can only discuss infertility for X number of minutes each day. Regardless of what the specific format is, people often feel comforted by these arrangements; they feel that their ability to reach an agreement is evidence that infertility has not simply overtaken their lives and overshadowed their relationship.

Couples must also sort out how to deal with the public nature of the infertility process. What began as a very private decision to have a child together becomes public once a couple enters into infertility diagnosis and treatment. This loss of privacy extends beyond the loss of sexual intimacy; it means that the couple must relinquish control over their schedules. Partners inevitably envy those friends who can advance in their careers, travel, or enjoy recreation without having to live lives marked by the monthly cycle.

As individuals—and as a couple—people must make decisions about privacy. Early in their experience they realize that there are consequences to keeping their infertility to themselves (upsetting questions from curious friends and family, invitations to baby showers or other events from people who have no idea how much discomfort the invitation brings), and there are other consequences that come from being open about their situation (unsolicited advice from people who tell them to "just relax," well-intentioned questions from people who ask, "how's it going?"). Couples also realize that it is probably best for them to reach some agreement regarding whom to tell and what to tell them.

Couples for whom treatment is not successful face what is, for most, the formidable task of considering other options. Those who find that they are

in agreement about a second choice, whether it be adoption, gamete donation, or resolving without children, are fortunate. There are still decisions
to be made, but it is quite comforting and reassuring to know that they are
basically "on the same page." For them, the task in moving forward will
be to identify a course of action that feels comfortable for both of them.

Unfortunately, all couples are not automatically in agreement about a
second choice. I have found that in most instances, apparent differences
may have more to do with timing and pacing than with real discrepancies
in second choices. However, there are couples who do find themselves in
the unenviable position of having different ideas about what to do if they
are unable to achieve a successful pregnancy together. These couples do
face a marital crisis that may not easily resolve. Nonetheless, it extremely
rare for a couple to be ultimately divided by this decision. Instead, many
find that love conquers even the extraordinary difficulties of infertility and
enables them to reach unanticipated compromises.

As I observed earlier, infertility tests marriages, but tends to strengthen
rather than destroy them. We are fortunate to have essays testifying to the
resiliency of strong relationships in the face of infertility and to the affec-
tion, concern, and compassion that partners can feel—and show—for each
other. In "Sad Music," Frank Neal captures the pain of a man as he watches
the woman emerge from a miscarriage. Carla Duffy, in "Stay to the Outside," draws on some versatile advice from her beloved grandfather to cope,
together with her husband, with disappointments and loss and, eventually,
with pregnancy. In "Keeping Faith" Barbara Silck talks about how her marriage, though tested, was able to remain strong throughout infertility and
adoption. In "We," Barry G. Cronin talks about his efforts—and those of
his wife, Nancy—to share their infertility treatment.

―――――――  o  ―――――――

## SAD MUSIC
### *Frank Neal III*

I am a man in my early fifties, and occasionally I look back on events in
my past with regret or sadness or even anger. But I can attest to the truth
of the old saying that time dulls tribulations and enhances victories. Such
is the case with my wife's and my experiences with infertility, pregnancy
loss, and, ultimately, adoption.

Some people remember moments connected psychologically by certain
smells and sounds. I often associate important things that happened in my

life with music—uplifting, romantic, contemplative, but especially sad music. Sad music cuts through time.

The infertility vignette that I remember with particular sadness occurred in the afternoon of an early spring day. Another pregnancy had failed; another D&C had just been performed. My wife, suffering deeply with this loss, and caught in a vice of spiritual and physical pain, was for a time trapped at the hospital. These buildings, filled with a sea of people, some doing their jobs—some helpful, some soulless—became symbols of futility and loss. I knew that I had to get her out and away from there. I had to get her safely reconnected, back to the rational place of our love and the physical safety of our home, where I could protect her.

When we were finally able to leave the hospital, we were sent out a side entrance. I pulled the car up and had my wife lie down in the back seat under a blanket. Her head rested on a pillow. As I pulled out into a busy street, I watched her through the rearview mirror. I drove as carefully as I could, trying not to jostle her, but determined to get us safely home as soon as possible. The music on the car stereo haunted me as I drove; it was by CheckField, and it was quite sad. One song, "The Hitchhiker," was about a person who felt lost, and the lyrics, given our situation, were extremely poignant.

We made it home, and I helped my wife upstairs to bed. When she was safely under the covers, I went to the kitchen and made her some chicken soup. Only when she had finished eating could I feel the unclenching of the muscles in my shoulders. I silently vowed that there would be no more treatments. We held each other, and she fell asleep in my arms, but before she did, she told me that the music in the car had been beautiful and soothing.

It was that. And quiet and terribly sad. I have listened to that album only once—recently—in five years since. And the feelings and images of that pathetic, yet loving, little van ride home swept over me suddenly, clear and sharp as leaded crystal.

○

## STAY TO THE OUTSIDE
### Carla Duffy

It has been five years now since my husband, Marko, and I started trying to have a baby. During those years we've gone through a number of very difficult experiences, and unfortunately we're still going through them. We lost one baby at twenty weeks, and I had a miscarriage at nine weeks. Even as I write this—now four and a half months pregnant—I am living in fear, as initial prenatal testing suggested that our baby has Down syndrome.

Although it has been hard—awful, I must say—I have learned a lot through this ordeal. First and foremost, I've learned that my relationship with Marko is the most important thing in my life. There were times when I didn't believe it, when I was convinced that we would split up. Instead, we seem not only to have survived the turbulence, but to have emerged with a stronger relationship. I would like to take credit for some of this, but I have to say that it is Marko who has been—and steadfastly remains—the rock.

There have been many times along the way when I thought I was losing my mind, as well as my marriage. At each juncture, Marko has been there to pull me back and to make me see that everything has a positive side. Even at the darkest moments, he has been able to find a "silver lining." I'll admit that sometimes his positive outlook has been frustrating; I would be in the depths of despair and he'd be there telling me that everything would turn out OK. At times I felt like throwing a cold drink at him, but I realize now that if it wasn't for him, our world would have crumbled.

Marko has not been the only one who has helped me survive infertility and pregnancy loss. I have met some wonderful women along the way, I've had kind doctors and nurses, and my friends have been terrific. However, the other person who was been central in this experience—and remains so even after his recent death at the age of ninety-three—is my grandfather.

My grandfather was very different from Marko in many ways, but they had one important similarity: a love of life. Like Marko, my grandfather taught me "not to sweat the small stuff" and to live more fully in the moment. Before infertility I was a big planner—someone who always knew what I was going to be doing long in advance—but now I've learned to take life as it comes. I am more patient and much stronger emotionally than I ever thought I was or could be. What these two incredible men have taught me is that the really important things in life are health and family and friends and that it is always better to focus on what I have rather than what I don't have.

Over the past year, my grandfather grew increasingly weak, and several months ago he had to leave his home of many years and go into a nursing home. This was all very painful to see, yet through it all he kept his spirits up and remained wonderful company. My friends would tell me, "You're so good to visit him so often," but what they failed to realize was that I *loved* visiting him. My grandfather always told great stories and did so with a flair, making me laugh. Even now, when I cry over missing him, I can smile inside and remember his stories and his warmth.

More than anything, I wanted my grandfather to live to see my child. When I became pregnant this past fall, I believed—for the first time—that that might really happen. I knew that he did not have long to live, and it seemed that my pregnancy might have come at this time for a special reason—to bring him his great-grandchild before he died. So when he died during my pregnancy, it was very difficult.

Now as I wait to find out whether I will have a child who will be able to carry on my grandfather's wit, spirit, and optimism, Marko waits with me and remains my rock. When things get really bad, he reminds me of something that my grandfather told him when he ran the Boston Marathon. As he entered the field of many thousand runners, my grandfather said to him—with a great twinkle in his eye—"Stay to the outside. Then you may have a chance of winning the race."

My long marathon to motherhood continues. I'm staying to the outside because I feel my grandfather watching over me and guiding me along the way—and because I have Marko at my side.

○

## KEEPING FAITH
### *Barbara Silck*

Recently I took my four-month-old baby daughter, Kristen, for a visit to the fertility center where my husband, Fred, and I were patients for many years. I was excited to see the staff there—many of whom now feel like old friends—and I was certainly eager to have them meet Kristen. I was a bit apprehensive about returning to a place where I had felt so much pain and disappointment, but it was something that I knew I wanted to do.

Kristen and I received a great welcome! We had no sooner entered the waiting room—the place where I had my *worst* memories—than the nurses, office staff, and physicians came bounding out. They all seemed so happy to see me and to meet Kristen. As they enthusiastically handed her from one person to another, a couple came in and took seats in the waiting room. Suddenly, my joy at showing Kristen off was tempered by my concern for this couple. It felt like yesterday (*and* like a million years ago!) that I had been in their place. I remembered how helpless, angry, bereft I had felt. I remembered, also, how hurt and enraged I felt when people would bring a child, especially a baby, into the waiting room. Now here I was delighting in my beautiful new baby. I wanted to go over to them and explain. I wanted them to know that Kristen—the most perfect baby in the world for us—joined our family through adoption. I wanted to let them know that things would work out.

My work involves a lot of telephone customer service. Yesterday I was talking with a woman—a total stranger—who commented, after just a very brief phone exchange, that I sounded like "such a happy person." I was struck by this comment, both because she was absolutely correct—I *am* a happy person—and because there is a certain irony to my being so openly happy that even a total stranger can pick it up on the telephone. If she had seen me only six months ago, a year ago, two years, three years. . . .

I was not always happy. While Fred and I were in infertility treatment and later, when we were waiting to adopt, I was downright miserable. For different reasons, each experience tested me—and our marriage—to the limit. Now as I look back on both experiences, I feel very grateful that we emerged from them with our personal lives and our marriage intact.

For me the infertility experience felt like a complete defeat. I was certainly young enough to become pregnant (early to mid-thirties), our infertility was essentially unexplained (thereby giving us a "good prognosis"), and we received good treatment (several IVF attempts at a good program). Still, for some reason that I may never understand, we never conceived. Or I should say, *I* never conceived. That was what it felt like—for some reason *I* was failing. It was a terrible feeling; I had wanted to be a mother for as long as I could remember.

Fred wanted very much to be a father, but he always seemed to have other things going on that helped him through the experience. For one thing, Fred is a marathon runner and that, quite literally, kept him moving. For another, he is very involved in the Special Olympics. He does some great things for people in need and gets a lot of satisfaction, as well as recognition, in the process. So there were times when I felt like I was standing still and doing nothing, while Fred was moving his life along in fruitful directions. Even in the midst of it all, he began a second career as a real estate agent.

For me, by contrast, infertility felt like an experience of standing still. I had worked for my company for many years and stayed there because I wanted the benefits and job security and because I basically enjoy my work. Nonetheless, it was difficult being in a job that involved helping and pleasing people when I myself was feeling so miserable. I did my best not to show my impatience on the telephone at work, but it came out at other times.

Once or twice I almost lost it in the waiting room of the fertility center—the very place that I recently returned to so jubilantly. The women there would inevitably chat about their treatment, their situation, their worries and fears. Some of the time I liked participating in the conversations or enjoyed eavesdropping on others, but there were some people who simply drove me crazy. I remember one woman in particular, who was all of about twenty-five years old and complained loudly that her mother gave birth to her at sixteen, so that made her nine years late already. She was loud and obnoxious and stupid. Still, I couldn't believe it when nice, kind, soft-spoken me stood up and said to her, "If you don't stop talking like that someone may punch you out, and it may be me."

Fred didn't know what to make of me at times like that, and I will always be grateful to him for his patience. He would listen, not say a whole lot, and then reassure me that things would turn out all right. Sometimes his optimism only made me feel worse and more frustrated, but I guess it would have been a sorry state of affairs if both of us had been so down.

And then there came the point when we decided to adopt. It's funny that I say it that way, referring to a point in time; in reality, it was probably a slow transition that occurred over time. Still, looking back, it feels like there was a turning point. We were infertility patients and then we were pre-adoptive parents. Neither was easy.

There were a few people who helped us a lot in the adoption process. One was my nephew Sean, who is now twenty-one and was adopted at birth. I have always felt very close to him and our relationship convinced me long ago that I could certainly love an adopted child. The other person who helped me immensely is a little girl named Erin. She is a neighbor of ours who sought Fred and me out. Erin quickly won our hearts and taught me how much I could care for a child.

In addition to my nephew and my little angel, Erin, there were others who helped me along the path to adoption. I attended a support group with wonderful women, one of whom adopted before I did. Another person who helped is my cousin Joannie, who adopted a little girl from China. Having people close to me adopting and seeing their happiness went a long way toward helping me—and us—make the decision. Still, once we got there we discovered that we were only at the beginning of yet another difficult process.

I won't tell our long, agonizing adoption story, except to say that it was long and agonizing and, as is evident from the beginning of this essay, had a very happy ending. A new beginning. What I want to focus on now is survival: to take a look at how Fred and I managed to survive infertility and to feel, at least at this juncture, that what didn't break us made us stronger.

As I said, there were important people along the way. There was also faith. My religion has always been a central part of my life and it remains so. Certainly there were many times when my faith in God was shaken and when I questioned why good people like us seemed to be being punished. Nonetheless, I was able to hold fast to my faith and ultimately be strengthened by it.

Still, when I look back and try to determine what it was that got me through, it was my relationship with Fred. There were many times during our infertility treatment when we were angry at each other, and there were certainly times when he was frustrated with me and tired of all my complaints and unhappiness. But he never gave up on me or on our relationship. Rather, he maintained hope and a resolve that all would work out. His optimism drove me crazy, but it also provided me with an anchor to hold fast to.

Soon after Kristen arrived, we were asked to be interviewed for an evening news report on adoption. The local news crew arrived at our house with trucks and cameras and lights and spent a good deal of time interviewing us. When all was said and done, they aired only a very brief segment of the interview. I have it on tape and love to watch it because we look so happy and content. I especially cherish the image of Fred's beaming face as he says, "It was all worth it."

I hope that we reached some TV viewers who are going through infertility. I hope that they found hope in our happiness.

○

## WE

### Barry G. Cronin

The shots have started again. This time there is a different kind of shot, with a smaller needle, injected into the thigh. A different needle, and a different location on my wife's body. Same burning sensation, but Nancy tells me it's nothing. She always says it's nothing. She is the trooper. I am the helper. These are our roles, it seems, on our difficult road to becoming parents.

From experience we have learned the key to giving shots: rotation. You don't want to puncture the same spot too many times in a row. So, we give a shot to the same area of Nancy's stomach two days in a row, then move to the other side for another two days. We then return to the original side, and so on, until our cycle of shots is complete. This round of shots ended with one large, ominous-looking needle filled with Profasi, an ovulation inducer, which was administered to the hip pocket of Nancy's backside. This was a one-time-only shot.

You notice that I am saying "we." "We" give the shots. "We" receive the shots. We do our best to keep it "we," despite the fact that it is Nancy who must go through so much and I who can only do what I can to help her through it.

Nancy and I have been trying to have a child for just over three years, most of the time that we have been married. The doctors say that there is nothing physically wrong with us. We are just old, and age makes it more difficult to conceive. At thirty-eight and forty-three, we don't *feel* old. Married four years ago, we waited a year before trying to have a child.

Our fertility efforts began with Nancy charting her temperature. For a year and a half, every morning began with the beeping sound of a digital thermometer. And for a year and a half, we didn't become pregnant. During that time, Nancy read books on fertility and learned all that she could about her body and the little things we might both do to enhance our chances of becoming pregnant. We both avoided alcohol and started taking vitamins every day. I wanted to do more, but there was little more that *I* could do.

This has been very difficult for me—this strange experience of "we" and "I." Although I cannot personally become pregnant, I am trying as hard to achieve pregnancy as Nancy is. And although it is Nancy who must receive the shots and undergo uncomfortable procedures, I wince with her pain and feel it deeply inside me. If infertility has done nothing else for us, it has convinced us of the "we-ness" of our relationship. Not a bad feeling at all for people who "married late."

After a year and a half of trying on our own, we consulted an infertility specialist. He recommended that I have a sperm test and that Nancy have a laparoscopy. We agreed to have both tests and were relieved when the results showed each of us to be physically able to have children. Still, I was concerned by Nancy's condition after the laparoscopy.

I had dropped Nancy off at the hospital for a one o'clock surgery, and I was to pick her up four hours later. When I arrived at her bed in the recovery room, she was drowsy and incoherent. We waited awhile, hoping she would begin to feel better, then a nurse wheeled her to the front door. I helped her lie down on the back seat of the car, and we drove away. It was a long, painfully quiet twenty-minute ride home. I felt terrible seeing my best friend lying there, so uncomfortable and having gone through so much.

During the long night following Nancy's surgery, I finally realized that she and I were in for a complicated journey if we were going to have a child. I wanted to have a son or daughter so badly, and I knew that Nancy dreamed of it all the time. I also wanted it to happen soon so that Nancy would not have to go through any more than she already had. She was doing almost all the work and making the sacrifices so that we both could have a family.

It was at that point that I began to turn more seriously to God through prayer. I prayed to God for a child and asked that if we could not have a child right away, we be given the strength to persevere. I told God that we would accept any path planned for us. I began to pray often and each time the thought of a child crossed my mind, I said a prayer. I prayed also for Nancy, hoping that she would not be too stressed by our complicated road to having a child.

The next test that we faced was the HSG. Again, Nancy would have to undergo an unpleasant procedure and I would again be the helpless bystander. The test went well and reconfirmed the finding that "all systems were go." Our doctor suggested we try a conservative approach to assisting our fertility—six months of Clomid. Again I prayed to God that this would work. It did not.

Our next step was IUI. This also meant moving on to injectable medications. Although I didn't like the idea of injecting my wife—when Nancy and I exchanged marriage vows I never thought that giving injections would be part of our relationship—I did take it very seriously. And as I said at the start, I became good at it. Then one day, it seemed that my efforts—our efforts—were being rewarded. Nancy greeted me at the door one beautiful May afternoon and asked me if I was ready to be a father. *Ready? Father!* I was speechless.

Neither Nancy nor I could believe that the treatment had worked this quickly. Once we came down to earth, I again turned to God. My prayers had been answered, and I now needed new prayers—of thanksgiving.

Two weeks after that initial test, Nancy and I went to the doctor for an ultrasound. It was an amazing experience. There it was—the tiny beating of our baby's heart. We decided then that we wanted to wait until the baby was born to know whether it was a boy or a girl. Looking back, I guess we felt that our efforts to have a child had already been so dominated by technology that we needed the pregnancy to remain as natural as possible.

Nancy and I loved being expectant parents. It felt wonderful. We were so proud and so excited. For several weeks it seemed that all we did was smile. We were especially thrilled to see Nancy's mother's reaction; she was so pleased that she could barely talk about being a grandmother for the first time.

I was away on a business trip when I received a call from Nancy. She was eleven weeks pregnant, and although we knew we were almost out of the riskiest period, she was worried. That night, she miscarried. She miscarried, and I was far away, unable to return until the following day.

If I had felt helpless in the past, I felt it even more so at the time of the miscarriage. "We" were pregnant and yet, again, it was Nancy going through it. Again, I was comforted by prayer. I prayed to God to take care of Nancy and to take care of our unborn—now never to be born—child.

Nancy recovered well from the miscarriage, and the doctor again assured us that we could have children. We took a nice vacation and, following doctors' advice, let Nancy rest her body for two months. During that time we were sad but also comforted to know that indeed we could get pregnant. Then it was time to try again.

Our second round of IUI did not go as well as the first, and we are now at the point of IVF. In some ways this feels like a big step, and in others, it does not. Experience has been a great teacher, and we both feel well equipped to handle the treatment, the needles, the ups and downs, the "we" and the "I." Experience has also taught us to be patient, and it has taught us that prayer helps.

I remain hopeful that Nancy and I will be parents together. I hope we do not have to wait too much longer, but in the meantime, I take comfort in knowing we can do it. Infertility has taught us both a great deal about sharing. About being a team. We are.

# 5

# INFERTILITY AND FAMILY

INFERTILITY IS ABOUT CREATING and building a family. Nonetheless, infertility also poses significant challenges to family life; relationships with parents, siblings, and in-laws can become strained as family members fail to understand each other's experiences. Hence, infertile couples are often struck by a strange irony: they feel distanced from their families at the very time that they have the strongest need for closeness.

A difficult family scenario occurs when one sibling becomes pregnant while another is struggling with infertility. Although this is almost always upsetting, it is especially trying when the woman who is pregnant is the younger sister (or sister-in-law) of the woman who is infertile. Another upsetting situation occurs when there are two or more expectant couples in a family, leaving the infertile couple feeling isolated and left out. There are instances in which one sibling has two, three, perhaps even four children during the time that another family member is trying to conceive. Relationships between fertile and infertile siblings are difficult because feelings of envy and competition inevitably arise, often evoking former childhood rivalries.

Although these situations—and certainly others—are inherently challenging, they become more or less so depending on how they are handled by the family members involved. Those who try to be sensitive to the feelings of their infertile siblings can significantly reduce the trauma of the situation. Simple things, such as telling the infertile sibling first—and in private—about the pregnancy, establish good will. Similarly, the pregnant sibling who encourages her infertile sister or sister-in-law to take care of her own needs—even if it means skipping a baby shower or not visiting new mother and child in the hospital—conveys a sense that she understands the pain of infertility and that she deeply values their relationship.

Relationships between infertile couples and their parents are difficult in different ways. Sometimes these difficulties arise because the would-be grandparents are actually experiencing "secondhand" infertility themselves: they long to be grandparents, and their children's losses are felt very personally. Alternatively, they may already be grandparents several times over, and though they would welcome more grandchildren, they may not have a personal longing for more. Perhaps because of this—or perhaps because they are trying to reduce the stress their children feel— they may say things that are unintentionally hurtful, such as "having children isn't so great after all" (tough to hear from one's parents) or "You should be happy to be together; you are lucky to have found each other." And of course, there are the presumably well-intentioned but blundering parents who say, "Relax, then it will happen" or "I heard from so-and-so about her daughter, who became pregnant by . . ."

For a variety of reasons, some couples do not tell their families about their infertility. Some feel that if they tell family members, people will worry, ask too many questions, or offer too much advice. Others do not tell because they feel that conception is a private matter, and they do not want to tell others—even those closest to them—such personal information. Still others keep silent because of feelings of shame; they feel that infertility is a shameful experience and don't want their loved ones to know this about them.

Some couples are not in agreement about whether family members should be told about the infertility and if so, what they should be told. This disagreement may have to do with differences in family styles or differences in their relationships with their families, or it may have to do with the diagnosis: the infertile partner may not want others to know that he or she has been identified as having the problem.

Regardless of their reasons for not telling, couples who do not share their infertility with their families almost always encounter painful experiences. Unknowingly, family members will make an array of difficult comments, ranging from "What are the two of you waiting for?" to "You should be thinking more about starting a family and less about your careers/traveling/having fun." In addition, there will be difficult family occasions such as baby showers or religious ceremonies celebrating a newborn's arrival. These events, focusing so intensely on babies, inevitably prompt comments and questions from well-intentioned but uninformed relatives who want to know when there will be other arrivals.

Occasionally, there are couples who decide to tell some family members but not others about their infertility. This may occur if one person feels strongly about telling his or her family and the other feels equally intensely about maintaining privacy. It may also occur if there are certain family members who would predictably make things more difficult for the infertile couple. In either event, it is hard to control the flow of this information, and efforts to do so may intensify the stress of infertility.

What is sadly missed in some of the interactions that occur between infertile people and their families—especially their parents—is the shared sense of loss. The couple is seeking to add a child to the *family,* not just to their couple relationship. Their failed cycles and other disappointments represent losses for all family members. For those whose parents are not yet grandparents, these losses are particularly significant. Just as the infertile couple must stand on the sidelines as friends announce pregnancies, so also must would-be grandparents stand by as their friends proudly show pictures and tell tales of grandchildren.

The shared losses in a family are especially compelling when parents age and become ill: their children, already struggling with their own losses, feel that their infertility is cheating their parents of the joy of grandparenting and, poignantly, their future children of grandparents. Although some couples are able to express these feelings to their parents and to gain comfort in their ability to experience infertility together, others withdraw into isolation and sometimes anger.

In addition to dealing with the disappointments and frustrations that occur during infertility treatment, some families face other tasks as well. Family members may learn from children or siblings that the couple plans to adopt. This news, which may come entirely unexpectedly if the couple was not open about their infertility, can be startling to family members. To the extent that they are unfamiliar or possibly uncomfortable with adoption, this news is unsettling, even upsetting. Family members who find themselves in this situation realize that they must begin to prepare for being part of an adoptive family.

Perhaps even more challenging are those instances in which gamete donation occurs within a family. Relatives may learn that one sister has offered to donate eggs to another. This scenario—and others involving third party reproduction—presents families with situations that, in all probability, they never anticipated. The tasks that they face range from adjusting to the news itself, which may seem very strange to them, to preparing to welcome a child into the family who may be the genetic offspring of one relative and the gestational offspring of another.

We live in a time of changing families. Interracial marriage, international adoption, single motherhood, and lesbian and gay parents have all created families that do not look like traditional two-parent families. Perhaps these other new kinds of families—many of whom are quite visible—are helpful to infertile couples trying to forge new paths. Being "out there" as they are, they remind all of us that a family can be shaped and defined in many ways.

In the pages that follow, we see family and infertility from two very different vantage points. In "Not in the Family Way," Maggie Rogers talks about her experience as the infertile member of a family of "Fertile Myrtles." Then, through a very different lens in "Random Acts of Love," Kathleen McKiernan Cormier tells of the special bonds that exist in a family built through two generations of adoption. In "Father and Sons," Sam Guckenheimer offers the compelling observations of an expectant father, waiting to meet his Cambodian-born son.

○

## NOT IN THE FAMILY WAY
### *Maggie Rogers*

My mother bore nine children in thirteen years, all by exhilarating natural childbirth. She was nicknamed "Fertile Myrtle," and she never confessed to a moment of discomfort during pregnancy, labor, or delivery. Other women may have had trouble conceiving or may have lost babies through miscarriage, but in our house, childbearing was one of life's greatest adventures, a heroic odyssey to be embraced and, yes, even enjoyed. Fertility was an unquestioned blessing, and motherhood was a woman's inevitable reward.

The childless aunts and cousins who gathered with us at holiday time were certainly odd fixtures in that rollicking household dominated by children. When my own sisters began having children, mostly unplanned, the family tradition of unbridled fertility continued. By now, I am an aunt thirteen times over, preparing to welcome the fourteenth baby. I have spent the last decade watching a parade of little ones burp and crawl and toddle and walk. Last Christmas, I held my three-month-old niece in my arms and sobbed uncontrollably—the sweetness was unbearable, the pain sublime.

Infertility. I am the first woman in my family or my husband's to travel this ground, so cold and strange. So it is not usually the family nest, the seven-sister brood, that comforts me on discouraging days; instead, it is the faces and voices of friends who have also had a rocky road to the distant dream of motherhood.

There is the friend and former coworker who suffered her first miscarriage at my wedding seven years ago. Two more miscarriages and much heartache later, she has adopted two Columbian children. There is the old hometown friend who has spent the last few years being injected, inspected, and dejected (as Arlo Guthrie would say) but who can't seem to get a clear diagnosis. And, of course, there are the brave and wondrous women of my RESOLVE infertility support group who have shared their stories—and listened to mine—for the last year and a half.

We have all surfaced in these last months from the depths of despair with the harrowing memories of nearly drowning—feeling alone, out of control, swallowed in salty, watery whirls. We know what it's like to feel victimized by fate, the medical establishment, insensitive remarks, and our own utter helplessness. No other part of our lives has brought so much chaos and frustration, yet all the parts of us have been somehow shattered and need repair: our marriages and careers, our passions and interests, our friends and families, our faith, our hope, our self-esteem. That we can laugh about the many indignities of infertility now—that we can swap advice on adoption and even listen to tales of new motherhood—is, to me, a remarkable sign that we are healing. But healing is a slow process, and the scars we bear are not always visible, or quick to fade.

I do have a real scar, a thick pink vertical ridge that slices my belly from navel to pubic bone, a lasting token of my laparotomy last June; I lost a tube in that operation. My surgeon told me that the bands of scar tissue, or adhesions, that she was attempting to remove resembled a Manhattan traffic jam. I can hardly blame her for sacrificing the tube. Or can I?

One of the peculiar quirks of infertility is that the patient is often as well-informed as the doctor, having researched her condition and explained it to countless internists, gynecologists, specialists, surgeons, and endocrinologists over the years. My general distrust of the medical profession is an inherited family characteristic, based in large part on my own woeful early experiences with those people in white. There was a botched tonsillectomy that resulted in messy hemorrhaging. (I can still see the doctor's once-white jacket splattered with my blood.) Far worse, there was the teenage trauma of a burst appendix that was difficult to diagnose. As I lay writhing and moaning, without pain medication, four male doctors carried out a horrible prolonged pelvic exam while a nurse begged them to put me out of my misery. No wonder I have so little tolerance for gynecological exams.

Since then, I have sacrificed my privacy and dignity on the examining table countless times because of infertility. So far, it has all proved, as they say, fruitless. Though some women lose their faith in God during this process, I have simply reaffirmed my lack of faith in those fallible humans who perform no medical miracles on me. Ah, how I wish believing in miracles could make them happen!

My problem can be directly traced to the ruptured appendix and the resulting emergency surgery that left extensive scarring, inside and out. Because the memories of that experience are so painful, I tucked them away in some remote corner of my unconscious, where they gathered dust for years. When I got married in 1980, I wrote to the surgeon whose scalpel and hands had so violated me during adolescence. Did he think that the emergency appendix operation could have in any way affected my childbearing capabilities? He responded in professional gobbledygook, hemming and hawing that he wasn't sure, but he thought, maybe, that it would not.

Somehow, that doctor's vague assurances were little consolation to me six years later as I lay in the pre-op ward of a Boston hospital, shivering in my skimpy green johnny, awaiting general anesthesia and the operation that would, perhaps, undo the damage caused by the ruptured appendix. As I trembled with anxiety and chill in that room last June, I could not have known that I would emerge from surgery with one Fallopian tube gone and no better than a 20 percent chance of ever becoming pregnant. I only knew that major surgery—that most dreaded of experiences for the person who likes to be in control of her life—was my only chance at all.

In the weeks of recuperation that followed my hospital stay, I relaxed in the comfort of my home, basking in the gifts, care, and attention of my husband, family, and friends. I also grappled with the odds—that the medical miracle I had secretly hoped for might never happen, that the magical presto! pregnancies of my mother and sisters might not be my path to motherhood. And yet, as I wrestled with those demons, I had the dim realization that another miracle had taken place. I was surrounded by people who had stood by me despite their confusion and embarrassment at my odd predicament. They had come through my infertility with me, had listened and learned and been transformed by it.

I will not easily forget the day my father carried a supper tray to my bed and stood, bewildered, as I burst into tears at the sight of that meal so lovingly prepared. And how reassuring it has been to see two mothers (my own and my husband's) leap across the gap in experience and understanding to lend their support, their strength, and their shoulders when I needed them. (I'd like to be able to muster half their loyalty and wisdom for my own children someday.) I am also finding new ways to approach those sisters and sisters-in-law who move into pregnancy and parenthood so effortlessly (or so it seems). Yes, I still ache over each new baby, but each new mom who acknowledges my pain helps to diminish it.

I must be making progress on this strange road. At New Year's, when I cradled my three-week-old nephew, I didn't feel my heart pound or my eyes water. Instead, I breathed deeply, indulged myself in the soft, sweet pleasure of his touch and smell, and wished for him a world full of promise.

Someday, the promise of motherhood will be fulfilled for me. I suppose we all have to hang onto that golden thread to get us through the tough times. Yes, I grow weary of the dashed hopes every month, but I grow with them, and so does my husband. There is a raw and intense intimacy that we share in those moments of disappointment that is showing me a new side to this commitment called marriage. Our most recent "communion" came during a tropical vacation last winter, when my always-reliable twenty-nine-day cycle lasted an agonizing thirty-six days. He openly wept with me as my period brought us crashing back to reality after days adrift in a fuzzy fantasy world of nursery chimes and baby-soft skin, all mixed up with the exotic setting of palm trees, surf, and sunshine.

By now, that episode has taken its place among the many ups and downs that make up my history of infertility. My husband and I are plugged back into the ordinary events of daily life, and we find some measure of challenge and comfort in the familiar—our jobs, our home, our friends and families, our dog. I find myself thinking less about pregnancy and fertility, instead seeking inspiration from life's tiny wonders: a spring snowfall, a call from some long-lost friend, the big hearts and tiny hands of neighborhood children. Each time a friend or sister or mother calls, I hear myself telling them things I didn't know I knew: that I'm getting better at playing this waiting game, that I'm ready for the next move—whatever it is, and that maybe I can even win, scars and all. Each day I seem to shed old skin. And, oddly enough, the bright pink scar on my belly begins to stretch as I grow into my new skin.

○

## RANDOM ACTS OF LOVE
### *Kathleen McKiernan Cormier*

Earlier this evening, my husband, Steve, our two young sons, my mother-in-law, my father-in-law, and I sat enjoying the food and company of our Sunday dinner, and a thought occurred to me. We are a very close and loving group who care deeply about each other and consider family our number one priority. Yet strangely, our sons—both of whom were adopted at birth by my husband and me—were the only two "blood relatives" seated at our table. I chuckled to myself and thought, how did we all get here?

The road to creating this family began with the years of infertility experienced by my in-laws. There was little treatment available thirty-five years ago, and they were lucky to resolve their infertility through adoption. My mother-in-law worked at a law office where a young girl, who would be the birthmother of their son, came into the office seeking assistance with placing her baby for adoption. My in-laws paid this woman's living and medical expenses for the final three months of her pregnancy, and they ended up with a son, who entered their family when he was five days old. They have been the best parents, and Steve has been the best son. I think they are all exceedingly lucky to have found each other, as I feel exceedingly lucky to have found my husband and, by extension, my in-laws.

Subsequently, for Steve and me, the road once again included years of infertility, including numerous attempts at conception through in vitro fertilization. Though our efforts were repeatedly unsuccessful, we felt grateful for having the opportunity to experience hope, even in short and erratic bursts. Yet as the cycles grew increasingly monotonous, these hopeful moments came with less frequency, and we somehow together found the nerve to say "enough." I have heard many horror stories about the quality of care received by infertility patients. We, however, worked with many wonderful, caring professionals and were treated with respect, dignity, and empathy. While we didn't—nor will we ever—regret the extraordinary means by which we attempted to conceive a baby, we found ourselves strangely relieved to regain some control over our lives as we turned our hopes of creating a family toward adoption. Though I never felt the need to mourn the "loss" of my biological child, I did spend some time getting over the fact that I would probably never experience pregnancy and childbirth. I also worried that Steve may have felt resentful for failing at his chance to create a blood relative. When I questioned him on this, he assured me that his goal was for us to become parents, not to produce a biological offspring. As Steve is perhaps the most honest and self-assured person I've ever known, I believed him.

Adoption seemed a very natural path to parenthood for both of us to pursue. My own mom battled infertility for years (I am an only child, as is Steve). I always had had, in the back of my mind, the thought that I would undergo a similar struggle that might perhaps someday lead to adoption. (Yet, like all optimistic infertility patients, I expected to have a "few" biological children and then adopt.) Steve says that because he was adopted, he suspected that adoption would play some part in the formation of his family. Hence, we shifted our attention, admittedly with some trepidation but with surprising ease, from our near-nightly injections to educating ourselves about the adoption process. We began preparing for our homestudy—the formal determination of our suitability as adoptive parents—with the usual mix of disbelief (are there really children to be adopted?), caution (let's be sure to protect a tiny corner of our hearts; everyone has heard the horror stories!), fear (so many unknowns, so little control!) and, above all, open hearts (neither of us doubted that we could immediately and completely love our adopted child). I armed myself with every available book on all aspects of adoption, and though I urged Steve to read these same books, he had little interest; he already felt equipped to jump right in.

We had no choice but to jump right in, as things began happening very, very quickly. Within a few months we commenced and completed the homestudy process. Soon thereafter, we were presented with a prospective match and, then, our son. We had the wonderful experience of meeting our son's birthparents, which was, undoubtedly, one of the most profoundly moving moments of our lives. Our meeting was not unlike our entire adoption experience, as it came about with little time for preparation—or internal struggle. We were suddenly thrown together and made an immediate connection. We asked why they had chosen us for their child and received this simple answer: "We knew you were the right ones. Steve was adopted. We are not ready to be parents, and we know that you are." We felt so blessed.

The bonding with our son was immediate and overwhelming, and our joy knew no bounds as we adjusted to our role as parents. We had defined ourselves by our infertility for such a seemingly long time, then later as prospective adoptive parents for a thankfully shorter time. Yet we soon were so sleep-deprived that we had little time or energy for introspection on how we had gotten to where we were. Then, as our son turned nine months old, and just as we seemed to be getting a handle on our new role (we were finally getting some sleep!), we received a call from the adoption agency informing us that our son's birthparents again found themselves expecting a baby; they desperately hoped we would consider adopting this baby, too. Two months later, we became parents for the second time in an eleven-month period when we were presented with another son—the biological and adoptive brother of our first child. We were able to spend some quality time with the birthparents, who once again proved themselves as remarkably selfless people. We felt doubly blessed.

Steve has always told me that he considers himself the luckiest person in the world for having birthparents who, in the ultimate act of selflessness, made a decision solely with his best interest at heart. Now, Steve finds himself an adopted son with two adopted sons of his own. We are truly a family whose collective lives have been dependent on numerous random acts of love. Our dinner conversation today revolved around unextraordinary events of the day: Who would win the Super Bowl? Had we seen the latest film? Did the babies have enough to eat? The extraordinary event is that we have all come together as a family, and we never take that for granted.

○

## FATHERS AND SONS
### Sam Guckenheimer

"Tomorrow is Saint Valentine's Day"—that's what Ophelia sings when she goes mad. It was almost Valentine's Day when we learned about Chetra. After a year and a half of waiting for a domestic adoption to materialize, we had applied for one from Cambodia. Things started happening instantly. We'd just Fed Ex'ed our papers in a few days before. First came a phone call: "We have an infant boy. Do you want him? Please give me an answer right away. We need to find a family." "Yes, of course, we want him."

Tomorrow is now Saint Patrick's Day. It's also my son's three-month birthday. The thing is, I've never met him. I was supposed to travel to Cambodia today to adopt him. I was supposed to have him in my arms by now. But I don't.

I had my tickets. Cambodia is on the other side of the earth. No country takes longer to get to. I had my bag full of prescriptions and diapers ready to go. My wife, Monica, was going to stay home, since we couldn't predict how long the trip would be. For the first time in ages, I was excited about traveling. I'd been reading my history and language books. Even changing planes in Saigon seemed like it would be exciting. But I'm not going now.

Someone in the government has better things to do than approve my adoption. I can understand that. There's a civil war, martial law, show trials and mock elections. Chetra's adoption won't influence the play of power one iota. No one will get wealthy or powerful or kill his enemies by giving Chetra a family any sooner. I know that.

After the stunning phone call, we got a faxed medical report, completed in Franglais on a UN form: "Very good developpement. Good weight, good measurements." A couple of weeks later, a postage-stamp-sized picture. Huge eyes. Alert. Can he smile yet? Who does he look like?

The travel arrangements. Touch and go every day. At the end, daily calls to Cambodia. Usually you don't get through. Often the circuits are down, probably because of power outages, who knows? Then the news last night: "Don't come. Papers aren't so far along." Yeah, I thought they were waiting for the prime minister's signature—imagine a country where the prime minister has to approve every adoption!—but no, they're not typed yet. Stuck in another office. "Well, could I come and wait if it's going to be a few days?" "You can come, sure, that's your decision, but it will be several weeks at least. Are you willing to stay in country that long? Maybe better to schedule when we know it will work, in two months." Oh, OK, we'll do that. I've been here before. Three years ago this month, something worse happened. A birthmother chose us to adopt her soon-to-be-born son. Then he was born. We confirmed the meeting, bought our tickets, packed our bags, and the night before traveling, heard she had changed her mind. Of course it wasn't about us. She'd just decided to parent. But to us it felt like she'd decided that *we* wouldn't get to parent.

And we'd been here before that. Five years ago, Monica was five months pregnant when we learned that our son would be crippled with Down syndrome, and we decided to abort. Our choice? Yes, we ideally could have given life to that fetus, but it would have been unfair. Children have enough strikes against them without having to be knowingly brought into the world handicapped. They might be cute kids, but when they grow up, the world no longer finds them so cute.

Why am I still thinking about that? There's a voice that says, *I should be over this. We did get a daughter, who's now two and delightful. Why am I complaining?* I think that's my father's voice; I'm not sure.

Father survived by reminding himself of all the bad things that didn't happen to him. He sheltered his mother in his house for thirty years. He hated her so much that they never spoke. Only his wife (my mother) spoke to her, in her only language, which the children didn't understand. I can't remember how many times my mother would talk about the past and say, "We had no choice." The thing is, I never remember asking the question, and when I did ask something, she always seemed to answer something else. Something about not having a choice.

Father didn't even answer that much. He was just silent, except when he got angry. I guess that's how he communicated. If he got angry, you knew you were doing the wrong thing. When I was a child, I wished that I could do something right, but I never found out how. Later, when I was grown up, my father began to talk about the past too, but only the really distant past. I guess that was the time for him before there were no more choices in the world.

Father was a great stockpiler. When he died, I thumbed through his closets. Of all the children, I was the only one who might be able to wear his clothes. I took some suits and a jacket. I'm not sure why. I didn't need them, and they were ugly, but it seemed that my father would want me to use them if I could. Most things I threw away. He kept every slip of paper he'd ever had. Twenty-year-old gas station receipts and canceled insurance policies were preserved equally with pictures and letters from his grandchildren. They were all in a locked strongbox, hidden in a drawer behind his socks.

Father was so numb that he could not make even the simple choices of life. His house was overflowing with paper, and he couldn't choose to throw any of it away. At his funeral, people I'd never met came up to me to say how much I resembled him. At the time I was flattered. Afterward, I wasn't. I didn't want to be like him—a numbed survivor.

I wanted to live life with feeling. I made as many choices as I could, easy ones, hard ones, unusual ones, and often wrong ones. I just didn't think that building a family would be one of the hard ones. I thought you stopped using contraception and it happened. I was wrong.

It took seven years of medical intervention, a failed pregnancy with late abortion, and a fallen-through adoption to get our daughter. Then we waited eighteen months in vain for a domestic baby before giving up and applying to Cambodia. Then we were ready to go, again. And now it's delayed.

I think about my father. He survived too, but he never *lived*. I want to live. I want my family to live and flourish and know that we *lived* together. We named our daughter Zoë—Greek for "life."

Abraham was a survivor, too. He was ninety-nine and Sarah ninety, when God taunted them with the promise of a child. They thought it was a cruel joke, until they conceived Isaac. The name means, "he laughs." "I will name him Isaac," Sara said, "because he makes me laugh." They learned what it was to live. We chose the name Isaac for our son, but he was the boy whose birthmother changed her mind. We don't know what she named him. We'll find a different name for Chetra. Maybe this time we'll use "life" again, perhaps from another language.

Chetra reminds me of all the choices we made that formed and failed to form our family. He *will* join us—eventually, just not for another two months. Sure, he won't know or remember that at three months he almost joined us, but that the event got delayed. He won't remember, but we will. And we'll love him every bit as much, whether tomorrow or in two months. It's still not fair, to him or to us.

I don't know whether he will be our first or third son. The other two were never ours to count, at least not in the socially accepted way. That didn't keep us from naming them and letting them into our hearts.

*You know, we're very spoiled. A hundred years ago, only half of infants survived childhood anyway. Infant mortality is a reality all humanity has faced and survived. It's much worse than these imaginary losses. Get over them.* That's my father's voice speaking inside me, again.

It's hard not to listen to Father, because he reasons so well. He knows a hundred ways to tell me that I'm wrong and a hundred subtler ways to dismiss my feelings.

Maybe Chetra can help me choose when not to listen. He'll be five months old when we meet. He should have a healthy cry by then.

## Update

Sam traveled to Phnom Penh on May 8 and arrived on May 10 (Mother's Day). He and his son returned home on May 14. Sam and Monica sent out announcements that read:

### ELIAS CHETRA GUCKENHEIMER

| Into this world | Dec. 17, 1997 |
| Into our hearts | Feb. 4, 1998 |
| Into our home | May 14, 1998 |

### A BLESSING

# 6

# INFERTILITY AND FRIENDSHIP

AS MANY PEOPLE HAVE OBSERVED, men and women tend to have different types of friendships, different feelings about their friendships, and different ways of establishing and maintaining these friendships. Often, though not always, infertility presents greater challenges to the friendships of women than it does to the friendships of men. Some of this is because women are the ones who are trying to become pregnant and they are the ones who must endure the grief, envy, and unexpected resentment that they feel when friends become pregnant. Some of this is also because women's friendships are often based more on shared conversation than on shared activity, and feelings about fertility and infertility tend to interrupt shared conversation more easily than shared activity.

## Women's Friendships and Infertility

There are several ways in which infertility challenges women's friendships. These challenges come when one friend becomes pregnant and another struggles with infertility; when an infertile friend is invited to a baby shower, a christening, or a bris; when one friend opens a letter or a holiday card and learns that an old friend is pregnant. These challenges recur when the friend later announces a second or even a third pregnancy or when other members of a group of friends announce that they, too, are pregnant.

Despite the multiple challenges that they face, friendships that matter—ones in which both women are resourceful and willing to sometimes put personal feelings aside for the good of the relationship—survive infertility. In fact, many such friendships are actually enhanced by the experience: friends learn, as marital partners do, that their relationship can withstand adversity. This is both satisfying and reassuring.

But how does this happen? How do two women manage to keep their friendship alive and well and solid when one is experiencing infertility and another is not? It seems that the key ingredients—not surprisingly—are communication and compromise.

The communication between friends regarding fertility and infertility is complicated. Given that both women begin the experience with little preparation for how divisive it will feel, there is often a difficult period in which each is feeling her way—and sometimes makes mistakes in the process. One common example is the friend that doesn't know how to tell her friend that she is pregnant, who then attempts either to avoid the subject or to avoid her friend entirely. In either event, her actions inadvertently hurt her infertile friend, who in most cases would prefer to be told the truth promptly and directly.

Infertile women also make mistakes in communication. Like their fertile friends who try to cope with a difficult subject by avoiding it, infertile women sometimes withdraw from their friends when they need them most. Many feel intense conflict: they want their friends to express interest and concern, but they are also unclear about what they want their friends to say and ask and offer. Rather than figure out what they need to say to a friend and what might be helpful for their friend to say to them, they withdraw, feeling injured and isolated.

Part of the difficulty in communication between infertile women and their friends involves education. Women who have not experienced infertility are unfamiliar with diagnoses, procedures, and treatment options, to say nothing of the accompanying feelings. Many say the wrong thing or ask the wrong question because of a lack of information. Their infertile friends must make some determination as to how much they want and need to teach their friends about infertility.

Fortunately, most enduring friendships overcome the awkwardness and the disconnections that occur during infertility diagnosis and treatment. Once friends begin to figure out ways to maintain their relationship, especially when one is pregnant, they are back on track. To their surprise, however, this track may actually involve less contact, fewer visits together, less apparent sharing and conversation. It is entirely normal for the pregnant friend to want to be with people who can celebrate her pregnancy, and it is normal for her to want to begin to meet other pregnant women and, after delivery, new mothers. Similarly, it is almost always helpful for infertile women to seek out the companionship of other women going through infertility.

Compromise joins communication in preserving friendship during infertility. These compromises are often most evident around the time when a fertile friend has her baby. Although it would be her wish—if circumstances were different—that her close friend attend (if not give) her baby shower, and although she would like to visit with her friend shortly after childbirth, neither may be possible. It is excruciatingly difficult for most infertile women to attend baby showers and equally distressing to visit a friend on a maternity floor or at home immediately after birth. Similarly, although it might be the infertile friend's wish to avoid seeing her friend at all in the weeks just prior to and immediately following the birth of her child, a total withdrawal often feels too potentially damaging to the relationship. Instead, many friends find a way to compromise: they go out to dinner together as a twosome instead of seeing each other in the joyous crowd of the baby shower, or they plan a visit a week or so after the baby is born, when it can, again, be just the two of them.

It is important, of course, for friends to recognize and respect that both pregnancy and infertility are experiences that heighten emotions and feelings of self-concern and self-centeredness. To the extent that each can cut her friend some slack in this regard, they are tending the friendship. Again, it is entirely normal for a pregnant woman to be absorbed in her pregnancy and intrigued by her changing body. Similarly, it is entirely understandable that someone going through infertility treatment is going to be focused on the changes in and demands on *her* body. No matter how close they are and how mutually concerned, it will be nearly impossible for them to listen to each other.

Sadly, though infrequently, there are friendships that do not survive infertility. They are few, but situations do exist in which one person or the other—or both—cannot tolerate the ways in which fertility and infertility are challenging their relationship. Such people tend to feel misunderstood and uncared for, and if they do not successfully communicate these feelings to their friend, they become estranged. Given the charged emotions during this time, it is easy, although sad, to understand how this estrangement can lead to a permanent rupture in the relationship.

In addition to relationships that begin long before infertility, there are those that begin because of infertility. Not surprisingly, infertility brings women together. They meet in their doctor's waiting room or in a support group or at a RESOLVE meeting.

Most are very grateful to meet someone who is feeling many of the same things they are. Information and experiences, as well as feelings, are exchanged and shared.

Although some of the new friendships that begin with infertility endure for many years, others do not. People meet, share, and move on. One of the most potentially disruptive events in an "infertile friendship" is when one of the women becomes pregnant: it is one thing when a fertile friend conceives but quite another when a fellow traveler through infertility is suddenly on another path. For this reason, some infertile friendships end soon after they begin; they don't have a long, solid history to draw on and can more easily be destroyed by news of a pregnancy. Other friendships grow over time, through pregnancy/adoption and early parenthood, and develop a rich and shared history.

## Men's Friendships

Men tend to have friendships that involve more doing than talking. Men like to participate in or attend a sporting event together. Or they will share a beer and talk about sports or investments or their jobs. It is less common for men to get together to talk about feelings. As a result, infertility—which involves so many feelings—may not have a great impact on their relationships. Infertility is certainly less likely to affect the format of friendship between men than that between women, who may need to spend less time together when one is pregnant.

Although men do not always talk about feelings, the feelings are there. Hence, infertility can also affect the underpinnings of male friendships. A man undergoing infertility diagnosis and treatment may still have a beer with the guys, but he may find it more difficult to laugh, to be enthusiastic and join in with what's happening. If he and his wife are in a high-tech treatment, it may also be more difficult to take the time to play tennis or racquetball or golf with his buddies.

Men have known for their whole lives that they cannot become pregnant, but most have assumed that they could impregnate their wives. It may be very difficult for a man to be with his friends when they have children or when their wives are pregnant. How stressful must it be, for example, for one man to listen to another complain about how demanding his wife is when she is pregnant when the infertile man would give anything to have his wife making similar demands? And because men tend to be more private about personal matters, a man going through infertility may be reluctant to tell even his closest friends about the problem. This is often the case when the man is the member of a couple who has been diagnosed with the problem.

Some men are surprised to discover that they feel relieved when they talk about their infertility. They may test the waters of conversation with a friend or perhaps with a colleague at work. Interestingly enough, some men choose to talk with a female colleague—perhaps someone also dealing with infertility—about their experiences. Most find that although it may be a new and unfamiliar experience, talking with others does help to reduce their feelings of helplessness and isolation.

## Couple's Friendships

A great pleasure for many couples is to have friendships—as a couple—with other couples. Perhaps it is this area of friendship that is most challenged by infertility, since it not only involves feelings between friends but also involves feelings between partners. For example, one member of a couple may want to tell their friends what they are going through, but the other partner may feel a need for great privacy. How difficult it then becomes to get together with other couples: either the more private partner—usually the man—gives in and agrees to reveal information, or the other partner— usually the woman—fears that others will ask questions ("So when are the two of you going to have a baby?") or make comments ("We get pregnant every time he blinks at me!") that are upsetting.

In order to maintain their couples friendships, infertile couples must decide how they will talk—or not talk—with others about their situation. Some decide together how they will respond when others ask them if they are planning to have children. Others agree to talk between themselves as situations arise and to try to remain in sync vis-à-vis their interactions with friends.

In short, infertility tests friendships, but it usually does not seriously damage or destroy them. This perspective is confirmed in the pages that follow. Both Debra Sherman Shrier in "My Friend Wendy" and Heidi Sisenwine in "No One Disappointed Me" speak to the significance and resiliency of enduring friendships. Mary Poole's "Ode to the Brave Women Who Dreamed Their Children into Being" captures the power of shared experience among infertile women. Here she chronicles the passage to motherhood of seven women in a RESOLVE group.

○

## MY FRIEND WENDY
### *Debra Sherman Shrier*

When my husband and I were undergoing infertility treatment, it was a terribly isolating experience. None of our close friends had gone through the disappointment, and no one understood why two healthy young people could not conceive. We could not understand it or believe it either, but we were living from appointment to appointment in search of parenthood.

Through my excitement and tears, I shared most of my heartache with my closest friend, Wendy. She listened. She wrote me encouraging notes and praised my commitment to pursue motherhood. She helped me to pick up and keep going when nothing seemed to work. And she subsequently wrote our letter to the agency when we decided to adopt.

Wendy and I had been friends since childhood. Our fathers had had a friendship that had begun over thirty years previously when her dad, Nelson, was my father's professor at night school. Years later, when my dad became a chiropractor, "Uncle Nellie" became his patient. Although they were very different in many ways, they remained friends for life.

Since our parents were close, our families were together at times. Wendy and I share some memories of sitting in the very back of their station wagon, being driven to Hebrew school on Sunday mornings. But it wasn't until I was twenty-four years old and had moved to a new state for a job in the town where Wendy lived that a true friendship developed. Not having any of our family members nearby, we each became the extended family that the other needed in difficult as well as happy times. Years later, after I was married, Wendy basically sat in the seat behind my husband and me as we rode the infertility roller coaster.

For me, my friend's deep compassion and understanding was what helped me feel that I was not alone; she was right there with me and would have done anything I needed. I was fortunate that Wendy also had a medical background, so she was able to appreciate the medical intervention on a more intricate level. She had experience as a nurse in the special care nursery of St. Margaret's Hospital as well as Massachusetts General. Eventually, at my suggestion and because of her outstanding credentials, Wendy accepted a position at an infertility clinic, where she could combine her professional skills as a nurse with her compassion in order to work with adults on a very intense level.

While my husband and I were awaiting news regarding our adoption, Wendy became pregnant. It was difficult for her to tell me; she felt guilty and afraid. She knew how painful it was for me when yet another friend or relative became pregnant. She didn't know if it would be uncomfortable for me to see her during this time or if she could talk to me about her thoughts and feelings. When she told me she was pregnant, I didn't have the same sad feeling I used to when other friends told me the same thing. I felt as though I had moved to a new place in my head and my heart about pregnancy, children, and parenthood. Maybe it was because Wendy understood where I was and had been as I struggled through my years of infertility. Perhaps I had changed, too, just knowing we were going to adopt. My husband and I felt we were getting on with our lives, and this feeling gave us a certain calmness after such turbulent times.

In a strange way, the timing was perfect, since my husband and I had submitted our paperwork to adopt a few months prior to Wendy's news. Knowing that at some point I was going to be a mother made me feel stronger in many ways. It allowed me to accept Wendy's pregnancy more easily, because I had stopped hoping for a medical miracle and begun praying for a child. Wendy and I secretly shared some of her nine months' experience because we (quite selfishly) both hoped that somewhere out there, someone else would also be pregnant, yet unable to parent.

Although I had thought it would be difficult to talk to Wendy about her pregnancy or even see her during this time, it wasn't. She was always sensitive about how I might feel. We didn't focus on her pregnancy as much as we shared our thoughts on how our futures as parents would be.

Even though I didn't know when we'd get the call from the adoption agency regarding placement, Wendy and I shopped for baby clothes. We looked at cute little outfits and soft blankets. I was finally able to walk into the infant section of a store, look around, and touch things, something I couldn't do before. Wendy's due date gave us a timetable, and it became fun for both of us.

Once we were shopping together, looking at newborn clothing, when a salesperson approached Wendy to see if she needed help. They chatted about items, what she'd need, how Wendy's pregnancy was going, and so on. Afterward, Wendy said to me that it was interesting that no one asked if I needed anything; it wasn't obvious that I, too, was about to become a mom. Sometimes I felt it was my special news that I didn't want or need to share. Other times I wished that complete strangers would make a fuss over my future child and me.

The day before her daughter was born, we had lunch together. We talked about how there were so many exciting things ahead for both of us—yet so much we just didn't know. I always think back on that last day as our final time for a leisurely lunch. I was glad, in so many ways, that I had allowed myself to deal with my own sadness at not conceiving and been able to share in this exciting time with my friend. I was grateful to Wendy for trying to consider where I was with my infertility and helping me work through it. Looking back on it, I realize that my infertility gave me a newfound strength.

I came home from the hospital after visiting Wendy and her beautiful daughter, and I announced to my husband that I was amazed at the sight of this new life. Holding little Emily made me hopeful that news regarding our child would arrive soon. I also realized that I hoped our child would also be a girl—a daughter for my husband and me and a friend for Emily. Our children could continue the generations of friendship between our two families. I went to bed that night somehow knowing that our call from the agency would come soon.

Five weeks later, I called Wendy to tell her I had just held my own incredibly beautiful daughter for the very first time.

○

# NO ONE DISAPPOINTED ME

## *Heidi Sisenwine*

When I first met Sally, I was twenty-three years old, had been married for one month, and, having just completed my master's degree in education, was about to begin my first teaching job. She and I clicked instantly. We had so much in common. She was married two weeks after I was, had just received her master's, and was going to be teaching second grade at the same school. It wasn't long before we began to plan our lessons together and share ideas and become close friends. In fact, at school others often confused us with each other, which had a great deal more to do with our parallel lives than with any physical similarity.

Three years after our first meeting, we both started thinking of "trying." In preparation, we switched to the same OB-Gyn and began taking prenatal vitamins. I remember telling her that each day as I looked at the pregnant woman on the cover of the jar I broke into a smile. Unfortunately, the smile did not last long. That July, after hoping that I would conceive during a vacation in Europe, I found out that I was not pregnant. To me London will always be a place of my lost innocence. It was there that I learned my dreams would be deferred.

When I returned home, I visited Sally's new house. But the house was not the only change that summer; she also told me she was six weeks pregnant. Being the good friend, I congratulated her with a huge smile. But in truth, I felt nauseated, fearful, and jealous. These emotions, which first infiltrated my soul on that hot August day, would possess me for the next three years of my life.

I responded to Sally's pregnancy and my lack thereof with the behavior of a good friend. I listened to her excitement over her changing body and her daily reports to our colleagues and friends. Finally I realized that I had no control over the pain I felt with each word of congratulation she received. In late fall, I confronted Sally and told her that I cared deeply about her, but I couldn't be with her every step of the way. I didn't want her to take it the wrong way. It wasn't her; it was my sadness, and if I might sometimes leave the teacher's room when the topic of pregnancy came up, it was simply because the situation was too painful for me. Fortunately, she was very understanding. By midwinter, I had physically separated myself from the situation. I began eating lunch in my classroom, telling other teachers that I needed to catch up on some work.

That year, in addition to beginning my first battery of fertility treatments, I put a tremendous amount of energy into being a good friend to Sally. I helped plan her baby shower and, harder still, attended it. I made a gift for her baby by hand and delivered a stuffed rabbit to the hospital only five hours after her daughter was born.

Three months later, my husband was transferred to a new job and we moved four hours away. I no longer spoke to Sally. The distance made it easier to force the separation. I began intense infertility treatment and joined a wonderful support group. I threw myself into my new life. But the self I threw was not the self I had been. Now, I was even more nauseated, fearful, and jealous. Sad feelings brought on by infertility were now experienced on a daily basis. It no longer took a friend's pregnancy to trigger feelings of jealousy. It could be a complete stranger that I passed on the street, even a television show.

I decided that the only way to prevent the pain was to build a wall around myself that was stronger than anything or anyone, even myself. Once settled into our new home, I now befriended only those whom I considered "safe." I sought friends who were single women or recently married couples. This frustrated my husband, as he was anxious to branch out and befriend many people, but I wasn't ready. If they were pregnant, had young children, or simply liked to talk about babies, I would point-blank refuse to meet them. I couldn't get past the walls of jealousy.

Not only did my pain limit my potential friendships, but worse, I completely stopped communication with old friends from home who were pregnant or who had young children. I wrote them from time to time and even sent gifts as their babies were born, but for three years I never saw or spoke to even one of them. This total self-isolation was in complete contrast to what I had tried to do for Sally. I could no longer falsely show interest; the charade was draining. I would now seek to protect myself by carefully limiting my interactions. I even curtailed discussions with my sister-in-law, whom I love like a sister. I only visited once during her pregnancy, when we were brought together for a family funeral. The void of life was gaping.

I knew that by cutting off all contacts, I was not doing what was best for lasting friendships, but it was all I could do. During those long, painful, and often lonely years, I always knew in my heart that those who truly were my friends and loved and understood me would eventually open their arms and welcome me back into their lives. But I knew it had to wait until my pain was over.

Three medical practices, countless procedures and surgeries, hundreds of shots, a miscarriage, and almost three years to the day from my terrible realization in London, I sat with my husband, parents, and a dear—and, of course, single—friend under a tree in my yard as I received the call I had thought would never come. "Heidi, it's Jen. The test was positive; you are four weeks pregnant!"

A few weeks later, I was sitting with my family discussing how and when I was going to share my news with the friends I had left behind. My sister-in-law was surprised. "I never realized all the people you've lost touch with," she said. "It must be hard to be your friend." And for the first time since receiving my miraculous news of pregnancy, I cried tears of pain and sorrow. She was right; it had been hard to be my friend.

The next week, I sent out five heart-wrenching letters to the friends I'd left behind. In the tear-stained letters, I shared my joy, guilt, love, and thanks for all their patience and understanding. I thanked them for having supported me with their understanding absence. But I wrote them, because I was too scared to call. I was scared that my faith in their unswerving support and understanding was nothing but a delusion.

A few short days after I mailed the letters, I received four phone calls and a letter. Each friend was there to share my joy. Many had newborn children; some even had had two since we last spoke. Finally, Sally called. Much time had passed, but she understood. She was thrilled for me.

A week ago, during my twenty-sixth week, Sally called again. This time, she simply called to chat and give me advice on best baby buys. It was just like old times; our lives were running parallel once again.

During my two years in self-imposed isolation, when I believed in so little, I always knew that true friendships never die. Emotional and physical distance is only temporary. I just needed my life to catch up. I always believed that my friends and their resilience would maintain our friendship despite my pain and jealousy. No one disappointed me.

○
_____

## AN ODE TO THE BRAVE WOMEN WHO
## DREAMED THEIR CHILDREN INTO BEING

### *Mary Poole*

From different walks of life we came
To talk and weep and feel less shame.
The fertile world, it seemed too cold
To help our precious dreams unfold.
Through IVF and operations,
And far too many ovulations,
Pergonal and Clomid, too,
Babies we lost or never knew.

All the heartache, all the fears,
Regret for all the passing years.
We struggled, week by week, to find
A way out of our childless bind.
Slowly we learned, "Enough is enough!"
We could walk away from the medical stuff.
When one of us moved into adoption,
It became more familiar, a promising option.

And then came Eric, in the fall,
A GROUPie baby, first of all!
Tyler arrived with winter's cold,
And in the spring, lo and behold,
A double blessing: Kelly and Kenny.
Our hearts were full, our joys were many.
A year passed by, another spring,
and Allison Robin came on wing.

Autumn winds brought Rusty home
(A future GROUPie, then unknown).
At last, one pregnancy didn't fail:
We all gave birth to Abigail.
And so we met on a Tuesday in May,
To share our joy that Mother's Day,

For we had all survived the pain,
And we'd made rainbows out of rain.

And now our rainbow coalition
Brightens with each new addition.
Rebecca, Patrick, Curtis, and Kyle
Brought double the trouble, triple the smiles.
Benjamin, Emily, Molly—make room!
We've got fourteen kids, our own baby boom.
These days, we're engaged in a noisier struggle.
It's diapers, sneakers, and lessons we juggle.

We are seven women, it's been seven years.
We've had more than our share of crises and tears.
We have our own families, our separate lives.
We try to be supermoms, workers and wives.
Wherever we go, we'll still remember when . . .

Being infertile was torture times ten.
When talking and listening brought out the good,
As we nurtured and birthed such a dream . . . Motherhood.

# 7

# INFERTILITY AND CAREER

WHEN A COUPLE encounter infertility, they inevitably have feelings and fears about how this experience will affect—and interface with—their life at work. Although this is especially true for women, who must take considerable time off to attend doctor's appointments, it is also true for men. In addition to the time they must take for their own appointments and their participation in various procedures, many men want to accompany their wives to appointments. Hence, infertility causes most people to lose time from work.

It is not only time but energy and enthusiasm for work that can be lost in the course of infertility. As people face disappointments and losses, it becomes increasingly difficult to keep such feelings out of the workplace. This is especially true for women, who often find themselves amid pregnant colleagues or coworkers. Conversations on the job and in the lunchroom about children and grandchildren are also very difficult for women struggling with infertility.

Infertility prompts many people to question their earlier feelings about the significance of their career. This is especially true for older women, who may feel that they have sacrificed the opportunity to have children in order to pursue an exciting career. Such women look back with regret at having postponed parenthood. For some, this regret is combined with anger and resentment toward other career women who seem to have it all, having built careers and families simultaneously. Anger may also be directed at physicians, for not pushing them to try to have children at a younger age, and at spouses, for their role in the postponement.

For other women, career regrets are reversed: rather than lamenting the decision to have a career and postpone motherhood, these women regret having made motherhood their primary career goal. Women who never pursued a career because they felt strongly that motherhood would be a full and satisfying vocation look back with regret and resentment, wondering why they did not go to graduate school or seize exciting job opportunities.

Men, too, may encounter career questions and regrets when they face infertility. Some who have worked very hard to get ahead and provide may wonder if their efforts were worthwhile. Others may feel that they would have taken a different path in life had they known that infertility would be part of their life experience. Many find that they now feel stuck in their career path. Sometimes this "stuckness" comes from real limitations: a man may have to stay in a position in order to maintain specific insurance coverage. Other times, the stuck feeling is more related to depression and to the fact that the man is in the throes of a life crisis.

Some jobs are easier to maintain than others in light of infertility. Jobs that require extensive travel—especially when it is unpredictable—and those that demand a rigid schedule are most difficult to manage during infertility. By contrast, a job may be very challenging and involving, but if it has flexible hours and few rigid guidelines, it can be adjusted to meet the rigors of infertility.

Sometimes it is not the schedule of a job but its nature that makes it difficult to maintain during infertility. Obstetricians, obstetrical nurses, pediatricians, pediatric nurses, preschool teachers, day care providers, adoption social workers, and others all face a formidable challenge when trying to keep their feelings about infertility out of the workplace. Nonetheless, many people in these fields have the remarkable ability to keep work and personal life separate. In fact, there are many who seem to actually thrive as they face this challenge. One woman, a labor and delivery nurse who endured several years of infertility and pregnancy loss before moving on to adoption, accounted for her reaction in this way: "I am glad that I do the work that I do. I don't feel like an outsider in the world of pregnancy and childbirth. My job keeps me intimately involved."

Privacy—a theme that runs throughout infertility and its aftermath—plays a central role in people's experience with infertility and career. Even those who are most open in their personal lives about their infertility, believing that it is best to let family and friends know what they are going through, often decide not to tell employers and colleagues about their experience. They have several compelling reasons for maintaining privacy.

First, many people decide to keep news of their infertility out of their workplace because they don't want to jeopardize their job advancement or mobility. Aware that the infertility could take several years to resolve, they recognize that it would be a mistake to make career decisions—or have them be made for them—based on the possibility of an upcoming pregnancy. They fear that if they tell others about their infertility, their employers or supervisors may give them promotions or new assignments more cautiously, fearing that training and other investments in the employee will be wasted.

Another reason that people do not tell employers about their infertility is because they actually fear job loss. Although it would be discriminatory to dismiss a pregnant worker because she was pregnant, an employer who wanted to avoid paying for a maternity leave or maternity benefits might be tempted to find another reason for letting someone go prior to pregnancy.

Finally, there is privacy for the sake of privacy. Many people simply feel that the workplace is not the place to discuss something as personal as infertility. It is not that they have a specific fear but rather that they feel some things—family planning among them—are best kept at home. Even if they enjoy very cordial relationships with their colleagues, they still may feel that they are best off not involving them in their infertility drama.

Although many elect to try to keep infertility separate from work, others decide that it is best to let coworkers or employers know what they are going through. One reason for this is pragmatic: they don't want to have to sneak around when they are going through a demanding treatment cycle. For them, it feels easier and safer to let people know in advance that they will be coming in late or missing some time because of treatment. They prefer to have the truth be known—and to face any consequences of that—rather than be perceived as lazy, depressed, or looking for another job when they are absent from work.

Another reason that some people decide to tell others at work about their infertility is so that they will not have to entirely camouflage their feelings when a coworker is pregnant. Inevitably this situation will be difficult, but they anticipate that it would be ever so much more so if they had to attend baby showers or other celebrations at work with no one aware of their quest. Although colleagues may not prove sensitive to the situation, presumably they won't make the mistake of saying, "So when are *you* going to have a baby?"

Even individuals who decide to tell others about their infertility and its treatment may conclude that it is best not to tell them the specifics. Talking about such things as an upcoming egg retrieval or an embryo transfer inevitably leads to questions or suppositions about the timing of a pregnancy test. When this occurs, all privacy is relinquished. Worse still, if the pregnancy test is positive, they find themselves in the position of having many potential onlookers in the long, draining weeks of early pregnancy.

Regardless of how it is approached, infertility and the workplace is a very difficult combination. Whether they tell a little about their situation to a few people or a lot to many, those going through infertility feel vulnerable. Job security and advancement come into question, and disconnection from other employees feels inevitable.

If a couple decides to move on to adoption, new questions arise regarding their employment. Even those who were open about their infertility treatments may feel a need to be more private when it comes to adoption. They may not want others to know their adoption plans because the timing of adoption is so uncertain and there can be many disappointments and plans that fall through before a successful adoption. Employees may not want coworkers asking, "How is the adoption going?" and they may not want employers passing over them for job opportunities because they think a placement is pending. Finally, there are those who want to remain quiet about their adoption plans because they feel so vulnerable: they are not quite sure how they feel about adoption and don't want to take the risk that others will make comments or have reactions to adoption that will upset them.

There are many workers who decide that it is essential they tell their employers about their plans to adopt. For some, this is a matter of being responsible: an adoption can occur anytime, and they feel it is only fair that their employer know that they may be traveling or on parental leave unexpectedly. Others decide to talk about adoption for the pragmatic reason of wanting to be sure that they get their adoption benefits. (As of this writing, 25 percent of U.S. companies have adoption benefits, usually a contribution of $2,000 to $10,000 toward an adoption.) Still others decide to tell employers, colleagues, and everyone else they know about their desire to adopt, hoping that this networking may actually lead to a baby.

Once people become parents, many find that their careers are affected by their "post-infertility" status. Having worked so hard to have a family, they may not want to return to work as soon—or as close to full time—as they had once anticipated. For some, this change of heart does not present a problem: they have the financial or professional security to allow them to take some time off or to cut back. However, there are others who have depleted their savings to pay for treatment or an adoption and who find themselves having to work to replenish their nest egg or simply to pay their bills. In such instances, an array of emotions arise: new parents after infertility feel deeply appreciative, but they may also may feel resentful of those for whom parenthood came easily—and inexpensively.

Some people make significant career changes as a result of infertility. Nurses, psychologists, and social workers may redirect their careers so that they are able to work in the field of infertility, helping others through the crisis that they themselves have recently emerged from (that was how I got into the field of infertility!). Others simply decide that former career goals are no longer applicable after infertility. Some change careers in order to have more time at home with their children, more flexibility, or less travel.

In the pages that follow, two women who have found themselves dealing with infertility in both their work and their personal life speak of their experiences. "Always Present" is Emma Stow's account of how concerns about reproduction are always present in her life: she is an infertile woman who is also a labor and delivery nurse. Her daily life involves working with women who are going through a passage—childbirth—that she sought for many years but never experienced. Ellen Jean Tepper, a clinical social worker who specializes in infertility counseling, talks about her feelings years after her own infertility experience in "An Old Friend."

○

# ALWAYS PRESENT
## *Emma Stow*

As I sit down to write about my experiences with infertility, we are fast approaching our daughter's fourth birthday. She came to us through adoption and her arrival brought incredible joy. Strangely, I sometimes have trouble drawing on the feelings of those six seemingly endless years of pain, injustice, and suffering that we went through in our twelve Clomid IUIs, twelve IVFs, six laparoscopies, one ectopic, and one early miscarriage. But that memory lapse does not last long!

The irony of my infertility was never far from the surface, not only because I came from a "Fertile Myrtle" family and because I had had an unwanted pregnancy as a teenager, but also because of my career: I am a labor and delivery nurse. On a daily basis I am faced with the culmination of pregnancy and the joy and miracle of birth. It's an odd position to be in when pregnancy is so elusive and its successful conclusion so seemingly impossible. Impossible and commonplace. On my job it happens every day and every night. On a busy shift, we will have several women in labor. How strange to always be confronting two realities: abundant fertility and seemingly unbeatable infertility.

My job is to coach and support women in labor—the very women that I have envied, judged, and hated. When I was in the midst of treatment there were times when I deeply resented hearing them complain about the pain of labor or, worse still, about having a second boy. Didn't they know that I would trade places with them in a minute? In a second? Didn't they know how lucky they were?

No, they didn't. And to my surprise and my relief, I found that I didn't (entirely) hold it against them. Instead, I realized that I had a choice: I could allow infertility to destroy the career that I love, or I could do everything possible to separate my personal feelings from my professional realities. I chose the latter, and although it has not always been easy, I am pleased that I was able to successfully make that choice.

One of the first steps was for me to confront a difficult truth: it is perfectly normal not to know how lucky you are when you are in labor. Once I acknowledged this, I was able to offer my patients support and guidance during what was for them, as well as for me, a very challenging time. This felt like a real victory for me; for once, I had taken some control over my infertility and had succeeded in diminishing some of its power.

This is not to say that it did not—and does not—remain difficult. Although the adoption of our daughter eased many of my most painful feelings, it is still hard when patients innocently ask, "Oh, where was your daughter born?" or "Was your labor long?" or "Did you have an epidural?" Personal questions are a natural part of the job that I do as a woman working in a very intimate way with other women, and I understand why people ask me these questions. Still, I feel that my truthful responses detract from my credibility with patients when they are in labor. Moreover, it is very difficult to be in the midst of helping someone else go through labor and be suddenly reminded that this is something that I never have and most likely never will experience myself. Because I love our daughter so much and feel so intensely connected to her, I am sometimes startled by how painful this realization remains.

My husband and I have been waiting several months to adopt our second child. Although comforted by the knowledge that a child *will* come and that we will once again find ourselves in the blissful state of new parenthood, I am also finding it difficult at work. It is again painful to watch couples welcome a child into the world and into their families in the way that we had anticipated—and assumed—we would welcome our children. It is hard to see the interaction between partners as they go through labor and delivery together and to know that despite all the injections, surgeries, and pregnancy losses, we will never have that experience.

Although I know and enjoy the breadth and depth of a mother's love, I remain but an active bystander in the process of creation. Sometimes the paradox of my situation is terribly upsetting. Other times, it is strangely heartening. Always, it is humbling. More than most people, I am deeply aware that creation is a mystery and a miracle.

○

## AN OLD FRIEND

*Ellen Jean Tepper*

Many years ago, when I was going through infertility treatment, I would often read Barbara Menning's book, *Infertility: A Guide for the Childless Couple*. In those days—the late 1970s—it was the only layperson's book on infertility, and my copy became ragged from many readings. Among the many amazing things that Barbara Menning, the founder of RESOLVE, included in her book was the following quote: "My infertility resides in my heart as an old friend. I do not hear from it for weeks at a time, and then, a moment, a thought, a baby announcement or some such thing, and I will feel the tug—maybe even be sad or shed a few tears. And I think, 'There's my old friend.' It will always be part of me."

Although it has been over twenty years since I first read this quote and seventeen years since I became a mother, the words remain ever with me. Infertility is, indeed, my old friend—one that can make a sudden, unexpected, and even startling visit. Infertility is also the language and the currency of my professional life; I now have the privilege of meeting countless individuals and couples immersed in a struggle that I once knew so intimately and now know primarily as an onlooker.

Take today for instance. This afternoon I had a dentist's appointment. My dentist, a woman, has two children, whom she tells me about while I am sitting there, mouth wide and unable to respond. I have enjoyed this, not only because it is a woman-to-woman rather than a dentist-to-patient interaction, but also because she experienced several years of infertility before her first pregnancy. My dentist is forty, and until this afternoon, I had assumed that her family was complete. Enter my old friend. . . .

I arrived at the office, unsuspecting that infertility would suddenly be paying me a visit, and noticed that my dentist looked a bit wide around the middle. Startled by what I knew I was seeing, I looked away quickly, trying to convince myself that I was wrong. There was a brief effort at reassurance; I reminded myself that she was forty, was very busy, had been infertile, and seemed overwhelmed by the two children she already had. Then I looked back for a moment, and she interrupted my internal chatter with a simple, "Yes, I am having another baby."

And yes, my old friend was back. My first impulse was to jump out of the chair, run out of the office, burst into tears, and return to a world where infertility was no longer able to sideswipe me. After all, I hear about pregnancies every day. I *celebrate* pregnancies every day. I spend my life trying to help people become parents, as well as survive the grief they feel when pregnancy fails. Why was I reacting so strongly and with such pain?

Because infertility never really goes away. As the quote says, it remains with us, in the recesses of our hearts, as a companion. Although my silent companion hit me over the head in the dentist's office, she spends most of her time being my true friend. She guides me in my work each day, enabling me to hear and understand my clients in ways that I don't believe someone who has never gone through infertility would.

I returned from the dentist's office to lead a group. These women have been together for the past five years. During that time, several members have become pregnant and have left the group. The six women who remain include three adoptive mothers, one woman who is pregnant after several pregnancy losses, and two women who are still going through treatment. The discussion this evening moved from initial chitchat about the new sale at Gymboree, where the three mothers love to shop, to poignant conversation about how the adoptive mothers feel around pregnant women. Each said that she adores her child—all have daughters—but that she still feels a deep, powerful longing to be pregnant and give birth.

I listened. No longer the suffering, still-infertile-after-all-these-years middle-aged mother of teenagers who nearly disintegrated in the dentist's chair, I was able to hear them, to comment, to help. I was again the professional, and infertility was again my old friend, my informant, my guide. I understood what the women were saying. I remembered the joy and the relief I had felt as a newly adoptive mother as well as the ongoing pain I had experienced around pregnant—and postpartum—women.

Today was unusual: my infertility pays me surprise visits only four or five—perhaps ten at most—times a year. By contrast, I retrieve old memories on almost a daily basis, "for professional use only."

Women frequently tell me of the pain they feel when a friend tells them she is pregnant. When I hear this, I immediately step into my time capsule and return to two conversations that occurred nineteen years ago but are in my mind always. In one, a friend (who remains one of my two closest friends) stood with me in front of the hospital that we both worked in and told me she was pregnant. I remember that I was wearing a red dress and that I felt both sadness and gratitude to her for the way that she told me. The other memory is similar, save that the friend called on the telephone and said, "There is something I need to tell you. I'm pregnant and I hope you are next." Again, I was both sad and grateful. Years later I told her how much I appreciated her caring and kindness in telling me. Her response then touched me even more deeply than her original call. She said, "I thought about it carefully before calling."

So one set of memories that I draw on are the "going through infertility" memories. Another set are of the adoption decision-making variety. When couples come to me with their doubts, their fears, their skepticism about adoption, I again reach into my memory bank. What fun it is, as an experienced adoptive mother of so many years, to revisit these old feelings. Remembering my own doubts gives me confidence to convey to others a belief that adoption *will* work for them. I know, from my own experiences, that negative feelings about adoption do not predict a bad outcome to an adoption process. In fact, I remember feeling once that I had reached a point at which I had "taken out my adoption garbage." Having rid my emotional house of all that clutter, I felt well equipped to move on toward adoption.

Memories of my own experience as an infertility patient are not my only helpers in my work with infertile individuals and couples. Even more helpful have been the years and years of hearing other people's stories. The rich range of experiences, of reactions, of perceptions has helped broaden and deepen my understanding of infertility. I have learned that there are many common themes in infertility, but that each person's experience of this crisis is unique.

Sometimes I wonder where I am going with this. I am now in my fifties, and my children are nearly grown. I am now the same age as the parents of many of my infertility patients. When I realize this—it always comes as a shock to me—I wonder how the patients perceive me. Do they see an old lady and doubt that she can really understand what they are going through? Or are they able to see in my face, now lined and wrinkled, that I *do* get it and that my infertility, which happened so long ago, is still with me?

Yes, it is my friend—I guess, for life.

# 8

# INFERTILITY AND RELIGION

*Give me children or I die.*

—Genesis 30:1

THE IMPORTANCE OF FERTILITY—and the anguish of infertility—date back to the Bible. Rachel's plaintive cry echoed the pain of Sarah and was echoed again by Leah, Hannah, and others who suffered the ache of childlessness in a world that both demanded and celebrated fertility. Now, several centuries later and in an era of assisted reproduction, infertile men and women continue to echo Rachel's cry. Many join her in prayer.

Childless individuals often find that infertility has a profound impact on their religious observance and, more important, on their faith. This contributes to their feelings of isolation, as there appears to be little place in organized religion for the childless couple. They look to major religious holidays, including Passover, Easter, Christmas, and Hanukkah, and find that each focuses on children. In fact, the central symbols of both Passover and Easter—eggs and greenery—are symbols of fertility. Similarly, many are troubled by the fact that church and synagogue services include christenings, namings, and other celebrations of the arrival of a child, but provide no prayer or ceremony for those who are infertile.

Frequently, a crisis of faith precipitates a questioning of one's beliefs; many are anguished to discover that their faith in God has been shaken. Especially vulnerable to a crisis of faith are those who have a strong belief in an all-powerful, all-knowing God, who rewards the righteous. In the face of this belief, they cannot understand why they have encountered infertility and are plagued by such questions as, "How can this torment be part of God's plan?" "What did I (or we) do to cause this punishment?" "Why are my prayers not answered?" Some are able to reconcile their belief in God by arriving at a different—less controlling, less punitive—concept of God.

Many people experience the crisis of infertility without an accompanying crisis of faith. Among these are not only those who do not have particularly strong religious beliefs to begin with but also individuals who have discovered that religious (or spiritual) beliefs sustain them, so that they continue to derive comfort from faith, prayer, and religious ceremony. Such individuals even experience a deepening or broadening of their religious beliefs, often discovering some spiritual meaning in their suffering. Those who believe that God acts in unexplainable ways can more easily maintain their faith than those who expect to understand God's actions.

Clergy can also play a central role in determining the impact that infertility will have on an individual's religious faith. Although some religions or denominations frown on certain reproductive options or alternatives, the vast majority do not. Many infertile people are fortunate to have a minister, priest, or rabbi who approaches infertility with compassion and who actively supports a couple's efforts to build a family. When individuals approach clergy seeking solace and are rebuffed, it is very painful. How difficult it is to be told that one's infertility is in God's plan or to be judged about one's method of reproduction.

Because infertility strikes people in all walks of life, there are also some members of the clergy who are infertile themselves. These individuals find themselves in the extraordinarily difficult position of having to balance their job responsibilities—which include ministering to fertile couples—with their personal feelings of loss and isolation. How difficult it must be to officiate at a ceremony celebrating the birth of a child when one has just learned that yet another treatment cycle has failed. How painful to have to talk with a congregant about an abortion and feel a deep inner longing to be expecting a child.

In recent years, efforts have been made to address the needs of the infertile in the context of organized religion. There are, for example, churches and synagogues that offer healing services, and both laypeople and clergy have created special prayers and rituals for infertility and for pregnancy loss. Nonetheless, most infertile couples continue to feel like outsiders in their religious communities, observing that many of the church or synagogue activities revolve around families with young children.

In a time of extensive intermarriage, many couples face the additional challenge of reconciling two religious faiths with infertility. In some instances, the history of intermarriage may ironically be somewhat helpful, because the couple is already familiar with feelings of being outsiders in their religious communities. However, for the most part, their history of intermarriage adds to the religious questions with which many couples grapple. Sadly, a few couples even wonder if they are somehow being punished for their decision to marry outside of their faiths.

For many couples, the crisis of faith that arises during their infertility experience actually serves to strengthen their religious connections. Just as infertility will challenge but usually not destroy strong friendships, so also it can shake but usually not destroy religious faith. Some couples end up leaving their church or synagogue because they are deeply hurt by the lack of compassion or the indifference of fellow congregants or clergy, but most are able to identify and affiliate with another church or synagogue, within which they find the community they seek. Rarely do people grapple with difficult theological and spiritual questions and decide to leave their religious tradition. Most tackle the questions—many of which have no answers—and emerge with a deeper and more enduring faith.

In the pages that follow, Rabbi Joel Sisenwine talks about how his experience with infertility reshaped his understanding of the Book of Genesis and heightened his appreciation for the miracle of creation. He approaches this from both a personal and a theological perspective, capturing some of the challenges he faced in going through infertility while commencing his career as a congregational rabbi. Then we hear from Marilyn Andrews, a Catholic who found that her employer, the Roman Catholic Church, restricted her insurance carrier's coverage of infertility for doctrinal reasons. Caught between her strong desire to have a child—and her need for assisted reproduction—and her devotion to both her religion and her career, she struggles with profound questions of faith in "My Faith and My Infertility." Lisa Shearer Wilkins expresses her struggles with faith in "Vatican Adds to Isolation."

---
o
---

## GENESIS AND INFERTILITY
### *Rabbi Joel Sisenwine*

Taking our cue from the biblical book of Genesis, my wife, Heidi, and I planned our first act of creation, the conception of a child. We had been married for more than two years, and the time seemed right for an addition to our neoteric family. "Start the countdown to conception," we exclaimed, thereby beginning the process of choosing a spring or summer baby, selecting an appropriate name, and finally snuggling under the covers to inaugurate this exciting journey. Life seemed so wonderfully simple. Sure, the decisions were considerable, but the task was inspiring, even divine.

Unfortunately, that was four years ago. Since then, springs and summers have passed, taking the hopes of a child with them. The names Benjamin, Jacob, and Rebekah have been painfully replaced by Clomid, Pergonal, Metrodin, and a number of other high-tech infertility drugs. To our dismay, our nights have never been interrupted with the high-pitched squeals of a baby, an apparent frustration for our fertile friends. Rather, our lives have been overwhelmed by laparoscopies, intrauterine inseminations, and hundreds of injections—hundreds and hundreds of injections. Overcoming infertility has become a full-time job.

It was not long ago that we childishly assumed that creation was in our charge, simply a matter of our youthful lust, an ovulation predictor, and a jar of prenatal vitamins. "Be fruitful and multiply," we were instructed. Conception was supposed to be easy. Even the fish and the birds were told to "replenish the earth" (Genesis 1:22). The news magazines reported that teens get pregnant without even trying. Overpopulation is a worldwide concern. But what about us? We never had the opportunity to watch the small plus sign mysteriously appear on the home pregnancy test. Our monthly reminders were depressing phone calls from consoling nurses. The test was negative. We were not having a child in nine months.

I guess the Rolling Stones were right, even though they always were closer in age to our parents than ourselves: you can't always get what you want. No one had ever explained this to us over the years. In fact, we were always hoodwinked into thinking that the decision to conceive was ours. "So when are you going to have a child?" family and friends would ask, as if the answer was in our domain. "When the time is right," we smugly replied, failing to recognize that the decision was not ours to make.

Conception, the miracle of life, proved beyond our control. Why did we think that we could create a world with a personal "big bang"? Why did we think that human beings have the power to create at will, when some things are clearly limited to the Ultimate Creator? Perhaps it was because our postwar parents raised us with the heartwarming knowledge that we could do anything we desired, that the world was ours to embrace and shape. We were blessed with economic fecundity, always expecting the best. But now, even our parents couldn't help. They could only cry amid our pain. We were infertile, barren of power. Even science couldn't help. The idols now lay shattered.

*Please God, grant us a child.*

Of course, we tried everything: worry dolls and trinkets, fertility charms, rocks, and incantations. We heeded the Jewish tradition and gave Heidi an additional Hebrew name, Chava, "mother of all life," hoping that she would be as fruitful as the Garden of Eden. Our families told us to sleep with a silver spoon in our pillow. When that didn't work, we resorted to an age-old Jewish superstition: we saved an *etrog,* a citrus fruit and central symbol of life during the holiday of Sukkot. We saved an etrog, ate an etrog, even slept with an etrog, but conception remained a distant dream. "So, *nu,* you've been married five years. When are you going to have a child?" well-meaning friends and rabbinic colleagues would ask. "Only God knows," we now replied. "Only God knows."

I've been a rabbi for over three years now. I have several years of religious study along with five years in seminary under my belt. Still, I must admit that despite my good grades in Bible class, I never fully realized the mystery of creation and the complexity of Genesis. The first book of the Bible not only includes the all-powerful, omniscient God, who created the world at will, but also records the fragility of our infertile matriarchs. Sarah was ninety-nine before giving birth to Isaac. As a young male, I never could identify with her predicament. But now I know why Sarah gave her son the Hebrew name Yitzchak, meaning "laughter." The news of her impending childbirth, after all of those years, must have seemed like a joke. Having experienced infertility, I now understand the biblical Rachel. Rachel not only had to confront the pain of monthly failure, she had to witness her sister give birth seven times. Thank God, Heidi and I had to suffer this great pain only once.

Finally, there is Heidi's namesake, Hannah, who received only one portion from Elkanah the priest because "the Lord made her barren." The Bible records, "Elkanah would say to her: Hannah, why do you weep? Why don't you eat? Why are you so unhappy? Am I not dearer to you than ten sons?"

Unfortunately, Elkanah's insensitivity is not a thing of the past. So few people understand the pain of infertility. "Just stop thinking about it," people would often suggest, causing us to think about it even more. "When we were kids we just had to *look* at each other," others asserted. "At least you're together. Just love each other," friends would say. But we were barren.

Like Hannah, we were in pain. In the Bible, Hannah prayed and prayed, hoping for a child, but people considered her drunk and delirious. The Bible reports, "Her lips moved without making a sound." In pain I now recognize Hannah, bent over in tears, crying forth, "Please God, grant us a child," but nobody is listening.

Even today, synagogues greet the infertile with apathy and insensitivity. Many congregations define "family" memberships as "for members with children." Oftentimes the socialization of a synagogue and its entry points for involvement are child-centered. But not all our members can have children. Our infertility taught me that the question, "So when are you having kids?" is as senseless as, "So when are you going to die?" We will never know.

There is an old Yiddish proverb that says, "Humans plan and plan, but God sits up in Heaven and laughs." I have thought about this proverb often during the past few years. How foolish any of us are to think that we control the world. We are not the Creator of all things.

And then it happened. On August 11 of this year, after three long and painful years of treatment, we received a phone call. Heidi's mouth dropped to the floor. She was pregnant. Was it the prayers recited in her name, the etrog, the new name, the exact mix of Pergonal and Metrodin? Only God knows.

All we knew at that time was that Heidi was pregnant, and we were to wait twelve weeks before sharing our news with the world. You see, twelve weeks was the end of the first trimester, the conclusion of a frightening, insecure period in which fetal life hovers in the balance. Twelve weeks is a common marker, understood by the entire world for its incredible significance. But in truth, we knew that life is always in the balance. Our infertility had taught us that we are not in control and had reconfirmed our belief that God is the ultimate decider of life and death.

Of course we welcomed the twelfth week with great joy. Every day was a miracle. And yet, once we shared our happy news, it was sad to see that everyone knew how to treat a pregnant woman but no one knew how to treat an infertile one.

Finally, Heidi, the teacher, had the courage to share the news with her fourth-grade Jewish day school class. Following the announcement, a mother approached her and blurted out, "How could you? As a teacher, why couldn't you wait until the summer to have the baby? A spring baby will interrupt the school year."

If she only knew.

○

# MY FAITH AND MY INFERTILITY

## Marilyn Andrews

I often think about a talk I attended by Rabbi Harold Kushner, the author of *When Bad Things Happen to Good People*. Rabbi Kushner spoke of his faith following the death of his young son and said, "God doesn't inflict sadness and pain on certain people, but He provides us with many loving hearts who will help us through many of life's challenges and celebrate the joys with us."

I was inspired by Rabbi Kushner's words and his message, but I must also acknowledge that there are many times when I feel that God *is* inflicting some pain or punishment on us. I don't want to believe this, but I am baffled as to why my husband, Ed, and I would be denied children. I was always a great babysitter. My chosen career is elementary education, and I work hard at it. I have always been a loving daughter, sister, aunt, and wife. Why me? Why us? Why infertility?

It is very interesting that I began by quoting a rabbi. I say it is interesting because I am a Catholic married to a Jew, and both of our religions have played an important part in our infertility. In Ed's case the role of his religion has been more straightforward; his rabbi is an adoptive father and has provided us with the hope that our infertility will have a successful resolution through adoption, if not through pregnancy. Also, Ed has become increasingly active in the synagogue, and this year he is its president, a nice distraction from the struggles of infertility. So Ed's Judaism and our infertility have not been a bad match.

For me, it has been much more difficult. I was raised a Catholic and have always had deep ties to the church. In fact, when it came time to take a teaching job, I chose to work in a Catholic school—and continue to do so. Although I love my job and feel close to the nuns I work with, being employed by the Catholic church has been a problem. Although I have full insurance coverage for all assisted reproductive technology, the church has specified limits to my insurance coverage. As a result, in vitro fertilization, which would be the treatment of choice for us, is not covered by our insurance. This fact not only raises financial questions for us, but it also raises questions of faith for me. Why would my religion and my employer choose to do anything that would limit my chances to bear a child? Wasn't I taught that bringing new life into the world is a blessed act?

I find that I struggle with my faith a great deal these days. When Ed and I married, we agreed to raise our children as Jews. That was fine with me at the time and remains so, but I remain a Catholic and want to maintain my strong Catholic faith. I try to do so, but find myself troubled when my prayers are not answered. It has become difficult to attend weekly mass when I am feeling like an outsider in my faith.

Although I have been prompted to reevaluate my faith and sometimes that reevaluation is disturbing, there are also ways in which I feel that my faith has been strengthened. For one thing, my pastor has been a great source of support and guidance. For another, our lives have been touched by many wonderful people throughout this process, and, in keeping with what Rabbi Kushner says, I have felt that God has sent them to us. Finally, there are the many ways in which my relationship with Ed has become richer, and I cannot help but believe that God has a strong role in this.

I believe that I will emerge from all of this a stronger person and a stronger Catholic, because my faith has been truly tested and I have also been given opportunities to leave my faith. The fact that I have stayed with it through this—the most challenging test of my life—convinces me that my faith will endure. In the deepest, darkest moments, this awareness offers me comfort.

○

## VATICAN ADDS TO ISOLATION
### *Lisa Shearer Wilkins*

Dear Pope John Paul II,

Because of the Vatican's recent ruling on artificial means of conception, I now find myself an alienated Catholic, a member of that new "immoral" group—infertile people. Pronouncements such as the one you recently made seem to serve only one purpose: to add more hurt to a situation that is already marked by incredible pain, isolation, frustration, loneliness, confusion, and helplessness.

Infertility is not something a couple would choose to have happen to them. Bearing and raising children is something most people take for granted. It is assumed that we are all fertile and that when we decide to start a family it is as simple as going off the pill, and pregnancy will soon follow. For many of us, it simply does not work that way. My husband and I have desperately wanted a child of our own for more than four years now. It is quite possible that the only way we will ever have a biological child is by using what you call artificial and immoral means. My reaction to this decree is one of anger and deep pain. The experience of infertility seems to be absorbing my whole life right now. This is the time in my life when I most need comfort, understanding, and love. Yet the church invariably labels my efforts to have a family immoral and refuses to support me and my husband in our quest for a child born to us.

The Vatican has said that no couple has an automatic right to a child, yet we do have an automatic right to seek medical attention for diseases, accidents, and illness. In fact, many of these diseases and illnesses are what cause infertility. You say we should just heed God's will and accept our fate in life. If the Catholic Church believes in a God who arbitrarily wishes infertility or any other such tragedy on people, then I have a hard time believing in such a God. God gave men and women incredible talents to use, and many people have used their God-given abilities to create medical technologies that help infertile couples. To ignore these gifts would be to laugh in the face of a God who expects his people to use the knowledge He has bestowed on them to help other people.

I have heard comments not only from you but also from other active church members, that our extreme efforts are acts of selfishness and that it is really not up to us to decide if we are to be biological parents or not. One of the responses to infertility that bothers me most is being told that we can always adopt. Adoption is not the easy process it once was. Many people wait three to four years—often longer—for a baby. The expenses associated with adoption can be a financial hardship for many couples. Adoption agencies investigate every detail of a couple's life. They are the ones who decide if you are to receive a child or not—not God. If everyone had to go through what adoptive parents have to, it is likely that many would be turned down as parents.

There is not a day that I don't think about infertility. It permeates every aspect of my life. If you or anyone else who is so quick to judge my efforts could catch even a glimmer of the pain I feel each month when my body once again reveals no sign of life, then perhaps some compassion might fill your heart and you might understand why, in our love, we would go to extremes in order to create a child together. I want to bear life and will probably never understand why this tragedy has happened to us.

I have tried to become more vocal about my infertility. My hope is to raise people's awareness that the pain of infertility is real—and as devastating as any life crisis can be. I want to let people know that what we need is support and understanding, a patient heart and a listening ear. Criticism in regard to our efforts to achieve a pregnancy only serves to alienate us more. I am hurt by your pronouncements about infertility, but mostly I am saddened by the fact that the church and her people are so quick to judge and to label, rather than to be what I think Jesus has asked each of us to be: compassionate, loving examples of himself.

Sincerely,
Lisa Shearer Wilkins

# 9

# PREGNANCY AFTER INFERTILITY

"YOU CAN'T BE a little bit pregnant"—at least, that is what infertile couples have been told. They—like their fertile friends—have grown up with the understanding that either a woman is pregnant or she is not pregnant, and there is nothing in between. However, many infertile couples learn otherwise. While they are in high-tech treatment or shortly after they receive a positive pregnancy test, they discover that assisted reproductive technologies have altered the old adage: now they *can* be a little bit pregnant.

Pregnancy after infertility is probably most accurately described as a series of steps toward the birth of a child. Researchers Sandelowski, Harris, and Holditch-Davis have captured this phenomenon in their article "Pregnant Moments: The Process of Conception in Infertile Couples" (*Research in Nursing and Health,* 1990, *13,* 273–282). Rather than being able to identify a specific moment in time when they went from not being pregnant to being with child, infertile couples experience a series of steps in their journey into—and through— pregnancy.

Some couples using assisted reproductive technologies (ART) perceive pregnancy as beginning with the news that there is fertilization in the laboratory setting. Others feel pregnant when embryos are transferred to the woman's uterus. Still others believe that pregnancy has been confirmed with a positive pregnancy test or with an ultrasound or at the end of the first trimester. Some women pregnant after infertility cannot quite believe that they are with child until several months into their pregnancy.

The ambiguity of early pregnancy is partly a result of the medical process. Unlike their fertile friends, who often do a home pregnancy test and proudly announce that they are expecting, infertile couples being followed at a clinic rarely receive such a definitive yes. Instead, their early blood test provides them with a quantitative measure of pregnancy hormones. Unfortunately, many couples soon learn that a very low number is deemed "a chemical pregnancy." This strange and confusing term informs them that they are technically pregnant, but that the pregnancy is not viable—a phenomenon that probably happens proportionately as often in the fertile population as in the infertile one. Although most are spared the torture of a "chemical pregnancy," many couples newly pregnant after infertility do have to endure a number of weeks in which the viability of their pregnancy is uncertain, due to the simple fact that approximately one in six pregnancies results in an early loss. (Losses are more common as women age.) When the initial hormone levels are low (but not too low to preclude a healthy pregnancy) or when those levels do not rise as expected, couples find themselves in a very stressful situation. Looking for signposts of hope, they discover that pregnancy—the blissful state that they have so long looked forward to—is actually another roller-coaster ride. In fact, it is often a much more intense and jolting ride than the roller coaster of infertility.

One of the most difficult aspects of pregnancy after infertility is isolation. Most couples find that there is considerable support available for them when they are undergoing infertility treatment, but that they are left feeling very much alone once they become pregnant. Now they are the envy of their infertile friends, so there is little support available from that community; even those people who want to offer support find it very hard to actually do so. Worse still is the lack of support from fertile friends and family, who have no way of comprehending the extraordinary stress of pregnancy after infertility.

Isolation is furthered by the fact that women who are pregnant after infertility feel as though they are in "no person's land," medically as well as socially. The transition from their infertility practice to an obstetrical practice can be very difficult in a number of ways. First, it is hard to leave a staff whom one trusts and with whom one has experienced success. Second, it can be difficult to know where to go for obstetrical care, since most pregnancies after infertility—especially after ART—feel "high risk" even though medically they are not. A woman who feels high risk needs to find a physician or a practice that understands what she has gone through and sees her anxiety as normal, not pathological.

For women pregnant after infertility, it is very difficult to be an ordinary obstetrical patient. Physicians and office staff cannot fully appreciate how vulnerable they feel. Staff will fail to realize that for newly fertile women, seemingly uneventful, healthy pregnancies are marked by a series of near-catastrophes: the absence of fetal movement for an hour, only a small weight gain between visits, or breasts feeling ever-so-slightly less full—all set off alarm signals. Newly fertile women's anxiety is heightened by the fact that most obstetricians see their patients every several weeks—and then only for brief exams. This stands in stark contrast to the frequent monitoring that they received at their infertility treatment program in the early weeks of pregnancy.

Women pregnant after infertility are truly confused as to what is cause for alarm. This confusion begins early in the pregnancy when they learn, much to their surprise, that a little bit of bleeding is not a cause for panic; many healthy, uneventful ART pregnancies begin with some bleeding. Conversely, they are stunned to learn that a pregnancy can be proceeding uneventfully, and then, without warning, a woman can go into hazardous premature labor.

Although most couples work hard to share the experience of infertility and certainly hope to share the experience of pregnancy, an equal sharing is never possible. It is the woman whose body is undergoing changes, it is she who is intensely tuned in to each change and its meaning, and it is she who probably develops an early attachment to the baby. Hence, a certain kind of isolation may develop within a couple, with each member feeling a bit estranged from his or her partner. Fortunately, this feeling diminishes once the pregnancy is more clearly established and once certain decisions, such as whether to have amniocentesis, are made.

There are certain types of patients who are likely to remain vigilant throughout most of their pregnancy. Perhaps the biggest challenge comes for those couples who learn that they are expecting multiples. Such couples discover that multiple pregnancy does not simply mean an instant family or "two for the price of one." It may mean the spontaneous loss of one or more fetuses, with the survival of another fetus or fetuses. It may mean that they face the excruciatingly difficult decision of whether to reduce a higher-risk multiple gestation to a singleton or twins. It may mean adjusting—and readjusting—their expectations about their family as they learn that they may be parenting more children than they had anticipated—or that their children's arrival may be more like a traffic jam than an unfolding journey.

Women are likely to be vigilant throughout their pregnancy if they have suffered earlier losses—miscarriages, ectopic pregnancies, or certainly stillbirths. For these couples, pregnancy is inextricably associated with loss. They may set milestones for themselves and hope to feel better when they pass them, but those who have endured significant losses cannot easily erase the imprint of those experiences from their minds.

There are also couples whose pregnancies are stressful because they conceived with donated gametes. Such couples inevitably feel additional isolation from others, since they may want to preserve their privacy during the pregnancy. Those who conceived with anonymous gametes inevitably have concerns about the identity of the donor, and they may wonder whether they will bond easily with their child or feel like a real parent. Those who formed their family with a known donor may worry about how the various relationships will play themselves out and whether the persons involved can separate the genetic role from the nurturing role.

Finally, there are couples who have a "last chance" pregnancy. They are often couples in which the woman is older or is clearly losing ovarian function, as well as those who are pregnant with cryopreserved sperm or embryos. These pregnancies, so precious and so irreplaceable, leave couples with a tremendous sense of vulnerability. Inevitably they feel isolated from others who are pregnant and seemingly carefree.

Some couples begin to enjoy pregnancy once they have passed such critical milestones as the first trimester, prenatal testing (if they opt for it), and, most significantly, the point of viability. Beyond these points, many couples finally feel that they are expecting.

Anxiety often returns in the final trimester of a post-infertility pregnancy. Couples report feelings of isolation in a childbirth class, where other couples may be focusing on such seemingly insignificant matters as pain control during labor or their fears about a cesarean. By contrast, parents-to-be after infertility remain vulnerable to significant fears of loss and continue to worry that something will happen to their baby. Although some have the benefit of a high-risk specialist who appreciates their fears and who takes active steps to ensure a safe arrival, others fear that their physician and childbirth educators are assuming too casual an approach to the upcoming arrival.

Although very anxious for a safe arrival, some women who are pregnant after infertility also feel a sense of sadness as the pregnancy nears its end. Having worked so long and hard to become pregnant and having spent so much time fearing that they would not stay pregnant, previously infertile women sometimes feel an unanticipated longing for a short extension of their pregnancy. Many assume—or fear—that this will be their only pregnancy and want to savor the feelings—of a baby kicking, of movement inside—a little longer.

The pages that follow contain a variety of accounts of pregnancy after infertility. In "Pregnancy Happens to Other People," Lisa Finneran Niden captures the emotional ups and downs, twists and contortions of someone happily, though quite anxiously, pregnant after infertility. Similar sentiments are conveyed in Karen Propp's essay, "Out of Step." Then, in the bittersweet "My First Pregnancy," Ellen Jean Tepper captures the irony that even a pregnancy that ends in miscarriage can feel like a gift—and an accomplishment—after years of infertility. And in "I Never Believed It," Rachel Lewis speaks to the power of disbelief. Many women pregnant after years of effort can identify with the difficulty she had believing that she was really with child. Finally, we have Andrea Horowitz's "Twist of Fate"—her reflections on becoming accidentally pregnant after infertility.

○

## PREGNANCY HAPPENS TO OTHER PEOPLE
### *Lisa Finneran Niden*

*April 1993*   A well-intentioned friend lends me *Without Child*. I get to the chapter "Pregnancy After Infertility." Lucky them. It's been five years. Pregnancy happens to other people. Not me.

*February 10, 1995*   I'm on hold. I watch *Oprah*—a woman has seen Jesus in a tortilla. I wait. Just give me the results, so I can have a glass of wine, a cup of coffee, an aspirin for the caffeine withdrawal. The nurse comes back on. Her name is Eileen. I'll never forget Eileen. "Lisa, yes, that test is positive." I'll never forget those words. I'm dizzy. I drink six glasses of orange juice for the folic acid, then throw up. I feel crystallized, pure, uncluttered joy. I am pregnant. Me. No more waiting. No more worrying. I think.

*February 24*   We have a heartbeat. I drive home in my Escort blaring Amy Grant. Hormonal.

*February 27*   On my calendar I draw a big face with big hair and a smile to mark the day of the news. I tell a close friend I'm pregnant.

*March 2*   I'm spotting. I must be miscarrying. My friend offers to order a pizza. I love pizza. I say no. I lie on the couch, in front of the TV, eating Velveeta cheese. I check for blood eighteen times. I cry.

*March 17*   I stop my car in the road to help a runaway terrier. I knock on doors in search of the owner. An elderly man with an oxygen tank answers the door, forever grateful. The dog holds my ankle with his mouth then runs inside. I go home. I look up "Rabies."

*March 22*   I have a migraine, I must be miscarrying. Can't take medication. I pour vinegar on a cool face cloth and breathe in. A trick from my grandmother.

*March 31*   I feel optimistic. I'm eleven weeks. My sister-in-law tells me she miscarried at twelve weeks.

*April 10* I buy three pregnancy books, bringing the total to eight under my bed. I look at the pictures and read the descriptions. The baby is a piece of rice. The baby is a Lima bean. The baby looks like something I'd find at a raw bar.

*April 13* I take a cooking course. We make tiramisu. I eat it. There's Kahlua in it. I look up "Fetal Alcohol Syndrome."

*April 15* We see the baby on ultrasound. We hear the baby on Doppler. I move, it moves. The hands are there. The feet. The fingers. Amazing. I tell the doctor my health history. She needs my records to rule out congenital something, something. What?

*April 16* I work frantically to find old blood test records. I call my second doctor, who has me call my first doctor, who sends me the results. I fax them to my sixth doctor who tells me to contact my fifth doctor to get the most recent ones: normal.

*April 28* I acknowledge the pregnancy and go to a maternity shop. The store is stupid. Pillows, crackers, cream. Purchase points for breast-feeding bras. I buy tights.

*May 1* "One month at a time." If people can advertise their alcoholism, why not their infertility? A thought. The light turns green.

*May 2* I'm spotting. I must be miscarrying. It's fourteen weeks. I drive myself to the hospital. I cry. The nurse is a little frantic. I cry more. She listens for the heart but just hears bowels. She insists it sounds like limbs. I don't believe her. She yells for an ultrasound cart. She hooks me up. The heartbeat is there.

*May 14* I have the alpha-fetoprotein test. I look up "Spina Bifida" and wait for the call.

*May 16* The critical ultrasound. Everything's normal. Heart. Brain. Fingers.

*May 27* At the bank. In the drive-through. I feel the fluttering.

*June 18* I wash the dog with dog shampoo. My husband is concerned. I cry. I look up "Pesticides." I call the doctor.

*June 25* In the aisle, at the butter, I listen to a woman. Unending pregnancy prattle. I don't know her. She thinks we are the same because we look the same. We are very different. She has no idea.

*July 4* For the first time in ten years, I'm the one pregnant at the barbecue. I have a hamburger.

*July 5* I look up "Toxoplasmosis." It comes from raw meat. My hamburger was rare. The baby will be deaf.

*July 7* I find solace in a grill book. It defines "rare."

*July 22* I feel tightening. Contractions. At the Cape, on vacation. It's ninety degrees. I'm the size of Detroit. More tightening, must be labor. Premature. We drive to the hospital. I stay for three hours. They monitor me. Braxton-Hicks contractions. Normal. I drink two quarts of Cran-Cherry.

*August 5* I walk through the metal detector at a government building. What was I thinking? I corner a security guard. He explains magnetic fields and refrigerator magnets. I drive home. I cry. I read the section on X rays.
*August 14* A surprise. A mistake. A set of twins. And us. It's our first class. I never thought I'd be here. One couple talks of too much wine on their honeymoon, eight months ago. Another wants a drug-free, dim-lit home birth in the tub. My turn. Yes, the baby was planned, and yes, I'll take drugs, light, a hospital bed, and the sound of elevators to get it here. They have no idea.

*September 3* I clean the house. Spray some Lysol. Leave the house for eight hours.
*September 20* I have the rugs cleaned. Leave the house for two weeks.

*October 1* My baby shower. I want it to end. It rains.
*October 12* I'm the size of Michigan. My blood pressure's up. I stay in bed. Why did I eat the Fritos?
*October 13* I'm at a birthday party. I eat squash soup, drink water. My shoes are off, my legs up. I leave early.
*October 14* I go into labor.
*October 16* At six fifty-nine, at seven pounds, six ounces, Emma is born. I cry.

o
_____

## OUT OF STEP
### *Karen Propp*

During the first few months of pregnancy after infertility, you are still tied to your clinic, still tethered as if by an umbilical cord to the nurses at the other end of the phone line. "Your HCG numbers look good," the nurse says in a voice better suited to offer condolences at a funeral. "Never expect good news; never expect good news to stay good" might be the reproductive clinic's motto. "Keep taking the progesterone as a precaution," she counsels.

When an in vitro pregnancy is realized, you must continue the hormonal injections until the end of the first trimester. The nightly alcohol swab and needle's stab remind you that you've embarked on a medical procedure, and as in all things medical, there are risks. Every time you draw into the syringe the thick, viscous progesterone meant to line the uterus with a thick tissue, you say a little prayer against miscarriage.

"What about sex?" you ask the nurse in a small, scared voice. "When is it all right?" You were advised to abstain for the first two weeks after the embryo transfer, but now it has been six weeks, and you and your husband are chafing at the imaginary barrier you've constructed down the center of your bed. The nurse clears her throat as if you had brought up a distasteful subject. You recognize this particular throat clearing. It does not belong to the efficient, the cutesy, or the empathic nurse, but to the bitchy one. "Am I right that you invested a lot of time and energy and money to get pregnant?" she asks.

She is right.

"Then doesn't it make sense to protect your investment?"

"But what's wrong with sex?"

"Orgasm sends the uterus into spasms and could dislodge the embryonic sac. Penetration can touch the cervix, and there's a slight possibility of infection if the cervix is still open." She wavers for a moment. "But there are other ways you can play around."

Great. Three months' worth of blow jobs.

"They have no use for sex," says your husband that night when you are lying in bed. "They got you knocked up without sex, so why not do away with it all together? Call them the reproductive police." He covers his eyes as if struck by a searing searchlight. "Oh no! They're policing our bedroom!"

I go to my first appointment with an obstetrician. Scattered on teak end tables in the waiting room are parenting magazines that feature pregnant women in fox gray leotards, their bodies both huge and supple, their hair lustrous, their smiles beatific. Anatomically correct posters of a baby in utero at six months, at eight months, at nine months hang on the wall. The obstetrician is bouncy with congratulations and good cheer. "We'll reserve a birthing room for your due date," she says. "And here's information about Lamaze classes, car seats, lactation instruction."

"Wait a minute," I want to say. "Just hold on. One day, one week at a time. How can you be so sure, so confident?"

"Of course, there is the amniocentesis," she says. "Will you be wanting to do an amnio?"

"Absolutely. And I'm still on progesterone. The infertility clinic wants you to check my levels at twelve weeks to see if it's OK to go off it."

A look of vague annoyance and impatience crosses her dimpled face. "Oh, that," she says. "Just check in with the lab downstairs for the blood test whenever you're ready."

"What about sex?" I ask. "Is it OK?"

She waves her hand as if to dismiss all doubts and infinitesimal percentiles. She nods her head vigorously up and down. "Shouldn't be a problem. No problem at all."

At home, Samuel and I carry a happiness that's as fragile as a Chinese porcelain bowl, a joy we watch for fear it might break. We don't tell many people our news. We're afraid it might go away, or that we'll attract the evil eye. What if something happens? Better keep it to ourselves until we are sure, until we have learned how to live with this new and unfamiliar elation.

One morning he wakes up singing *"ce chambre sans berceau,"* a phrase from Jacques Brel's "Song of Old Lovers."

"It just hit me that we don't have to be that song," he exclaims. "We don't have to be old lovers in a room without a cradle. That's not us!"

Who are we then? Not yet cradle rockers. It's too early to think of ourselves as expectant parents, but we're no longer *trying* to become pregnant. It will take us—and me—some time to become comfortable with this new identity.

After twelve weeks, I make my first foray into the world of the fertile: a prenatal exercise class. Even the infertility clinic, everlastingly protective, did not prohibit exercise.

Everyone in the exercise room has a differently shaped belly protruding under her T-shirt. Bulky, substantial, massive, or gigantic. In comparison I feel flat as a paper doll. I'm wearing loose-fitting sweatpants that conceal my body—a throwback to how I dressed as a teenager—while the other women wear spandex shorts and close-fitting T-shirts that reveal. Do I really belong here? Could these optimistic, rosy-cheeked women be my new peer group?

Before class begins, we congregate in twos and threes; clearly the center of attention is an enormously pregnant woman with glowing skin, long blond hair, mascara eyes.

"I'm due in three weeks," she tells us. "But I guess it could be any day now." She gives the top of her stomach a friendly pat. "My first baby was ten pounds."

*My first baby.* How easily that phrase slips off her tongue. In my new and hard-won state, it hasn't occurred to me that anyone could be pregnant for the *second* time. The blond woman continues: "My OB keeps teasing me, 'Now, are we going to do that again?' I don't know how I get so big. But everywhere I go now, people stare. I literally watch them turn their heads and bug out their eyes."

She laughs an easy, jolly laugh, a laugh that belies no difficulty or self-consciousness about fertility, a laugh suggesting that pregnancy and childbirth have been a series of effortless surprises. Underneath black leggings, her thick thighs are muscular pistons. I take a step back and find my place before the mirror that runs across the front of the room. This woman, I realize, is an infertility patient's worst nightmare: fecund, celebratory, confident.

"Squat," the aerobics instructor barks at us once the music begins. "Squat deep and step left. You're going to need those thighs strong."

Suddenly, I am in the world of the pregnant. Obstetricians, fullness, delivery due dates. We are eight women in the room and eight babies on the way. The miracle that was private and singular to Samuel and me is becoming public and even ordinary. No one seems worried about an incompetent cervix, miscarriage, toxemia, gestational diabetes—all high-risk pregnancy problems that I hear about regularly on the counseling center help line that I work on. Can it be, I ask myself as I bend right, then left, that everything will be all right?

"Push your arms forward," the instructor shouts. We bend our elbows, hands to shoulders, then straighten our arms front, wrists bent and palms facing the mirror. "Push the baby in the stroller," she says. "Push the baby uphill."

Friends with children, relatives, and even acquaintances begin to initiate me into this new world of the pregnant. Unbidden, they begin to offer advice and opinions about episiotomies, changing tables, raising boys versus raising girls. And I am an eager listener, wanting to learn and master the information in this new realm much as I had recently learned the vocabulary of egg fertilization and hormonal fluctuations. But I am a skeptical listener, too. I have lived for so many years of my life outside this world of calcium supplements and diaper rashes that I'm not quite sure how to walk down its roads.

An old friend, who is the mother of three small boys, sends me two large boxes of her maternity clothes. When Samuel walks in the door and sees the boxes in our front hall and I tell him what they contain, a dark and worried look crosses his face. "Already?" he asks. "It could be bad luck. Put them in the basement."

Ordinarily my Samuel is a rational rather than a superstitious man. But infertility leaves its trace on even the most levelheaded, and I think he, like me, is unnerved by moving quickly into this new identity.

I call my friend to thank her for the clothes. Right away, she wants to discuss each outfit—the black cotton jumper with three buttons, the sleeveless summer blouses, the turquoise tunic. In her jubilant voice I hear how she is remembering her own three pregnancies and her happiness for mine.

I pull soft jersey from the box. "I like the striped shirt with a zipper," I tell my generous friend. I hold it out at arm's length as if she could see. "This looks like me." I hold it against my front and smooth the folds against my tender belly. The shirt seems huge, too billowy, almost misshapen. In truth, I can't see myself in any of it yet.

From nature's point of view, fertility is always an uphill struggle. A woman is fertile for only thirty-six hours each month and for at most thirty years of her much longer life span. You might say that the normal female state is actually nonchildbearing. As the weeks passed and my stomach swelled and I entered more fully the world of the pregnant, I realized that my extended experience with trying to become pregnant had made me more aware of the range of reproductive issues nearly every woman faces.

Perhaps naively, I was unprepared to hear one particular line of commentary. Here and there, I pieced together conversational snippets to form a court of maternal judgment that went something like this:

"Did you hear that Tanya's pregnant?"

"Her second, right?"

"Due in August."

"I forget how old her first child is now."

"Her little girl will be three in June."

"Oh, only three. I thought she'd taken much longer. Three years isn't too far apart."

And, like this:

"Eileen had another boy in December."

"Another one! How many is it now?"

"Six. Her sixth kid, fourth boy."

"Six kids! In what, eight, nine, years?"

"It's shocking how closely they're spaced. No one does that anymore. Catholics, you know. It's not as if they can afford them all."

What surprised me was that these were educated, professional women speaking. Everyone, it seemed, had an opinion on other people's reproductive histories, an opinion that betrayed their own insecurities as to what was expected and what they wanted.

On the counseling line and at my reproductive clinic, I was a woman to be envied, one of the few and the lucky. When I broke the news of my pregnancy to infertile friends, I made an effort to sound offhand and temper my joy. But in the wider world of motherhood, on whose entrance I stood poised, I was unlucky and late. Older, medically assisted, unlikely to have more than one. In my prenatal exercise class, I didn't mention the circumstances of how I had become pregnant. No one did.

The robust blond woman disappeared from class, presumably to have her baby. No one else in the group was as noticeably far along as she had been, and the title for most pregnant woman lay, for the time being, unclaimed. A couple of months passed, and then it became apparent that two more women were about to give birth—by coincidence, due on the exact same date. Before and after class, the buzz grew louder around their gigantic bellies. What hospital was each one using? Did she think the baby would be early or late? Was the overnight bag packed yet?

"It's such a rite of passage," one of the most pregnant said to me as she opened her locker to change back into her street clothes. "Becoming a mother, I mean." And then, under her breath, the sentence I had been dreading to hear ever since I'd joined. "Even if you hadn't planned it to happen so soon."

I nodded, said nothing, and busied myself with something inside my locker. Oh, well, I rationalized to myself, so she had to deal with pregnancy and having a kid earlier than she'd anticipated. Everyone has their own challenges. A lot of things don't work out the way one expects. Although I soothed myself with these thoughts, I had no wish to continue the conversation. She, however, seemed intent on drawing me out. "What do you do for work?" She was rubbing lotion onto the taut mass of her naked belly.

I swallowed a few times, and then I said, trying to make light of things: "I've just been through this whole in vitro experience, and I'm writing a book about it."

"Oh," she said, and drew in her breath and turned away, then turned back and said "Oh" once again.

I sat down on a low bench. "Yes," I said. "It's been quite an experience."

Another woman in the class, her locker directly across from mine, whipped around, black ponytail flying, eyes open wide. "In vitro!" she exclaimed. "I did in vitro and just about everything else. Two and a half years. Unexplained infertility. And then, you know what?" She waved her hands in excitement. "I got so fed up with nothing working that I took a month off. Started smoking cigarettes, drinking coffee, staying up late. I was angry. Angry at all the treatments that hadn't worked. And you know what? That was the month I got pregnant." She sat down and began to slip her bra straps onto her shoulders. "It's a miracle."

And then, like graduates of some august institution who meet in a foreign country, she and I sat, half-naked, our knees nearly touching in the narrow space between lockers, and talked doctors, drug protocols, egg retrievals. Suddenly, the pregnant world seemed less perfect and therefore less threatening; having found this opening, I felt more at home.

She told me her doctors had been extremely optimistic about the chances for success with what they'd called her "beautiful" eggs, and that was part of the reason she'd been so angry when the treatment failed. My doctors, on the other hand, were pessimistic about my chances of conceiving with eggs that were few and only "fair." I told her how depressed I'd been during the two weeks between the embryo transfer and the pregnancy test.

"Just goes to show you," she said.

"Isn't it strange how things turned out?" I replied. The sauna door opened just then, and several sweating women walked out through the warm steam that filtered into the room. They walked slowly, as if emerging from a deep dream, and I realized that I, too, had just emerged from a cloud as enveloping as the one that made their figures fuzzy and difficult to discern. I, too, had sweated it out by hot coals, and now I felt somehow purified, released.

"With you, the doctors were optimistic," I continued, "but treatment didn't work. With me, they were pessimistic and treatment did finally work. Their affect really affects you, doesn't it?" My new friend laughed and nodded in agreement. "And all those damned statistics," I said. "If I had one thing to say to someone who's beginning treatment, it would be, 'You never know.'"

She pointed her finger at me as if at a bull's-eye. "Put that in your book."

I turned to the woman who'd conceived accidentally. She'd been listening with interest and curiosity to the infertility conversation and was dressed now, ready to leave. "You're the one we used to hate." I could joke now.

She nodded rather kindly, as if she understood.

"Not anymore!" cried out my colleague from the infertility wars. From her locker she drew a ceramic brooch and strung it around her neck, where it hung glistening like a medal against her olive skin. "Not anymore."

○

# MY FIRST PREGNANCY
## *Ellen Jean Tepper*

My first pregnancy ended in a first-trimester miscarriage. The "products" of a six-year effort at conception landed in Dr. P's trash can along with the mail-order catalogues that Dave brought along to distract me. In many ways it was a very sad experience. Still, I look back on those weeks of early pregnancy as a time of great excitement—and of affirmation. I remember the first week with particular pleasure.

I first suspected that I was pregnant on a beach at Cape Cod. I was there for the day with friends, but after years of infertility, I was more focused on my soon-to-arrive period than on our outing. It was twelve days after ovulation, and since a short luteal phase always causes me to menstruate two or three days early, that July Tuesday was right about time.

Traditionally, I spent days twenty-five and twenty-six in the bathroom, checking for blood. For me it was easier that way. The thermometer told the news too harshly, with no room for error. But a little blood could mean many things—implantation bleeding, perhaps some spotting. I always gave myself a few hours to accept that it meant what it meant: failed conception.

But I was in a predicament that sunny July day; there were no toilets on the beach. Fortunately, infertility had taught me to approach situations creatively, and this one was no exception. Cautiously, I slipped my finger through the crotch of my bathing suit. Quickly, as though I were scratching. Then I took a discreet look. Clean. Safe on first.

The finger-up-the-vagina quick-check test served me well over the next several hours. Again and again, in quick, out clean. Day twenty-six was nearing an end, and I was beginning to wonder.

On Wednesday morning I went out running. I have a group of friends that I meet at six A.M. For an hour each day we share the most intimate details of our lives, as well as exchange recipes and movie reviews. But that Wednesday, day twenty-seven, I led two lives. There was regular old infertile me, running along and talking about my day at the Cape, and there was quick-checking, almost-convinced-I-was-pregnant me, now one day early—or one day late.

By Wednesday afternoon, I could stand it no longer. I drove to a pharmacy in a neighboring town, willing to go out of my way so that no one would see me buying a home pregnancy test. Still, I felt exposed. What would the cashier think? The pharmacist? Would they take a look at me and say to themselves, "not her"? Or might they mistake me for someone who had happened, quite by accident, into pregnancy?

As it turned out, I never got as far as the cashier. I examined each test kit and found that none would work until I was at least nine days late. Since I could barely wait nine hours, I had to find a better way. But what? I couldn't ask for a blood test when I was still officially one day early. And I couldn't ask Dr. P what to do, because he'd declared me hopelessly infertile.

By Thursday, day twenty-eight, now on time or two days late, I knew that something was different. I told Wendy while we were running that I suspected I might be pregnant, and swore her to secrecy. Later I phoned Rena and promised myself to stop there. But then there was Sylvia; we'd been through her first pregnancy together, and she'd been there when we'd adopted Emily. She was pregnant again, and now I was imagining that we might have the chance to do it together. By day's end, six friends knew that I was waiting and hoping.

On Friday I began to think more about those who didn't know what was going on, namely my husband, Dave, and my doctor, than about those who did. I had very mixed feelings about telling each of them. With Dave, I felt it was too much joy to bear. If it were really true, I wanted to save it for his birthday, now eight days away. Also, as long as I held off, I could fantasize over and over again about how I would tell him. There were countless scenarios, each more splendid than the one before. I knew that once I told him, I would have to surrender possibilities.

With Dr. P it was different. It wasn't that I wanted to save the news, but rather that I wanted to be sure I was really pregnant before I called him and embarrassed myself. He had been so certain that I was hopelessly infertile when he told us to adopt. Now I wondered how he would react if I professed pregnancy.

"Hello, Dr. P, I know that you are going to think I'm psychotic, but I think I might be pregnant."

"What makes you think that?"

"Well, I'm fifteen days past ovulation, and I've never made it for more than twelve."

"Congratulations. You've treated yourself. But have a blood test on Monday just to be sure."

Somehow I made it through the long, slow weekend. Finger quick-checks took up most of the time, and the rest was spent deciding who to tell next. Meanwhile, Dave's birthday was still a good six days off, and I was about to burst. Monday morning I could stand it no longer.

"Let's tell Mommy the news." Dave and Emily greeted me when I came in from my running. Some major event, like a poop in the toilet, must have just occurred.

"Well, Mommy has something to tell you." And there it was, spilled out with none of the splendor I'd imagined. Dave just sat there and stared at me in disbelief.

I did have a pregnancy test that day, and what I had suspected but dared not believe for nearly a week became official.

In my seventh week, I had an ultrasound "just to make sure everything was all right." Until that point, things had seemed to be going well. I was still checking for blood, but I was also craving chopped liver—a hopeful sign, I felt, for someone who had been a vegetarian for twenty years. So when that first ultrasound was inconclusive, I didn't know how to react. I worried, but I was also very busy being pregnant.

But the ultrasound one week later was a different matter. This time it was conclusive, and it revealed that there was no fetal development. A "blighted ovum," they called it, to be kind, but the hard, cold facts spoke for themselves. There was a little sac in my uterus, and it was empty.

Dr. P preferred to "wait and see," rather than to actively terminate the pregnancy. I suppose he hoped that I would begin to bleed on my own, and in retrospect, I think it would have been easier had it happened that way. But the blood did not come, and I continued to have some hope—though it grew dimmer and dimmer—that everything was all right after all.

At twelve weeks something had to be done. I was now convinced that I was no longer pregnant, but it looked unlikely that I would miscarry spontaneously. So we made plans to remove it. What I did not realize ahead of time was that the bloodless, physically painless, antiseptic procedure would seem like an abortion.

Dave and I went to Dr. P's office late one September afternoon. While we waited, I paced about, and Dave tried to entertain me with his mailorder catalogues.

"How about a plastic cole slaw dish? This one's in the shape of a cabbage."

"This is no time to joke about cole slaw dishes." Actually I thought he was pretty funny, but I think I wanted to be sure that the other people in the waiting room knew I wasn't there for just another Pergonal shot or PK test.

Eventually the waiting room cleared out, and Dr. P was ready to end his day—and my pregnancy. He made quick work of it, vacuuming me out in just a few minutes. Dave saw the placenta, but I saw nothing—no tissue, no blood. A day later I was sorry that I hadn't asked to see it.

With the suspense gone, I was surprised to find that I was not devastated by the loss. Certainly sadness and emptiness were there, but those feelings were also accompanied by a feeling of pride and accomplishment. Whatever would happen in the future, I had now been pregnant. Barren for so long, I now knew that something could begin to grow inside me. I had had a pregnancy test, and it had been positive. Yes, for a brief magical moment in time, I had enjoyed chopped liver.

## Update

My first pregnancy was not my last. I was blessed with another—and successful—pregnancy just a few months after my first loss. Although anxious throughout, I "enjoyed" an uneventful pregnancy, labor, and delivery. That was nearly fifteen years ago. I am now thoroughly enjoying adolescence—through fifty-year-old eyes!

○

## I NEVER BELIEVED IT
### Rachel Lewis

I seemed to have had a miscarriage about two months before I conceived my first child, almost a year and a half after we began trying to conceive. My period was ten days late, later than it had ever been. What came out of me did not look like the usual contents of menstruation. After I described it to my reproductive endocrinologist (I didn't have the foresight to save it), he concurred that it was probably a very early miscarriage. He called it a spontaneous abortion.

I was crushed. How could this happen to me? My doctor tried to be reassuring. He said that it was really a very positive sign, that at least I knew I could conceive. I tried to be optimistic and see things his way, though it was difficult to suppress my sadness. It seemed as if I had been trying to get pregnant forever. In retrospect, having worked for ten years with infertile couples, I now know that I was one of the lucky ones. A year and a half is small potatoes in the cosmic realm of infertility.

Two months after that probable miscarriage, I conceived. When my period was twelve days late I had a beta sub (blood) test for pregnancy. I listened in disbelief when my doctor got on the telephone and said, "Congratulations, pregnant lady!" I can remember asking him if it was possible the lab had made a mistake or switched my blood with someone else's.

He assured me there was no mistake (I imagine he had been asked that question many times before) and also mentioned that the beta sub count was high, indicating a strong pregnancy.

I didn't believe him, not because I am untrusting by nature, or because I had any reason not to trust him; I just didn't believe that I was actually pregnant. Unconsciously, I believed that infertility would be my punishment for having had a relatively easy life. It was also the worst punishment I could imagine, one I felt incapable of surviving.

I also remembered the miscarriage two months earlier and became certain that even if I were pregnant, I would lose it. I checked periodically for blood. My worries, to some extent, were based on reality. For one thing, I had none of the usual pregnancy symptoms that I had read or heard about: no sore breasts, no fatigue, and no nausea. I kept trying to conjure up those symptoms so I could reassure myself that everything was OK, but no matter how much I poked them, my breasts did not feel tender, and I could not fall asleep in the afternoon. The one change in my body was that I needed to urinate constantly. I did not know that that was common in early pregnancy, so I convinced myself that I had a bladder infection, which was somehow affecting my reproductive system and causing my menses to be suppressed. I thus alternated between anticipating a miscarriage and convincing myself that my bladder was in trouble.

So I drove myself crazy all during my first trimester. When the doctor examined me in my eighth week of pregnancy and told me that everything was progressing normally, I still did not believe him. I clung fast to the bladder infection theory and reasoned that my uterus was enlarged because I was not able to menstruate due to the infection.

When I was in my tenth week of pregnancy, the doctor heard the heartbeat, or so he said. To me it sounded like a child's choo-choo train. My husband and I were leaving the following week to go on a two-week vacation. I asked the doctor if perhaps he was just telling me he heard the heartbeat so we could enjoy our vacation. He looked directly at me and, in a kind way, assured me that he would never do that. It seemed there was no way to convince me that not only was there a fetus, but also that it was developing normally.

I did have moments during which I began to believe I might really be pregnant. During my tenth week of pregnancy, I actually experienced about an hour of nausea around lunchtime. I was thrilled! The timing was unfortunate, however, as I was meeting some colleagues who were taking me out to lunch. When I began to feel better, I didn't know whether to be happy that I could enjoy my meal or worried that the fleeting nausea was really a fluke and had nothing to do with any pregnancy. I seemed to be getting fatter; certainly I was gaining weight, but that phenomenon was not unknown to me either.

We had told people about the pregnancy early on, though now it seems strange to have done that when I did not believe it myself. I felt like an imposter when friends and family members asked me about my pregnancy or about our plans for the birth. I went through the motions of a pregnant woman: doctor's visits, looking into childbirth classes, even buying maternity clothes. Yet none of it seemed real.

I felt movement in my nineteenth week. At first it felt like a goldfish fluttering around, so I convinced myself that I was wrong about the bladder infection. I decided that I must really have a parasite growing inside me. By the time I was in the middle of my seventh month, the movements began to feel like body parts poking me or limbs moving. At that point, even my very strong denial (perhaps it was fear) began to fade. I realized that any woman in my condition who did not believe she was pregnant belonged in a mental hospital.

I began to enjoy my pregnancy more once I believed it was real, though I must admit that when my son's head emerged from me during delivery, I burst into tears. The moment was highly emotional, but beyond that, I cried because the last ounce of denial I had been harboring had been removed. I finally had the baby for whom I longed and whom I had never believed would be mine.

<hr>

○

<hr>

## A TWIST OF FATE
### *Andrea Horowitz*

"Are you using birth control?" he asked.

*Are you crazy?* I thought, but simply answered, "No."

"Well that's up to you, but I have known a number of women who have found themselves very fertile after successful infertility treatment."

*Them, not me,* I thought, but said, "I'll take my chances."

Two months later I was staring at a home pregnancy test in disbelief. I couldn't believe that after five years of infertility and after being told that I would never conceive, I was now pregnant! But I didn't have time to stare at the test very long, because our twins starting crying in unison.

Three years have passed, and I am now the busy mother of four-year-old twin sons, Josh and Max, and a three-year-old daughter, Hannah.

Each of my children is deeply loved and appreciated, and life for all of us is good. My husband, Dan, and I have so much to be thankful for. Our lives are very busy with the kids and work and seeing our parents and siblings. There is not a whole lot of time for quiet reflection, but occasionally, when I have thirty seconds or more of spare time, I think back on our infertility and our fertility and the way in which they collided.

In my day, I was one of the most infertile of the infertile. Not that that was any great accomplishment, but each physician we saw reacted with more doom and gloom than the one before. Although we were relatively young for infertility circles (thirty-two and thirty-three at the time the twins were born, after six years of trying), I had an assortment of seemingly insurmountable fertility impairments. Physicians tried to be gentle and kind with us, but all made it clear that we were most unlikely to have a child together.

Although we were actively investigating adoption, I persuaded Dan to try "just one more cycle" at "just one more center." That would make six cycles at three centers. Not surprisingly, he wasn't enthused about the idea, but he did agree to go along with it. By this time I was a walking encyclopedia of infertility, and I had ideas about how the cycle could be done differently to ensure its success. Dan and our new physician looked skeptically at each other when I announced my recommended protocol, but both agreed to go along with it. "But this is it," they said. This would be the last try. And it was.

My pregnancy with the twins was fairly uneventful at the beginning, but became increasingly stressful as time went on. I developed problems at twenty-one weeks, and there was some concern that I was headed for severe toxemia. As it turned out, that was not a problem, but other things were. I had early contractions and was put on strict bed rest from twenty-three weeks on. Although I eventually made it to thirty-five weeks, there were several scares along the way. And by this time, we knew that we were having boys and that boys born early tend not to do as well as girls.

Despite our worry, Josh and Max were both born healthy, at 4 pounds, one ounce, and four pounds, three ounces, respectively. They came out crying loudly and didn't let up for at least six months. But I can't say I minded, after all that we had been through. I remember lying there in the hospital after giving birth and pinching myself. I couldn't believe that it was me. I couldn't believe that my body, which had been such a major failure in the baby-making department, had actually given birth. I couldn't believe that I, Ms. Infertility, had become a mother. Me, an infertile woman, a mother.

And so it was a great shock to me that I conceived naturally when the boys were just five months old. First of all, I had pretty much forgotten that people actually conceived through sexual intercourse. Second, I can't say that I remember even having sex during those exhausting first few months. Third, I was nursing, and that is supposed to make it difficult to become pregnant. And finally, and most important, I believed myself to be seriously and permanently infertile.

So there I was, pregnant against all odds. I felt a strange mixture of emotions. Upset (I wasn't ready for another pregnancy, let alone another baby). Cheated (I wanted to have time with the twins). Frightened (Would everything be OK, and would I be able to handle it all?). Guilty (So many of my infertile friends would have given anything for one pregnancy, and here I was having another baby after twins). But most of all, I felt ecstasy. Here I was, accidentally pregnant. That made me a fertile woman. My infertility was really behind me.

Or was it? In the years since Hannah's birth I have thought a lot about my two pregnancies—the one that we forced and the one that forced itself on us—and I have thought about the strange way in which my infertility and my fertility bumped up against each other. When I was pregnant with Hannah, I felt that my surprise pregnancy was a cure—that I would no longer feel infertile. Afterward, I felt that my surprise pregnancy was actually an extension of my infertility; if I hadn't felt so completely infertile, we would have used birth control. And then there are times when I see a pregnant woman and feel a pang of envy, almost forgetting that I have been twice blessed with that awesome experience.

I guess that where this has led me is to believe that infertility—at least the serious kind that we had—never really goes away. I became pregnant. We became parents. We are thrice blessed, but I don't forget. Perhaps that is the greatest blessing of all?

# 10

# PREGNANCY LOSS

OF THE MANY INJUSTICES associated with infertility, perhaps none is as profound as pregnancy loss after infertility. It can feel like a cruel hoax: a couple spends time, energy, and often large amounts of money to achieve a pregnancy, only to have their hopes and dreams dashed. Even though many, probably most, who suffer pregnancy loss will go on to have successful pregnancies, the loss of a wanted child is often deeply felt for years to come.

Although each pregnancy loss is the loss of a life that is loved, wanted, and to some extent known, the type of pregnancy loss that a couple experiences—chemical pregnancy, miscarriage, ectopic pregnancy, stillbirth, or loss in multiple gestation—does shape some aspects of their loss experience and subsequent grief. Following are some observations of people's experiences within each category of pregnancy loss.

## Chemical Pregnancy

Being told that they have "just a chemical pregnancy" is one of the most confusing experiences that a couple can encounter in their journey through infertility. What does this mean? Is she really pregnant and is this simply another way of identifying a very early miscarriage, or is this not really a pregnancy? Is it a good thing in that it represents a step closer to their goal, or is it evidence of yet another problem? And how soon can they try again? Will this nonpregnancy resolve itself quickly, or will it delay their renewed treatment efforts? These and other questions plague those who experience chemical pregnancy.

The experience of chemical pregnancy is made more complicated by the fact that it is a "disenfranchised" loss: a loss that is not acknowledged as a loss; physicians make little of it, and most others in the would-be parents' lives do not even know that it has occurred. If they learn about it at all, it is usually after the fact, at a time when they are unable to offer appropriate support.

## Miscarriage

When most people think of a miscarriage, they assume that a pregnant woman discovers that she is bleeding vaginally and that that bleeding will intensify. Couples undergoing high-tech infertility treatment are surprised and often confused to learn that many miscarriages after infertility are actually announced in a much more scientific way. Blood test results may indicate that the pregnancy hormones are dropping or are not increasing at an adequate rate, or an ultrasound may reveal the absence—or disappearance—of a fetal heartbeat. Although there are some women for whom a miscarriage is signaled by vaginal blood, there are many successful pregnancies after infertility that involve considerable bleeding.

Miscarriage after infertility is almost always accompanied by regret and self-blame. Women look back on their pregnancy and torture themselves with questions about what they did wrong. Although those who miscarry without a history of infertility are also inclined to self-blame, women seem to take a far more torturous approach when they've had infertility treatment. Women feel especially responsible for pregnancies that were collaboratively established; with elegant synchronization, their husbands, their physicians, and the laboratory personnel all did their part. Once a woman has been inseminated or has had embryos transferred, she feels that she is responsible for the outcome of the pregnancy.

After a miscarriage a woman can almost always identify her "transgressions." Some women focus on one thing, such as an earlier elective abortion, and conclude that they are now being punished. Other women consider several possible causes for their loss—perhaps they exercised too much, failed to pray adequately, drank a glass of wine, remained on their feet too long at work, or lifted heavy packages. Whatever the specific "cause," the self-blame is excruciating.

Another key feature of miscarriage—especially miscarriage after infertility treatment—is isolation. Couples who experience a loss feel isolated from friends and family, who may not have even known about the pregnancy and who are certainly ill equipped to grasp the significance of the loss. Couples are also isolated from their physicians, who may have discharged them to an obstetrical practice or who may have difficulty expressing the true sadness *they* feel over the loss. Indeed, the partners may feel isolated from each other, since it is she who was pregnant and who felt early attachment. He may attempt to share the pregnancy in every way, but ultimately the loss occurred in her body.

## Ectopic Pregnancy

When an ectopic pregnancy occurs after infertility treatment—especially after in vitro fertilization—couples begin to feel they are in a no-win situation. Those who have a preexisting tubal blockage begin to wonder if there is any way of getting around it (and indeed, there are women who are advised to have their fallopian tubes removed or burned off at the ends to avoid any possibility of additional ectopics). Others, who had no history of tubal disease, wonder how it is that they, who were being treated for another infertility problem (including unexplained infertility), ever ended up with an ectopic. Some begin to fear that the treatment is doing more harm than good.

Regardless of how and why it happens, an ectopic pregnancy is almost always a traumatic experience. It often brings excruciating pain not only to the woman, who must endure the physical loss, but also to her partner, who feels devastated by his wife's suffering. Men have told me that they were even afraid to have intercourse with their wives following an ectopic, for fear that they would again impregnate her, thereby placing her in a serious—or even life-threatening—situation.

In addition to the trauma of diagnosis—which occurs either because a woman is in excruciating pain or because she has been monitored closely and an ectopic has been identified—there is the trauma of treatment. Surgical treatment of ectopic pregnancies has been partially replaced by the use of Methotrexate, a form of chemotherapy that can be effective in treating an unruptured ectopic. Unfortunately, many patients are no more prepared for this option than they are for facing emergency surgery. The news that they must undergo a dose or more of chemotherapy—followed by several weeks of slow resolution—is bewildering and often upsetting.

All ectopic pregnancies do not occur in the fallopian tubes. Occasionally a woman will have a startling—and potentially lethal—pregnancy on an ovary or in some other place outside the uterine cavity. It is also important to note that some ectopic pregnancies are accompanied by one or more uterine pregnancies. In fact, one woman carrying quadruplets was recently seen for severe abdominal pain. When her physician did exploratory surgery, expecting to find another pregnancy in a tube, she was surprised to discover a fifth pregnancy on an ovary. (This life-threatening condition, which resulted in significant blood loss, was surgically resolved, and the woman went on to successfully carry her quadruplets.)

## Stillbirth

Although it seems unfathomable that anyone who has suffered infertility will go on to face the devastation of stillbirth, this tragic experience does occur. Some women who go into premature labor and lose their babies after twenty to twenty-four weeks of pregnancy (babies born after twenty-four weeks usually survive), and some suffer the incredible misfortune of cord deaths, obstetrical errors, or full-term nightmares. Perhaps those in this group, more than any others who travel the road of infertility, experience a loss of faith in themselves, in the ability of medicine to overcome their problems, and perhaps even in God. As I said, they have suffered a loss that is unfathomable.

Despite the enormity of their loss, infertile couples who suffer a stillbirth usually manage to find the strength to go on. After a period of grieving, many say that they are ready to try again. They may even refer to their loss as part of their inspiration for returning to treatment; now they *know* that they can conceive.

## Loss in Multiple Gestation

Losses have always occurred in multiple gestation, but it was not until the advent of assisted reproductive technology that they became a common event. In part this is because early ultrasounds reveal twin and triplet pregnancies that are spontaneously reduced to singleton or twin gestations. As a result, some couples experience a loss they would not otherwise have known about.

The preponderance of multiple gestations as a result of assisted reproductive technologies has certainly added to the number of couples who suffer losses, both partial and complete, in multiple pregnancy. Although there is recognition that the loss of a twin or triplet pregnancy is devastating, few appreciate the magnitude of grief that a couple feels when they experience partial loss. Most often, they are expected to feel gratitude for the child or children that survive, rather than grief over the child or children that did not.

High-level multiple gestations—usually more than three babies—often lead to recommendation of a multifetal reduction. This extraordinarily upsetting process seeks to abort one or more fetuses so that the others will be able to survive and thrive. Although all infertility patients are informed of the possibility that they will face this decision, very few are prepared for it when they confront it. Many feel angry at themselves for tampering with nature, and some feel angry at their physicians, whose treatment is perceived as causing this painful situation.

## Repeated Pregnancy Loss

As devastating as a pregnancy loss is, infertile couples often experience one loss, especially an early miscarriage, as "progress." They are relieved to know that they can conceive and feel optimistic that the next pregnancy will be different. Indeed, this is very often the case, and survivors of pregnancy loss go on to have successful pregnancies.

Sadly, there are some couples who go from one painful journey to another. Their infertility becomes—or is interspersed with—a series of pregnancy losses. When this occurs, people feel defeated, bewildered, and certainly cheated. Repeated pregnancy loss after infertility is perhaps the most isolating of experiences. People in this situation find that they now fear pregnancy—because of its potential for loss—at the same time that they are using all their resources to achieve it. In addition, it is hard for them not to feel great disappointment in medical science, which has somehow figured out how to help them conceive, but which cannot seem to help them stay pregnant.

Some couples experience repeated miscarriages after infertility; others encounter an assortment of losses, which may include ectopics and even stillbirths. The latter experience is especially traumatic, because it leaves people with the sense that nothing is working. As difficult as a series of miscarriages is, the miscarriages may be somewhat less traumatic because people have learned, through their infertility treatment, that an identified problem may have a solution. It feels next to impossible to identify a problem when a couple has a range of pregnancy losses in addition to infertility.

Couples who suffer pregnancy loss after infertility can maintain no illusion that life is fair. They have endured one crisis only to have it followed by yet another. Some find that it is followed by several devastating losses. Although it seems logical that many would conclude that pregnancy loss on top of infertility is too much to bear, this rarely seems to be the case. Instead, many couples discover that they have remarkable courage and resilience. The stories and poems that follow are testimony to both the courage and the resilience. Poet Barbara Crooker provides eloquent testimony to the significance of lost lives in her poems "The

Lost Children" and "Stillbirth." Lisa W. Horn conveys the same message in her personal narrative "Andrew and Rebecca." We turn again to poetry with Vanessa Burgess's sweet and tender poem "A Borrowed Breath," then grapple with the unthinkable—loss after a bad amniocentesis result. Monica and Sam Guckenheimer generously share their extraordinarily painful experiences in two separate essays, Monica's "My First Child" and Sam's "When There's No More Waiting." Finally, we hear from Daniel S. Cohn, who, in "A Father's Grief," captures the feelings of isolation and helplessness that expectant fathers often feel following a pregnancy loss or a neonatal loss.

○

## THE LOST CHILDREN
### *Barbara Crooker*

The ones we never speak of—
miscarried, unborn,
removed by decree,
taken too soon, crossed over.
They slip red mittens in our hands,
smell of warm wet wool,
are always out of sight.
We glimpse them on escalators,
over the shoulders of dark-haired women;
they return to us in dreams.
We hold them, as they evanesce
we never speak their names.
How many children do you have?
Two, we answer, thinking three,
or three, thinking four;
they are always with us.

The lost children come to us at night
and whisper in the shells of our ears.
They are waving good-bye on schoolbuses,
separated from us in stadiums,
they are lost in shopping malls
with their unspeakable pools,
they shine at night in the stars.

○

## STILLBIRTH
*Barbara Crooker*

She said, "Your daughters
are so beautiful.
One's a copper penny,
the other's a chestnut colt."
But what about
my first daughter,
stillborn
at term,
cause
unknown?

Ten years later
and I sift the ground
for clues: what was
it I did?
Guilt is part
of my patchwork;
grief folds me up
like an envelope.

In the hospital,
the doctors turned
their eyes, told me
not to leave
my room.
But I heard them,
those babies in the night,
saw women from Lamaze
in the corridor.
They would be wheeled home
with blossoms & blankets,
while I bled the same,
tore the same,
and came home, alone.

Later,
women showered me
with stories
of babies lost:
to crib death,
    abortion,
    miscarriage;
    lost;
    the baby
    that my best friend
    gave up
    at fourteen.

They wouldn't let me hold her:
all I saw were fragments:
    a dark head,
    a doll's foot,
    skin like a bruise.
They wouldn't let me name her,
    or bury her,
    or mourn her.
Ten years later
and I do not have
the distance:
I carry her death
like an egg
in my pocket.

---
o
---

## ANDREW AND REBECCA
### Lisa W. Horn

As I look back with amusement on my wedding day, I wonder if our vows shouldn't have been, "to love, honor, and get through infertility treatment." I had already had six surgeries for endometriosis in six years, so we knew that having a baby was not going to be easy. But we never imagined how difficult it would be!

About six months after our wedding, I had microsurgery to repair my fallopian tubes, which had been severely damaged by the endometriosis. The surgery was successful, and three months later I was pregnant. Our baby's due date was New Year's Day, and we looked forward to it with great hope and excitement. I enjoyed a wonderful pregnancy and delighted in the joy that we were bringing to both sets of parents. This was going to be the first grandchild on both sides. Since several people knew how lucky we were to have conceived, they celebrated with us throughout.

My water broke while I was lying in bed at ten A.M. on December 30, 1993. I called Steve and told him to meet me at the hospital. He called me back to say that the guys at work had told him to come and pick me up.

When we arrived at the hospital, the nurse put the fetal heart monitor on my stomach. She said that the baby must be in a strange position, because she couldn't get the heartbeat; then she went for a doctor and an ultrasound machine. The doctor tried with the ultrasound machine for five minutes, then turned to us and said, "I'm not a trained ultrasound technician, but I cannot detect any heartbeat"—twelve words that turned our dream into a nightmare—a nightmare that I could not have imagined participating in. I remember at that moment hearing the baby's heartbeat from the woman in the next bed and experiencing the sound as deafening. The nurse quickly removed her from the room, but the heartbeat seemed to continue echoing off the walls.

My obstetrician, Dr. Cook, was called and came to us immediately. When she arrived, the first words out of her mouth were, "I'm so sorry, baby." I thought to myself that there was no baby to feel sorry for anymore. In the blink of an eye our baby was taken from us, yet he was still to be born. That put us in a very strange place—a place where very few people have been. It was sort of like being suspended between life and death. As long as my baby was still in my uterus, my body would keep him warm and, seemingly, sustain life. But that wasn't reality: our baby was no longer alive. Who's to say where the line of reality is in these situations?

The nurses brought me into a labor and delivery room to induce me. We called our parents, and the only words we said were that our baby had died. They all came to the hospital immediately, not realizing that he had still not actually been born. I slept through most of that afternoon with my doctor holding my hand. Steve would periodically go out and keep our parents informed. They sat in the waiting room full of other expectant grandparents and friends. Everyone knew what our situation was, and they gave their sympathies to our parents. Surely this changed their experience there.

Then the time came for me to start pushing our child into a world that he would never be part of. I was amazed that the doctor and nurse were able to motivate me to actually push. An hour and a half later, Andrew Thompson Horn quietly entered our lives. As soon as his head appeared, Dr. Cook told us that it was a cord accident. She unwrapped the cord from his neck three times and said it had been tucked under his arm, so there had been no give. There had not been any struggle because there was no meconium in the fluid. I guess that Dr. Cook told us that in an effort to help us feel better, but it didn't help. All I felt was empty as I held my son who was perfect in every other way. We held Andrew for two hours and stopped only when his skin began changing color. We wanted to remember him the way he looked when he was born.

Because the staff didn't want me to have to be on the maternity floor, I went to geriatrics. There I had a male nurse, who told me that he had been assigned to me because the female nurses were all too sad to take care of me after what had happened. That night was the longest and loneliest of my life. Both Steve and Dr. Cook had offered to stay with me through the night, but it had been my decision to be alone. I blamed myself for not saying anything when I noticed his movement slowing down two days earlier. Now I felt that I had been foolish to listen to others who had told me that that was what happened right before a baby was born. I lay there, tormented by the thought that Andrew would be with us if I had done things differently.

We buried Andrew in a private service during a snowstorm. I appeared strong and in control. I think I was trying to make everyone else feel better by letting them think I was OK. Needless to say, I was not. The service was very painful, and deciding on a headstone was so difficult. I had imagined doing many things for my child, but this was not one of them. I felt as though I was burying my future as well as his.

No one knew what to say to us, because none of our family members or friends had been through this experience. When I came home from the hospital, the recently completed nursery had been dismantled. Everything for the baby was gone. Steve and my brothers had taken the things to my father's house, because they thought it would be too painful for me to come home to so many reminders of Andrew. I know that they meant well, but I think that packing the things away myself would have been easier than sitting in that empty room. Every time I passed the room, it seemed to be mocking the emptiness that I felt in my life.

I returned to my job as an elementary school teacher a few weeks after we lost Andrew. It was difficult being there at a time when I had anticipated I would be home adjusting to new motherhood. However, the kindness of the other teachers, as well as many parents, meant a great deal to me. I learned that the teachers had collected money to buy books that they would donate to the school library in Andrew's name. Steve and I designed a bookplate together with Andrew's name, birth date, and a quote from a poem: "A lifetime of joy in an instant." That phrase summed it up for both of us.

The months following Andrew's death remained very painful. Steve and I grieved both together and separately. We joined a support group with three other couples who had lost babies at birth, and I spent time alone, filling Andrew's baby book with everything we had been given. During this time we also had to go through the difficult experience of hearing that some of our friends were expecting. I had to struggle with whether to attend their baby showers (I did manage to get to a few), but I never went to visit any of them at the hospital after birth.

When we got the go-ahead, we began to try again. When another surgery was not successful, we decided to try in vitro fertilization, but even then, things did not go well for us. After two additional surgeries and unsuccessful cycles, Steve wanted to take a break. I was able to convince him to stick with it a little longer, and then I faced yet another hurdle: my FSH level was over 10. I convinced my doctor to let us proceed with the cycle, and two weeks later we learned that I was pregnant. We were pleased with the news, but hardly thrilled in the way that we had been four years before, when I was first pregnant with Andrew. We were soon to learn that many things were going to be dramatically different this time.

At six weeks, I awoke at five A.M. and ran to the bathroom. I was bleeding heavily and assumed it was a miscarriage. I went to the doctor's office at noon, expecting the worst, but was told that the fetal sac was fine and that it was a blood clot next to my uterus that was causing the bleeding. The doctor sent me home, saying that I had a fifty-fifty chance of carrying the pregnancy. Hearing this, I felt like I was going out of my mind. Still, I managed to follow his instructions to stay in bed, and after six weeks the clot had reabsorbed and the baby was doing fine.

At the end of the first trimester, my pregnancy was deemed normal. Still, there was no way that it was going to feel normal. Anger. As I look back over those nine months, that was the emotion I felt most often. I had some friends and coworkers who were expecting at the same time, and I saw them so happy and excited. By contrast, I was so scared. I became very angry that other people could enjoy being pregnant, and I felt like I was the only person who had seen the dark side. There were no showers, gifts, or nursery preparations at all. If I didn't feel the baby move every hour, my heart dropped. Steve did not want to discuss anything about the future for this child. He said that he'd been caught in that trap once before and he wouldn't let it happen again. Occasionally we allowed ourselves to discuss names, but I think that was because we knew that every baby, whether dead or alive, needs a name.

My doctor decided to induce me at thirty-eight weeks so there would not be a chance of tragedy repeating itself. I will never forget the drive to the hospital because it was so terrifying. We didn't talk much, and I hoped that the memories of the first time were not going to become overwhelming. Fortunately, I began to feel much better as soon as we got to the hospital and the heart monitor went on. Instead of the darkness and quiet of the first time, the sun was shining and the TV was blaring. Then they induced me.

Seven hours after I was induced, Rebecca MacNeill Horn announced herself into the world at the top of her lungs. Seeing her for the first time, I knew that everything we had been through had better prepared us for this moment. We would never take a day with her for granted, and that was Andrew's gift to his sister. He had made us more compassionate and mature people. He had made our marriage stronger by defining us as individuals and as a partnership. Rebecca would reap the benefits of those life-altering experiences. I know that I am not the same mother to her that I would have been to Andrew.

Having another baby has not made me less sad about losing Andrew. There is a bittersweetness in watching Becca with all of her "firsts." Would Andrew have crawled earlier, or would he have liked peas so much? I was supposed to be the mother of a son; having the worms and hockey rink experiences. But the anger has dissipated. I know that I am the mother of a son, but I have to wait a lifetime to be with him. In the meantime, I am so grateful to have a daughter who is happy and easygoing. I think there is a peacefulness in her that comes from another place—a place that most people are traveling their whole lives to get to.

Every year on Andrew's birthday, Steve and I go to a bookstore and buy a few additional books to donate in his memory. I have come to enjoy this annual event; it gives me a sense that I am keeping his memory alive. When I see one of his books being enjoyed by one of my students, I feel that he is nearby.

○
_____

## A BORROWED BREATH
### Vanessa Burgess

Smoothly carefully and folded gently,
I packed away the sweet smell
that surrounded your yesterday.

The feel of soft fabric,
faded flannel from your shirt
I held you but I held her the same.

Hands that healed my own
lost baby blanket cover my
stomach where I'd kept you
safe like your sister before.

The sound of your breath
is a rhythmic reminder of the
air that cannot remain no matter how sweet she was.

I breathed her in for such a short
time and, relishing the remains of sweet lullabies
and angels, I released her last breath as my own.

○
_____

## MY FIRST CHILD
### Monica Guckenheimer

I was ten when my best friend Kate got a baby sister and I fell in love. I'd beg Kate's mom to let me feed Jessica, steal her away for walks, change her diaper, burp her, or just hold her. I knew then that I desperately wanted to be a mom.

It was devastating to find at the age of thirty-five that we could not have children the old-fashioned way. We would need to go to a clinic and have medical help to try to become pregnant. But I approached this problem as I had approached others in life; if I just tried hard enough and was earnest enough, we'd overcome it. I believed that my destiny was a product of my tenacity. I would become the best fertility patient there ever was. And I would be successful.

I was brave but emotionally demolished. How could God, whoever she is, have done this to me? Why? We doggedly continued to be good patients despite one failed attempt after another. On the fourth try, we were rewarded with a positive pregnancy test. All was forgiven. I was right. I knew I could get pregnant. I was sixteen and a half weeks pregnant when I went for my amniocentesis. The doctor was unable to aspirate any amniotic fluid, but he reassured me that if I came back in two weeks it would be a cinch. I never gave it another thought. I knew that our chances of having a baby with Down syndrome were one in one hundred at my age. These struck me as great odds, and when the day came for the second amniocentesis attempt, I told Sam I wasn't going. We were scheduled to move in three days, and I had a lot to do. Besides, I felt great, the pregnancy was easy and going well, and I knew that the outcome of the test would be fine.

We had been back in the States for two weeks when we got the call. I'm sorry to have to tell you, but your baby has Down syndrome. One sentence changed our lives forever, another cruel stroke. We were one of those few couples who had talked about what we would do if we got a positive amnio result. We felt firmly that there was no point in undergoing amniocentesis if we did not plan to terminate. For one week a twenty-two-week-old fetus continued to grow in my womb as we scrambled to make the plans. My first and possibly my only pregnancy, I felt my baby kick and roll over and hiccup inside of me. I couldn't believe it. How was I supposed to disengage and stop loving this little being that had been my constant companion and best buddy for five months? I stopped enjoying my pregnancy. It was hard to touch my lovely swollen belly anymore.

Making the decision was so much easier than following through with it. The abortion was as bloody and painful and gut-wrenching as anyone can imagine, and when it was over the emotional tidal wave I had been holding back burst. I started smoking. I drove the car around endlessly with the radio blaring to drown out my sobs. All summer long the top hit song was Michael Bolton's "How Am I Supposed to Live Without You?" For me the song was about our little boy. How was I going to live without him? How could I go on living? I wanted to die. Who was next? I'd challenge God: "Go ahead take Sam, take my parents, my brothers and sisters, and everyone I have ever loved. Go ahead."

It seemed that if I never discussed our diagnosis and subsequent decision, it would be because I was ashamed. I didn't want to bear a mantle of shame. I also know that there is room in the world for children and adults who are challenged physically or mentally. Our son was a desperately wanted baby. If I had skipped amniocentesis, his Down syndrome status would have been a surprise and we would be raising our four-year-old son today. Medical technology gave me a pregnancy I never would have achieved and gave me a diagnosis and an option I had never dreamt I'd exercise. It is a double-edged sword, a blessing and a curse.

I talked about it. I talked to almost anyone. I refused to feel ashamed. We went to a support group with three other couples who had terminated pregnancy after an amniocentesis result. It seemed like all the strikes were against us. We were the only couple who had conceived through artificial means. We could not just make love and expect to become pregnant again. We were the oldest couple. We had the pregnancy with the longest gestation. This made the fetus bigger and the abortion much more difficult. Some of the terminations were because the fetus would not have been able to live once born. I thought my grief was worse by far because our situation was so much more grueling. I felt terribly alone. Even Sam didn't feel as I did. I was alone in my grief, and so was he. His story was one of an observer and participant watching the wife he loved and the baby he loved go through an abortion. His story is about helplessness and rage. It happened in and to my body. The tremendous plummet of hormones, the sweating, the diarrhea, and finally the milk that gushed and greeted me as a cruel reminder every morning set me apart from Sam.

No one had warned me about the milk. The milk that came in to nourish a new life. The milk that made my breasts so hard and painful that I screamed. The days of swollen breasts and the accompanying pain were as difficult to bear as the abortion itself. It was God socking it to me again. I was alone and bereft.

But as I found out, there is no measure of grief. There is no comparing. There is no knowing someone else's loss. It is absolute and it is personal.

And so I continued to talk about it all and cry, and as I talked, a strange thing began to happen. Women confided in me their stories of babies lost, of babies gone, of babies dead. Whether it was by miscarriage, by abortion, by stillbirth, by SIDS, by an ectopic pregnancy, by selective reduction, by a molar pregnancy, by illness, by adoption fallen through, or by the relinquishment of a child to adoption, each woman remembered her child and could tell me exactly how old that child would have been on that day. Women talked about their feelings of grief for the child never conceived. Whether it was recent or long ago, each of those children lived on in the heart and soul of each woman. Each was treasured and never forgotten, each honored in their own way. I began to feel that I belonged to this group of women who all carried empty places in their hearts and wombs where a child had been. I began to feel that I was Everywoman. Slowly the chronicle changed from isolation, secrecy, and who had suffered more to seeing a common spirit among us.

Our child lives on within me. He is a boy. He has a name. He has a diagnosis. I talk to him every day. Two years later when his sister was born, I was aware that his little spirit lived on in her. They and they alone have shared my womb. I sometimes have a strange but comforting image of the two of them holding hands. The tears continue not as grief unabated, but as a process of honoring my boy and healing just a little. When people ask me if my daughter is my only child, sometimes I say, "She is my second child." Sometimes I don't, but I always *think* it.

---

o

---

## WHEN THERE'S NO MORE WAITING
### *Sam Guckenheimer*

We were happier and busier than we'd been in years. We were finally having a baby. After three and a half years of fertility investigations and treatment, it had finally happened. We were so excited that we told everyone. We had actually beaten the biological clock.

We rearranged our lives completely. After five years in England, we had just moved back to the United States, so we could be closer to family and friends. We had everything lined up. We had sold our house overseas and left the week before; we would be able to move into a house in Boston in two weeks; I had an exciting job. And Monica was showing. She was twenty-two weeks pregnant and proud as a goddess that we would soon be parents.

That's when we got our call. We were loading the car to take Monica's father to the airport, so that he could fly home after a short visit. We would still be staying with friends for another couple weeks until our house was available. It was Fourth of July weekend, Monday, six-thirty A.M. Our best friend called from London, where it was the middle of the workday. She just had a message for us to call Dr. Julian Norman Taylor at Queen Mary's Hospital and have him paged. Monica knew instantly what that meant. She was right—bad amniocentesis results. Down syndrome. Any possibility of an error? No, I'm sorry. Amnio is the golden standard. Well, can you send us a fax with the test results? OK; I'm so sorry.

The drive to the airport, like so many details of the next week, is engraved in my memory: Monica sitting next to me biting her lip, her father crying silently in the back seat, me trying to focus on the road. Then I had to deal with a surly toll attendant. Her passing rudeness filled me with red anger. I should have understood what was happening to me, but I didn't. I had to hold it together now, handle the arrangements, stay in charge, get everything organized for Monica.

When we returned from the airport the fax was waiting: trisomy-21. We knew what that meant. By the way, it was a boy.

Making the decision wasn't hard. To this day, few people seem to understand this. We had talked about it months before. Why have amniocentesis if you're not prepared to face up to the results? The hard parts were the biology, the grief, and the change in our lives.

THE BIOLOGY. As quickly as we could, we organized an abortion. I spent another day of rage, this time with insurance executives, who had to be cajoled into approving the procedure. (It had been such a hassle just getting insurance coverage before we moved back to the United States, because, after all, pregnancy is a "preexisting condition." So much for the industry's stance on family values.) Monica and I filled our days with friends and phone calls, trying to cope.

Wednesday we went to the hospital for preparation. There was no genetic counselor, just an incompetent social worker, used to dealing with teenagers half our age. She had no comprehension of what it meant to end the pregnancy we had spent years trying to achieve. Her assisting us with informed consent seemed grotesque.

Thursday we checked in before seven A.M. We both wanted to be conscious and present for the full procedure. Soon Monica was given a saline injection in her womb, in the hopes of inducing labor. I had never seen such a large syringe. The day was marked with visits from the doctor and procedures every hour or two. Monica's body stubbornly held on to its fetus, now dead for many hours, as though echoing our years of determination in creating it. All day we waited.

During the afternoon, the weather outside became miserable, with torrential rains and record-breaking tornadoes. At five-thirty we agreed to proceed with an evacuation. I held Monica's hand and forehead during the procedure, which was long and bloody.

Afterward, the doctor called me into his office. He had carefully copied the best statistical research on chromosomal abnormalities and their recurrence. The odds had been one hundred to one in our favor before this pregnancy. They were still one hundred to one in our favor against recurrence. But how do we interpret this, when we have been that one?

THE GRIEF. We had arranged to spend the next week in the care of friends on Cape Cod. Going away didn't help much. Having focused so hard on the logistical order of the previous days, I now fell apart. Every normal inconsequential event would fill me with rage. Ordinary conversation was a struggle. I would get angry at everyone, including Monica.

How could we share with others the grief for a baby that we alone had known? Because of the assisted pregnancy and complications in the first trimester, we had seen our baby on ultrasound seven times. The ultrasound at twenty weeks had lasted forty-five minutes. Through most of the exam, the baby seemed to hold up its right hand and wave to us. All the measurements had been normal.

Biology was definitely taunting us, making our feelings of loss more acute. Nothing had prepared us for the milk. This was the ultimate irony. Monica had not had a normal menstrual cycle for three years, as she underwent one hormone treatment after another. Now her body believed that she had given birth. Her breasts were hard and sore and incessantly expressed milk.

Monica seemed to spot Down syndrome people everywhere. A couple days after the abortion, we stopped in a store. One of the other shoppers was yelling at her adult Down syndrome daughter. We had to leave. Then we saw parents with young Down syndrome children at the beach. The kids can be cute, but difficult, and increasingly so with age.

In the midst of this, we moved into our house. We put the baby's room to other use. Monica remained sick for a long time. Even after she stopped producing milk and showing symptoms of a recent birth, she still had lingering diarrhea as a complication from antibiotics. There was nothing I could do to share the physical symptoms, a helplessness that made me more irritable and angry. The next months, unlike that first July week, have faded into a blur.

Some friends and most family members recognized our grief. Some didn't. We largely stopped socializing, except with a very few close friends who could empathize with our loss. Small talk continues to be very difficult.

THE CHANGE IN OUR LIVES. We resolved to try as soon as we could for another pregnancy. Then we discovered that we would have to wait three months for Monica's body to realize that she was not nursing a baby and resume menstruation. (That biology, again.)

Waiting now has a whole new meaning, as do statistics. Monica is forty years old. Month after month we're back at the "futility clinic," as we now call it. Monica goes every morning for blood tests and injects herself with hormones. And every month the treatment plays biological tricks on her body, giving her morning sickness without the pregnancy. And even if and when we succeed and learn that she is pregnant, we will be afraid to discover which "one in a hundred" we are this time.

Seven months have passed since the phone call. We still get cards asking about our nonexistent newborn baby. I'm still not sure how to tell people what happened. What's the correct etiquette for sending nonbirth announcements?

When asked, we no longer have room for euphemism. We tell people that we had an abortion, not a "termination." We believe that we made the right choice, and we want anyone who would have precluded that right to think twice. When asked, we describe our fertility treatment in detail, lest anyone try further to impede reproductive science.

No one else knew our baby, and few people ask about our feelings anymore. When they do, we tell them that there's a private corner in our bedroom. On that wall there is a cast of a nameless angel from a child's tombstone. Above the plaque hangs a lithograph of an empty chair. That corner belongs to our son, to whom we could not offer a full life. We continue to hope that he may have a brother or sister to whom we can.

We know many people who have waited anxiously for prenatal test results and for whom the second phone call has brought wonderful news. For one in a hundred of us, however, the news is different. For us, those weeks of waiting don't fade away.

○

## A FATHER'S GRIEF

### Daniel S. Cohn

As a father, grieving for a stillborn twin has been a strange experience. I have found that so much of the grief process and the community response seem geared to the mother.

Most support groups—at least those that I have found—are for mothers. Some encourage couples to come, but most report that very few fathers attend. I've been unable to find a support group only for fathers, and although I have been lucky in that I've found a couples' support group that does have participating fathers, so far the discussion has focused primarily on the mothers' needs. Because the pain of grieving mothers is so compelling, it seems that our needs, as fathers, get lost.

I have found that the community at large doesn't seem to know how to deal with a grieving father. Most people ask me how my wife is doing, somehow assuming that because I did not carry the babies, I am doing just fine. I suppose part of it is due to society's image of the man as the strong support in the family, taking care of the physical and economic needs of the family and letting the woman handle the emotional and child-rearing aspects. Part of it is also that most people are uncomfortable around grief in general; dealing with a man's emotions is even more difficult. Even in today's "sensitive" culture, a truly sensitive man is still considered somewhat wimpy and less of a man. The sensitive man should still be tough and gritty and only sensitive when dealing with a woman—a Clint Eastwood who can understand the needs of a woman and can open up when she wants to talk. Thus, it is hard for a man to ask another man how he is feeling emotionally, especially where grieving is concerned. Couple this with the fact that most women don't ask about a man's emotions because discussing such things can breed sexual undercurrents, and you get a very lonely environment for a grieving father.

Much of my grieving has come from the fact that I've lost the ability to "always make things right" in my family. I used to be able to promise that everything would be OK—and I could always arrange it so that it really would be OK. But Marissa's death is something I cannot fix. And when I tell my wife that nothing bad will happen in a difficult situation, she no longer believes me. That loss of trust and power is a terrible blow to a father.

Another difficult aspect of the grieving process is that I seem to be grieving for everything except Marissa. I don't mean this as coldly as it sounds; I truly do grieve for my daughter. But I did not carry her, nor did I get a chance to know her the way that my wife did. The blow to me was much more conceptual than physical or real. The carrying of twins was a reality for my wife; for me, it was a happy concept, demonstrated in ultrasounds and OB visits and my wife's growing belly. But I couldn't really feel it or experience it. In the same way that it takes fathers longer to bond with their newborn children than it does for mothers, it has taken longer for me to feel my grief for Marissa as the loss of a child than it has for Sheri, my wife. When Marissa died, only my concept of her died, at least initially. What I lost most was the fantasy of life with twins. When Marissa died, I saw the death of my being a parent of twins, of me having three children instead of two. I saw the end of a happy pregnancy and the beginning of a time of turmoil in my life, family, and marriage. I saw the difficulty in raising a twinless twin, in dealing with a wife who had lost a child. I saw the end of the celebrity of being a parent of twins and the end of my ability to always make things turn out right. All of these conflicting feelings of loss make it harder to grieve for the loss of a child in and of itself.

It is hard to work through all of this with Sheri for two reasons. On the one hand, she is grieving as well and has little left to support me. (The reverse is also true.) On the other hand, we are both almost overwhelmed with the day-to-day tasks of raising two children, one of whom is a newborn, and juggling our business and home lives. This leaves precious little time and energy to discuss such weighty issues as grief. That is not to say that we don't try, but it is very hard. We feel that we give as much attention as we can to the subject and to each other within the limits of our lives.

Much of this makes me feel guilty. In one sense, I'm not treated as if I am grieving as much as my wife. And most of the time, I don't feel as if I am grieving enough. In another sense, I seem to be grieving for the wrong things. And last, I have little support and few outlets for discussing my grief. I am assured by those who do support me, including my wife, that these feelings are normal and that I shouldn't feel guilty, but I do nonetheless.

Thus it is strange to be a daddy who is grieving. It is such an odd mixture of societal stereotypes, personal grief, and misplaced guilt. I sometimes feel all mixed up, with no outlets for talking it out. Yet other times, I hardly feel as if I am grieving at all.

Having said all this, I want to be sure to also say how much I love and cherish Rachel, Marissa's surviving twin, as well as our two-year-old son, Brian. The joy and love I have for our children is not diminished by my grief for Marissa. Her loss colors and affects my life but does not define it. We will always grieve the loss of Marissa, but we will always celebrate the lives of Rachel and Brian and the life that we all share as a family.

## 11

# MULTIPLE BIRTHS

ALL COUPLES undergoing assisted reproduction are aware that they are using medications and procedures that increase the possibility of multiple births. They are also aware that a multiple gestation can culminate in great joy and celebration or it can lead to painful, tragic losses. Multiple births—especially triplets or more—are a much more complicated venture than a singleton.

Many couples who feel barren—who have never achieved a pregnancy—have great difficulty "conceiving" of a multiple conception. Unable to imagine themselves having one baby, it feels nearly impossible to believe that they could actually become pregnant with two or three or even more. Understandably, some carry this disbelief into treatment, responding to cautionary words about a multiple with, "Multiples would be great. As far as we're concerned, the more the merrier."

Unfortunately, for some, the "merrier" becomes the "scarier." Some of the same people who hoped to be thrilled with news that they were expecting twins are terrified to learn that they are pregnant with three or more. They find that their bodies have played yet another trick on them: they have gone from being barren to suddenly being too much "with *children*." And perhaps the hardest part of this experience is the sense that their dilemma is not a fluke of nature. Rather, they feel—often with tremendous regret and shame—that they have tampered with fate and must now pay the price.

The price for carrying multiples can be high indeed. Even twin pregnancies require some special care, often including bed rest, in order to carry to term. Triplet pregnancies certainly demand more caution, and it is not unusual for a woman carrying triplets to spend several weeks in bed and to deliver several weeks early. Higher-level multiple pregnancies—more than three—are so hazardous that couples are often strongly advised to consider undergoing multifetal reduction (which is also generally offered, though not urged, in a triplet pregnancy).

Although almost everyone employing assisted reproductive technologies (ART) is told about multifetal reduction and is cautioned about how painful the experience is, few are prepared to face this difficult decision. Most people seem to assume that they will not have to face it—that having too many babies is simply not something that could happen to them. After all, theirs are very much wanted and sought-after pregnancies. The prospect of electively aborting a deeply loved baby is nearly impossible for most people to fathom.

Another aspect of multiple gestation for which couples are often ill prepared is spontaneous loss: early or late, partial or total. Certainly any pregnancy loss after ART is devastating, but when it occurs in multiple gestation, its impact can feel all the more significant.

Many pregnancies that are initially identified as multiples spontaneously reduce to singleton gestations early in the first trimester. While this is thought to occur often in the general population, when it occurs after ART and the couple is made aware of the loss, it gains significance. Most couples—even those who were hoping for a singleton—find that they become rapidly attached to their twins or triplets as well as to the idea of being parents of multiples. When they return for a subsequent ultrasound and learn that they have lost one or more fetuses they are startled and saddened, fearing that they will return for the next ultrasound and learn that all have vanished.

Early loss of an entire multiple pregnancy is another loss whose magnitude is rarely appreciated. Other people tend to regard this like any other miscarriage, failing to recognize that for many expectant parents the loss of more than one baby is actually experienced as double or triple the loss of a singleton. Couples who sought an instant family—especially those who were limited in the number of times they could try ART—have suffered the loss of that possibility on top of the loss of the pregnancy. Even those who feel optimistic about achieving another pregnancy anticipate that they will feel disappointed if end up carrying only one baby.

When loss occurs late in multiple gestation, it is all the more devastating. Again, this includes both partial loss and total loss. Even when a pregnancy is far advanced, others tend to minimize the impact of a partial loss. The assumption is always that the couple is getting what they set out for—a baby. The fact that they may have also lost one or more along the way is easily disregarded.

Although it is increasingly unusual, since even babies born tiny and several weeks premature are surviving, there remain some couples who face the enormous and devastating loss of an entire multiple pregnancy. When this happens, the grief is enormous—parents mourn two, three, or more babies whose voices they will never hear, whose lives were lost before they really began. It is not at all unusual for parents to spend several months grieving, and it is also not unusual for others to underestimate the magnitude of their grief.

Fortunately, many multiple pregnancies do not result in loss, but rather in the successful birth of two or more healthy babies. These babies are often small, and many are born several weeks premature, but advances in neonatal medical care have resulted in a good outcome for most of them. Some spend several days, weeks, or even months in a neonatal intensive care unit, but then go home to their parents and, possibly, older siblings.

Parents of multiples say that one of the main challenges they face when their children are very young is that of maintaining privacy. They observe that wherever they go and whatever they do, people intrude on their lives. Some are simply curious onlookers who enjoy looking at the twins or triplets because they find two or three babies doubly or triply cute. Others are more objectionable, asking personal questions about fertility treatments, for example. It becomes a real challenge for parents of multiples to figure out ways that they can go out in public, enjoy themselves, accomplish what they want to accomplish, and not feel bombarded by curious strangers.

Another challenge faced by parents of multiples involves family planning. If a family begins with twins conceived through ART and the parents wish to have another child, the question inevitably arises about whether it will be twins—or even more—the second time around. Parents face dilemmas about how many embryos to transfer in order to maximize the chance of another successful pregnancy but minimize the chance of another multiple gestation.

Perhaps the biggest challenge faced by parents of multiples is the task of parenting two or more babies who arrive at the same time. Things have gotten easier in recent years, with well-designed double and triple strollers and with car seats and other infant equipment that is more efficient and easy to operate. Nonetheless, as one father I spoke to put it, "You should never have more babies than you have pairs of hands." Some families do.

Once they make it past the stressful final months of pregnancy and the tiring early months of parenting multiples, parents of twins and triplets usually return to a "more the merrier" philosophy. Having been "without child" for so long, their bounty brings them great delight. One woman said, "We had both had empty arms for so long that we were pleased to have two babies to hold. We each needed to have our arms full."

In the pages that follow, Lidia Garofalo, the mother of triplets (two of whom are identical twin boys), captures some of the challenges—and triumphs—of multiple gestation.

o

## AS LONG AS ALL THREE ARE OK
### *Lidia Garofalo*

"Maybe we'll have triplets," John joked, as we went through our fourth IVF cycle.

"Be careful what you wish for," Marie, our favorite nurse, commented.

"We should be so lucky!" I snapped, wishing both of them would understand how discouraged I felt.

"Be careful what you wish for," Marie repeated.

We wished. We were careful. We got triplets.

I will never forget that first ultrasound. The technician immediately found a fetal sac, and to our great relief, there was a strong heartbeat evident. I remember looking at John and seeing sheer delight in his eyes and a big smile on his face.

"There's your baby," the technician declared. "There probably isn't another, because your levels are not high—but I'll take a look just to be sure." John and I grinned at each other, thrilled that we were finally expecting. Then I saw a concerned look come over the technician's face.

"What's wrong?" I asked.

"There's another sac here and . . ."

"And what?" Was she telling me there was no heartbeat? Was she telling me that we had been expecting twins and now there was only one? It's amazing how I had gone from the joyful mother-to-be of one baby to the anxiously expectant mom of two in a flash of an instant.

"And I think there are two heartbeats there."

At first John didn't understand. "So we're having twins?"

"No," she said as she turned to the two of us. "You are having identical twins and a triplet."

With that news, John and I laughed and laughed and laughed some more.

And that is how we first learned of Alessia, Christopher, and Daniel, our triplets. Although we had longed for one child, as soon as we learned that we were expecting three, the health and well-being of each of them became a priority for us. That was not something that most people understood, and it was their lack of understanding that became the most difficult part of our pregnancy.

From a medical standpoint, things went well. However, we learned early on that our sons Christopher and Daniel—or Baby A and Baby B as they were known at the time—were in one sac, sharing a placenta, and this meant that they were at risk for twin-to-twin transfusion. Twin-to-twin transfusion is a condition in which one fetus receives too much fluid and the other, too little. It can be very dangerous and can put one or both babies' lives at risk. We were told that if we made it to twenty-five weeks or more without significant evidence of twin-to-twin transfusion, the boys should be OK. At that point, I made twenty-eight weeks my goal.

I was twenty weeks pregnant when there was initial evidence of twin-to-twin transfusion. I tried to remain calm, but the news put me into something of a panic. I worried that we would lose a baby or that one would be born with serious health problems. I found it difficult to talk with others about my concerns because, with the exception of John, people didn't seem to understand.

"At least you'll have one," they would say. "That was what you wanted."

One day I was talking with a close friend. I was trying to keep my mind off the boys by focusing on other, less important matters. She picked up on this and asked why I was talking about seemingly trivial matters. I then told her of my concern about twin-to-twin transfusion, and she responded with what turned out to be the harshest of comments.

"Your goal was one baby, wasn't it? Remember that goal."

My goal had become three babies, and I was hurt that she could not understand it. Like others, she did not seem to understand that each of our children—Baby A, Baby B, and Baby C—was already an individual that I knew and deeply loved. Each one had his or her position in my uterus, and each had a personality. Baby C, who is now our daughter, Alessia, was quiet and reserved because she was positioned behind the boys. Baby B, who became Daniel, was very active and a solid kicker. Baby A, now Christopher, was more laid-back than Daniel but more active than his seemingly demure sister.

What my friend and others did not know was that I talked to each of our babies. Just as they had their own personalities, each with his or her own special kick, so also did I have a unique relationship with each of them. Although I spoke lovingly to each of them, my words reflected my feelings about who they were. Alessia seemed to need a gentler, calmer mom; the boys were more spirited, and I was more spirited in return.

The most important and satisfying time of each day came in the evening, when John and I sat down together and read to our children. This was our way of letting them know how much we wanted all three of them and how much we were looking forward to being their parents. I would touch the spot where each baby was and say something to each of them as an individual. John did much of the reading, something that enabled him to feel very actively involved in the pregnancy.

Weeks twenty through twenty-six were very difficult for me because I felt that the boys were in jeopardy and that there was nothing I could do about it. I felt well and moderated my activity, but other than praying, there wasn't much I could do to affect the outcome. Then, at twenty-seven weeks, we received some wonderful news: the fluid imbalance had corrected itself. Both boys were doing well, and we could anticipate a less eventful pregnancy from then on.

Although I had a day-to-day, week-to-week goal of remaining pregnant, my real goal became thirty-four weeks. I felt confident that if I could make it that far, the kids would all have a great start in life. I knew that I could probably safely deliver at an earlier point, but that was my goal.

At thirty-two weeks I went into preterm labor and was hospitalized. My doctor was able to stop the labor, and the triplets remained safely in utero for another three weeks. Then, at my thirty-five-week checkup, the doctor found that Alessia's umbilical cord was weakening. He advised an immediate C-section, which John and I of course agreed to. I'll never forget the fun we had walking into the operating room, knowing that we would soon be holding the children that we had longed for for so long. However, I'll admit that it was a very strange feeling seeing the three bassinets set up, awaiting their residents!

Throughout my pregnancy, I was moved by how close I felt to John. We had been through years of difficult infertility together and were thrilled beyond words to finally be pregnant. What I could never have anticipated, however, was how connected I would feel to John during the delivery. I remember lying there and asking him to tell me what was happening. He was a wonderful guide! First Christopher was born, then Daniel, and finally Alessia. I remember, with great pleasure, John's beaming face when the doctor asked him if he wanted to cut Daniel's cord. I realized then that we were sharing the most important moments of our marriage.

Christopher, Daniel, and Alessia are now nearly a year old. Each has abandoned his or her prenatal personality—or, more accurately, the personality that I imagined him or her to have. In place of those imagined personalities are their real selves. Daniel, the original kicker, is now a very mellow, laid-back child. Alessia, formerly the quiet, sweet little girl, is active and feisty. And Christopher, who was in the middle before, remains so.

Life has been full of wondrous surprises.

# MOVING ON

How will we ever know when to end treatment? Will we be forever tempted—and tormented—by the availability of new treatment options? Will we ever conclude that enough is enough?

These are the questions that couples struggle with as they make their way through infertility diagnosis and treatment. With a never-ending array of options available, they wonder if they will ever be able to identify an end point. More important, they wonder if they will be able to identify the *correct* end point. Some fear that they will leave treatment too soon, perhaps missing out on the opportunity to achieve pregnancy. Others fear that they will pursue treatment endlessly, only to be left with empty arms and depleted emotional, financial, and physical resources.

Remarkably, the vast majority of couples *do* know when enough is enough. To their great surprise—and relief—most arrive at a point when it feels right to end treatment. Often this decision comes somewhat unexpectedly: a couple may try and try to schedule and predict an end point, then find that it comes unexpectedly. Sometimes this is following a particular treatment failure—a cycle may be canceled for poor stimulation, or there may be no fertilization. Other times it comes because something else happens—a friend has a happy adoption experience or a family member becomes ill, and energies are directed elsewhere. And there are couples who decide that enough is enough without any apparent precipitating event or stimulus: the time has simply come to move on.

Regardless of how the decision to end treatment appears to come about, most couples draw guidance from both mind and heart.

# Guidance from the Mind

As they make their way through infertility diagnosis and treatment, most people make repeated attempts to assess the likelihood that they will be successful. Although this process is a subjective one and surely draws on guidance from the heart, certain information plays a significant role in shaping people's outlook for the future.

One thing that most people look at in determining whether—and how long—to remain in treatment is the woman's age. Aware that fertility declines after age thirty-five and much more dramatically after forty, many couples take age into account in their decision making. Some couples in which the woman is "older"—around forty—decide that their time, energy, and financial resources would be best spent on adoption or another alternative. By contrast, others feel that this is their last shot, and that treatment will help them maximize their chances.

Another piece of information that provides guidance from the mind is the couple's diagnosis and prognosis. Some couples have diagnoses, such as tubal blockage or severe male infertility, which make treatment imperative. Other couples have diagnoses that are far more ambiguous, especially those with unexplained infertility; these couples have the option of leaving treatment and trying on their own, concluding that enough is enough in terms of high-tech interventions. Still, they continue to have some hope for spontaneous conception.

Financial resources—both personal and through insurance—also play a significant role in determining who remains in treatment and who moves on. A couple with limited resources may conclude that they are better off committing the funds they have to adoption—a sure bet—than to treatments that may or may not work. By contrast, a couple that has insurance coverage for treatment but not for adoption may elect to remain in their treatment program longer, hoping that their continued efforts will eventually be fruitful.

Guidance from the mind also takes into account the availability and accessibility of alternatives such as adoption or ovum donation. For example, if a couple is aware of an adoption agency that is placing healthy babies in a timely and affordable way, they may be attracted to this option sooner than a couple that has little or only negative information about adoption. Similarly, a woman whose sister has just had her last pregnancy and has now offered to donate eggs may decide to accept this offer rather than to remain in costly treatment with little apparent likelihood of success.

Physicians also play an important role in providing guidance from the mind. Although no one has a crystal ball that accurately predicts pregnancy, physicians can help couples make educated decisions for themselves. Undoubtedly they must be very cautious about what they say and how they say it, but physicians should see it as part of their role to begin to guide patients away from treatment and toward other options. Those patients who are ready to hear it appreciate guidance from a physician who is able to let them know that she or he holds little hope for a successful pregnancy. Those who are not ready to hear it may still benefit from having the subject introduced.

Finally, couples draw guidance from the mind by having ethical conversations with themselves: Is it morally correct to bring a child into the world who will not be raised by both of his or her genetic parents? Is it morally correct to try so hard to create a child when there exist so many children looking for homes? Is assisted reproductive technology a medical advance like all others, or does it interfere with nature in some unacceptable—or unapplaudable—way? Couples ask themselves these and other questions and use the responses to guide them in their decision making.

## Guidance from the Heart

Although the decision to end treatment is in many ways a rational decision, in other ways it is not. Two people can accumulate similar information regarding age, diagnosis, prognosis, and availability and accessibility of alternatives, yet reach very different conclusions. There are a variety of reasons why this occurs.

First, people have perceptions about their fertility that may be based more on feelings than facts. For example, a woman who has never been pregnant may become convinced that she will never be pregnant, despite the fact that she has a favorable prognosis. Another woman may have the reverse situation: she may have become pregnant with ease, perhaps even unexpectedly, in the past but now have little likelihood of conception. However, because her history of fertility has left her feeling fertile, she may be more likely to persist in treatment.

A second reason that guidance from the heart can carry force equal to that of the mind involves the interaction between marital partners. As much as people may want to go through the process together, in most instances partners move at different paces. One partner may want to consider—and even pursue—alternative paths to parenthood, while his or her partner feels that they have many remaining options for infertility treatment. Perhaps one of the most difficult things a couple will ever have to do is to try to find balance between their conflicting interests. Sometimes this means that one or the other will have to put his or her rational perspective aside and listen carefully to the needs and desires of the partner.

Guidance from the heart is significant for other reasons. People's feelings about having a genetic connection to their child and about the alternative paths to parenthood available to them also shape their decisions. Those who feel a strong need for a child that is their full genetic offspring may remain in treatment even after they seem to have exhausted their chances for success. By contrast, those who feel comfortable with or even drawn to an alternative may move on easily, perhaps long before they run out of treatment options.

Feelings about the significance of pregnancy, labor, and delivery also provide guidance from the heart. There are some women who have waited their entire lives to be pregnant and who feel that it would be a major loss for them to never be pregnant. Similarly, there are men who have looked forward to what one man called "the nine-month countdown to parenthood." Other couples regard pregnancy as a means to an end and feel that they could comfortably miss this experience as long as they reach the desired goal. The relative significance of pregnancy to an individual and a couple will play a role in the decisions they make regarding treatment.

Guidance from the heart also takes stamina into consideration. Those who are exhausted and who feel depleted by their efforts to have a child may decide that it is in their personal and marital best interests to move on. Others, though tired, recognize that they retain the energy and motivation to pursue treatment.

People move through infertility treatment in different ways and at different paces. There is no right or wrong way to navigate this process. Rather, each couple searches for and ultimately finds the point at which they are ready to move on.

In "How We Finally Did It," Pam Freedman talks about how she and her husband made the transition to adoption in unanticipated ways. Then in the eloquent and poignant poem "Mother's Day," Margaret Rampton Munk uses images of gardening to capture another feature of moving on—the fact that new life can be nurtured and grown in other ways.

○

## HOW WE FINALLY DID IT
*Pam Freedman*

I had a dream, about five years into our infertility treatment, that I was sitting with a cane and a walker in the waiting room of my infertility doctor's office. It was not an unhappy dream. Rather, it was a sort of comfortable, expectant, hopeful dream. That is, until I woke up. When I did, I was horrified! Was this how long it would go on? Would I spend the rest of my life waiting to have a baby? Would I grow old and gray still expecting that it would happen?

The dream horrified me, but I can't say that it changed anything. My husband, Jeff, and I remained in treatment, dividing our lives into twenty-eight segments of ups and downs. Each time we met with defeat we crashed, stayed low for a few days, then returned to the world of the living with renewed hope. As they say, it springs eternal.

We are blessed and cursed to live in Massachusetts, where insurance covers almost all the costs of infertility treatment, so although it was a rough ride, it was a free ride. Sometimes I wonder if we would have been better off having to pay for our treatment. Of course I know that not to be true, but I also know that we would have stopped earlier had it not been free.

But it was free, and we did keep going. First, we did the obligatory six IUIs, then we moved on to four IVFs, and we topped the whole thing off with two GIFTs (gamete intrafallopian transfers) and one we-might-as-well-try-it ZIFT (zygote intrafallopian transfer). For these efforts we earned all of one chemical pregnancy and a delightful nine-week, after-a-heartbeat miscarriage. All the while, our friends were popping babies out. Naturally.

So I suppose I could say that we ended treatment because we simply ran out of things to try. That is one interpretation, and perhaps it is the most accurate. However, I think that even if there had been something else for us to try, we would have stopped. We were ready, and as such we were awaiting a sign.

The sign did not come to me in a dream; it came in a park. I was there with a friend and her toddler (simply being able to go there with them signified progress!) when I saw a mom with her severely disabled son in a wheelchair. I remember looking at them and realizing—perhaps for the first time—that pregnancy was not the be-all and end-all. Here was a woman who had been pregnant, who had probably assumed all was well, and who was now forever tied to a child who needed total care. At that moment it hit me: we could adopt a healthy child. There are no guarantees in life, but adoption was a pretty sure route to parenthood. That was my sign. There was our path.

Writing it now, it all sounds so simple, but it was not simple at the time. For one thing, Jeff was not with me in the park, and even if he had been, there is no saying that he would have received the sign simultaneously. When I realized what I needed to do—what *we* needed to do—I feared that I would have to convince Jeff. Like me, he had his heart set on having a biological child, and it would be hard to pry him away from that dream.

I rehearsed what I was going to say to Jeff and tried to figure out the perfect time to say it. I was so afraid that he would want to push forward with medical treatment and that even if he agreed to stop, it would be because he was acquiescing to me. So I picked my words and time, then did my presentation for him. It turned out to have a surprise twist!

"I've been thinking."

"About what?"

"Well, about . . . about . . . maybe beginning to look into adoption. I mean, not exactly stopping right now, but . . . you know . . . maybe visiting an adoption agency or something." I was about to pass out by the time I finished that sentence. Then came the shocker.

Instead of looking sullen or suggesting we talk about it again later, Jeff grinned. Unbeknownst to me, he had been talking with his friend Keith at work about Keith's brother's recent Chinese adoption. Apparently Keith was all excited about it as well, and his excitement seemed to have inspired Jeff.

I was dumbfounded. Completely surprised. Then not sure how to react. Although I'd been thinking about adoption, I hadn't been thinking about adopting a child from another country, another culture.

Several conversations about adoption followed, over the course of a few weeks. We talked a lot about how we would feel with a child of another race (fine), and we talked about how we thought our families would react (maybe not so fine). We talked about how important it was to have a newborn (more important than we'd originally thought) and about whether we wanted to meet the birthparents (yes). In the end, we realized that although China sounded tempting, a newborn domestic adoption felt right for us.

As I write this, we are in waiting mode. We are with an agency that makes no promises but says that it generally takes about a year for a placement. We've been waiting eight months and one week, but who's counting?! The wait isn't easy, but I can say that it beats all the waiting we did during our infertility treatment. We know that *this* wait will lead to good news.

Although I am excited and have reached a point where adoption feels really right, I'll admit that I still feel pangs of sadness. They come when I see pregnant women or parents with a child that looks just like them. The pangs are particularly strong when someone that I met through infertility becomes pregnant. I always feel a pang of envy on top of the pang of sadness.

But most of the time I am happy to be moving on. We did enough treatment. I know that now.

○

## MOTHER'S DAY

### *Margaret Rampton Munk*

I am afraid
To plant this seed.

The sun is warm,
The earth is rich and ready,
But the days go by,
And still no planting.
Why?

The springtime of my life
Is passing, too.
And ten years' planting
In a willing soil
Have borne no living fruit.
So many times I've waited,
Hoped,
Believed,
That God and nature
Would perform
A miracle
Incredible but common.

Nothing grew.
And oftentimes I feel
The mystery of life and growth
Is known to all but me,
Or that reality
Is not as it appears to be.

I have a choice:
To put aside this seed,
Leaving the planting
To the proven growers,
Pretending not to care
For gardening,
And knowing
If I do not try
I cannot fail.

Or plant,
and risk again
The well-known pain
of watching
For the first brave green
And seeing only
Barren ground.

He also spoke
About a seed,
The mustard's tiny grain,
Almost too small to see,
But, oh—the possibilities!
Those who doubt,
Who fear,
Are not inclined to cultivate it.
But it was to them He spoke.

And God remembered Sarah . . .
Rachel . . .
Hannah . . .
Elizabeth . . .

The seed is in my hand,
The trowel in the other;
I am going to the garden
and the Gardener,
Once more.

# 13

# ADOPTION

FOR SOME INFERTILE COUPLES, the journey through infertility treatment ends with the decision to commence a second and sometimes equally arduous journey: adoption. Those who go through the adoption process and become adoptive parents realize that they are now participants in a lifelong journey. For all members of the triad (birthparents, adoptive parents, and the adoptee), adoption is an experience that will forever alter and reshape their lives.

Infertile couples come to adoption with a range of perspectives. Some couples approach adoption with relative ease; they are comfortable with it as a family-building option, often because their nuclear family, extended family, or friends' families were formed in part by adoption. For those with this positive perspective, the idea of building their own family through adoption seems natural.

Other couples—in fact, most couples—do not come to adoption with such ease. Many are unfamiliar with the process and know few adoptive families. Their thoughts about it are encumbered with negative input from the media and from our culture at large. This input impresses on them the idea that adoption is not a normal way to form a family, that adopted people have problems, and that adoptive parents are not real parents. By and large, they receive the message that adoption is a last choice and that people consider it only out of desperation. Fortunately, most of these couples still find the courage to enter the adoption world. There they meet members of the adoption triad and discover for themselves that adoption is a means of forming families that are happy and thriving.

Unfortunately, there are some couples who have difficulty approaching adoption because one or both partners have negative associations about it. They may have a family member or friend who was adopted and who had significant problems in life or a tumultuous relationship with her family. It is hard for these potential adoptive parents to put those associations aside and consider the possibility that most adoptions do not end with misfortune.

Often marital partners have different perspectives on adoption. One may look on it with excitement and comfort, while the other feels fear and caution. Although these differences can pose substantial roadblocks, for most couples such differences in approach prove helpful. Differences help them move forward toward adoption at a reasonable pace; one partner's enthusiasm and eagerness to move ahead is tempered by the other's caution and restraint.

What is important for anyone considering adoption to know is that a history of doubt, fear, and negativity toward adoption does not predict a poor outcome in the adoption journey. In fact, I have found that many of the couples who struggle the longest, who doubt the most, and who take one step backward for every two steps forward, end up happiest when they adopt. Such couples firmly believe that their decision is right for them, and they move forward with confidence.

Regardless of the ease or difficulty with which they make the decision to adopt, all couples must grapple with the complex choices that they have in the process. Currently these choices involve decisions about whether to adopt a child domestically or internationally, whether to pursue a same-race or an interracial adoption, whether to adopt an infant or seek an older child, whether to hope for openness in their adoption or to seek a more closed process. Couples must also decide whether to adopt through a public or private agency or to do a private adoption through a lawyer or other adoption facilitator. A comprehensive discussion of each of these forks in the road is beyond the scope of this brief chapter introduction; however, the following sections present some observations about how and why people make each of the decisions.

## The Decision to Adopt Domestically or Internationally

Couples who seek a domestic adoption generally do so because they would like to meet the birthparents and have information about them, because they seek a newborn baby, and because they see domestic adoption as a simpler, more familiar process, both at the time of the adoption and in years to come. By contrast, couples who seek international adoption are drawn to the idea of having a multicultural family and look forward to bringing their child's native culture into their home. Such couples may also wish to avoid the openness that prevails in many domestic adoptions, perhaps out of fear that if they meet the birthparents, they will never feel that the child is really theirs. Some couples seek international adoption for humanitarian reasons: they want to provide a home for a child who would otherwise not have one.

Although most couples are clear early in the process about whether they prefer domestic or international adoption, some are not. Some, for example, may prefer an international adoption because they are drawn to the idea of having a multicultural family but ultimately decide against it because they fear that members of their extended family would not share their enthusiasm. Others might give up this idea because they know that they want a newborn baby and they recognize that most international adoptions occur after a child is six months old.

There are couples who prefer domestic adoption but seek an international adoption for reasons of gender. Those who have strong feelings about adopting a child of a specific gender—either because they have a biological child of the other gender or for some other personal reason—usually conclude that they must adopt internationally. Since most domestic adoptions involve prebirth matches and few birthmothers would be comfortable with couples who specify gender, some people turn to international adoption, where programs often honor gender preferences.

Finally, there are some couples who have had some adoption options closed to them. These include couples who do not qualify for an adoption in a particular country because of their age (domestic adoption usually has fewer age limitations than international adoption) and couples who have limited finances and must seek the most affordable adoption (which is most often a domestic adoption through a public agency).

## The Decision to Adopt a Child of the Same Race or of a Different Race

International adoption was once almost synonymous with interracial adoption, but this is no longer the case. White couples can adopt same-race children from Russia and Eastern Europe. Similarly, Asian American couples can adopt baby girls from China. As a result of these changes, adoption decisions regarding race have been separated to some extent from decisions regarding culture. However, in most instances, couples adopting domestically are seeking a child of their own race.

Whether they are adopting locally or from a distance, couples who decide to adopt interracially recognize that they are making a decision that will, quite literally, alter the complexion of their family. Grandparents, aunts, uncles, cousins, and the couple's other children—both existing and future—will become part of an interracial family. The couple needs to consider how others are likely to react and to try to anticipate ways to facilitate the child's acceptance into the family.

In addition to considering their extended family, couples adopting interracially need to consider the community in which they live. Some live in communities that are already racially and ethnically diverse, but others look around them and see only people who look like they do. How will a child of another race be accepted in the community, and equally important, how will he or she feel about being different?

Couples who decide to move ahead with an interracial adoption feel that despite the challenges it presents, it is the best option for them. They are usually people who welcome and embrace difference and who see this as an opportunity to create a very special family unit.

## The Decision to Adopt an Infant or an Older Child

It has been my experience that most couples adopting after infertility have a strong desire for an infant. Having missed the opportunity to share a pregnancy together, they look forward to actively participating in their child's growth and development. Most want to be involved in their son or daughter's life from the earliest possible point, and many welcome the opportunity to be present at the birth.

Couples adopting internationally recognize and presumably accept the fact that it is unlikely they will be able to adopt a newborn. Children adopted internationally are almost always at least six months old at the time they are adopted, and most are older. Hence, couples who prefer an international adoption are usually willing to miss out on their child's infancy in order to have the pleasures and enrichment they anticipate will come from adopting a child with a different ethnic heritage.

There are some couples who elect to adopt an older child from this country. These couples include those who are drawn to the humanitarian aspect of this choice: they will be offering a home to a child who might not otherwise have one. Other couples may not be planning on an older child, but unexpectedly a child comes along who captures their hearts. Finally, there are those who cannot afford an infant adoption and who decide to adopt an older child because this option is available to them.

## Decisions Regarding Openness in Adoption

Prior to the early 1980s, most adoptions between unrelated families in the United States were conducted in a closed manner, meaning that the birthparents and the adoptive parents learned little, if anything, about each other. Perhaps more significantly, the adoptee was denied any information about his or her birthfamily. Closed adoption was seen as being in the best interests of all members of the adoption triad. Birthmothers could "forget" that the adoption had ever occurred and move on with their lives; the adoptive parents could pretend that their family was no different from any other family; and the adoptee would not have to wonder about his or her birthparents because they could never be found. Only after adoptees and birthparents—and, to some extent, adoptive parents—came forward and spoke of the pain caused by the closed system, did things begin to change. As a result of those efforts, adoption professionals now recognize that adoptees have a right to know where they came from, that birthparents have a right to know where their birthchildren are, and that adoptive parents often feel more secure knowing that they have not snatched their children away from unwilling mothers and fathers. In recent years the closed system has gradually been replaced by one that is more open, though the degree of openness can vary significantly from one adoption to the next.

Couples usually enter the adoption process with questions and hesitation about openness. Initially, they are frightened by the prospect of meeting and talking with birthparents. They may fear that if they remain in contact with the birthparents, they will never feel a sense of authenticity as parents because there will always be other parents in the background. Some also fear that the birthparents will be tempted to try to reclaim the child or that the child will feel an attachment to the birthparents that will diminish his or her attachment to the adoptive parents.

Most couples who allow themselves to explore the concept behind open adoption discover that they are quite comfortable with some degree of openness. Once they begin to understand who birthparents are and how and why they make the decision to place a child for adoption, adoptive parents are able to understand and embrace the advantages that come with openness. These include the ability to provide their child with updated information about their birthfamily, the ability to have current medical information, and the ability to better foster their child's identity as an individual who truly comes from two (or more) heritages.

Although many couples appreciate openness in adoption once they become acquainted with it, others do not. There are couples who have deep and abiding belief in the benefits of a closed adoption. Such couples discover that their options are limited within the United States but that international adoption offers them some of the distance that they desire. It is important to note, however, that just as all domestic adoptions are not open, all international adoptions are not closed. There are instances in which a couple adopts internationally and learns the identity of the birthparents.

## Agency Versus Private Adoption

Adoption practices are governed by state laws, and these laws vary from one state to the next. It is important that couples consult an adoption attorney in their state so that they understand the regulations regarding private adoption. For example, some states allow private advertising for a birthmother, and others do not.

Assuming that a couple has the choice between an agency and a private, independent, or parent-initiated adoption, the following are some reasons that people lean towards one versus the other. Those who hope for predictability of the timing and cost of their adoption or prefer to have others handle advertising, phone calls, and legal work generally seek an agency adoption. These adoptions sometimes end up taking longer or costing more than independent adoptions, but adoptive couples appreciate the reliability that agencies offer. Moreover, some couples feel that by turning the process over to an agency, they are free to live their lives without having to be constantly focused on adoption.

Couples who seek an independent adoption generally do so because they prefer to feel that they are in charge. Although the process of finding a birthmother—on their own or with the help of a facilitator—can be frustrating and disappointing, such couples are willing to ride this rocky road in order to be sure that they are the ones who determine whether a situation is right for them. Couples who have the time and energy to spend on this process may also seek it because their active participation may help make it happen sooner and at a lower cost.

Some couples seek an adoption through a public agency. Such couples do so either for humanitarian reasons (they know that there are older children waiting for homes) or for cost reasons (public agency adoptions involve few costs). Public agency adoptions can occur quickly, as in instances where a waiting child is advertised on TV or in a newspaper, or it can take several years for the adoption of an infant.

Once couples have grappled with the key decisions that they face in adoption, most feel ready to move ahead with the process. This process usually begins with a homestudy—a generally benign series of interviews designed to confirm that they are responsible and stable individuals who genuinely want to parent a child through adoption. Then, depending on their chosen route to adoption, couples embark on advertising, immigration applications, or conversations with an agency, attorney, or facilitator.

The journey of adoption does not end with the arrival of a child; in many ways, that is where it begins. The lifelong experience of being part of an adoptive family comes with an assortment of rewards and challenges. Many of these are captured in the pages that follow. In "Our Family," Teri Sousa, an adoptive mom of three and now an adoption social worker, tells of her ongoing and evolving relationship with her son Tyler's birthmother. Shelly Tenenbaum chronicles her journey through four adoption agencies in "In the Best Interests of the Child." From there we turn to two of my own essays of several years ago, "A Child of One's Own: Some Thoughts About Birth and Adoption" and "Love That Grows," followed by a brief update. Rika Smith McNally presents the powerful and poignant story of her daughter's adoption from China; next we hear of another long journey when Katherine Thomas tells of her trip to Russia to adopt her daughter, Aleksa, in "Life's Journeys." Then, Mary Terhune, a birthmother, relates how her life was transformed many years after the placement of her firstborn daughter. Her title, "Finding the Sugar," could apply to many of the stories in this book. The poem "The Mother of My Child" by Judith Steinbergh captures the power of one woman transferring motherhood to another.

○

## OUR FAMILY
### Teri Sousa

I remember the first time I heard her voice, a soft-spoken, southern accent with an air of intensity and maturity that reached beyond her twenty years. Who would have known that eleven years later I would consider this person one of my best friends, a sister, the mother of my son.

Christina and I met for the first time over the phone before our son, Tyler, was born. She had heard about our hopes of adopting a child through a mutual friend. That friend, Cheryl, agreed to be the liaison between us. We would send pictures and letters via Cheryl. At that time we made no plans to meet in person, but looking back, I realize that that was always my hope—and my intent.

When Tyler was three years old, we planned a trip to Florida, where Christina lives. I had been thinking a lot about Christina and wanted very much to meet her. This seemed like an ideal time, so I asked Cheryl to contact her. To my delight, Christina agreed to a meeting.

When we arrived in Florida, we called Christina and arranged to meet her at Sea World. We were very nervous and excited. Since I felt that Tyler was too young to understand, I told him that Christina was a friend. Our first meeting was incredible. We spent the whole day together. Christina was wonderful with Tyler. We began to truly get to know each other, and I believe the process was healing for Christina and for me as well.

At the end of our day together, it was very difficult for us to say good-bye. Christina and I both cried and held each other in a hug that seemed to last forever. I knew, at that moment, that we would always be united. I realized also that we were family members and that, in a sense, she was as important to me as Tyler.

After the Sea World meeting, Christina and I began communicating directly with each other—not frequently, but we did maintain a close connection. As I said earlier, we were family members and as such did not need to see each other or even speak or write often to maintain our relationship. It was a given that we would remain close.

Our second visit took place when Tyler was seven; we invited Christina to his first communion. I had been talking a lot with Tyler about his adoption and his birthmom. I shared photos with him from our Florida trip. He had a good sense of who she was, but he didn't remember her. I asked Tyler's permission before inviting Christina to his communion. He was initially very happy to hear that she was coming, but as her visit approached he became anxious. I began to realize that he was afraid she would not like him.

Christina was anxious, too. Not only would she be meeting more people this time, but she would be returning to the place where she had left her baby seven years ago. There must have been many painful memories for her on this trip. Nonetheless, our reunion was a joyous one. Tyler was very happy about meeting her again, and she and I shared great joy as we held hands and watched our son receive his first communion. Extended family were there as well. Christina's father came from Florida, so Tyler got to meet his Grandpa Manny. We all celebrated with dinner at a nice restaurant. Although initially my family members were hesitant and a bit fearful because they did not understand how someone could place a child for adoption and then see the child only on occasion, things ended up going very well. Once they met Christina and spent some time with her, all their fears were allayed.

The day after Tyler's communion, Christina and our friend, Cheryl, came and picked Tyler up so that he could spend the night with her at Cheryl's house. It was another opportunity for them to get to know each other and spend some time alone. Then it was time for her to return home to Florida. Once again, the leave-taking was difficult for all of us; we wished we could be together longer.

Christina and I continued to communicate by telephone, and Tyler joined us, calling her whenever he wanted to. Christina in turn became close to Tyler's brother and sister, who also joined our family through adoption. If she sent gifts to Tyler, she would always include presents for them. She would also talk to them on the phone. Christina was indeed a member of our family.

When he was nine, Tyler again visited Christina in Florida. I was attending a conference for work, and Tyler flew down with me. We had arranged for Christina to meet us at the airport and to take Tyler for four days while I was at the conference. I remember tucking my phone number at the hotel into Tyler's pocket in case he missed me or wanted to talk. I asked Tyler what he thought it was going to be like spending four whole days all alone with his birthmom. He was nervous but also very happy. This time he would be meeting more of his family. Aunts, uncles, and cousins all anxiously awaited his arrival.

Although I speak of it now in a straightforward way, this visit was actually quite difficult for me. It was my first time letting Tyler go alone with his birthmother. Although it is not the same, I imagined what it must have been like for Christina to leave Tyler that first time with perfect strangers. All she had known of us was what she read on paper. She trusted Cheryl when Cheryl told her we were good people. She trusted us with her child. How could I not trust her at this moment? What helped me through this was the fact that I am secure in my parenting of Tyler. I know that I am raising him—that he is my son. I also know that he is hers as well. They belong to each other. This visit and all the others we have had and will have are in Tyler's best interest.

I thought of Tyler constantly when he was with Christina, and I called him twice each day. I was happy to hear him sounding relaxed, and I could tell he was enjoying himself. Had he sounded stressed, I would have gone and picked him up right away. Tyler was then and always has been very clear about the roles that Christina and I have. She is the woman who gave him life. I am the woman that sustains it. I am his mother, and so is she. Our son will always have two mothers and two fathers.

Tyler is now nearly eleven years old. Last summer, when he was ten, he flew to Florida with our friend and her family. Again he spent time with Christina, and once again all went well. I hope that this will become a yearly event for both of them. Each time he returns I feel all the more confidence in myself as his mother, in Christina, his loving birthmother, and in Tyler, who is thriving.

I have chosen to tell my story here for two reasons. The first is that, as with many happy personal stories, great pleasure comes simply from the telling. I love to take these precious memories out and enjoy them again. I love to savor them in a way that I am not often able to amid the hectic pace of daily life.

My second—and more important—reason for telling this story is that I hope I am helping readers to understand how and why open adoption works. We hear a lot about it these days—that it is a good thing—but people rarely get to hear how it really works. I hope that I have captured what I believe to be the essence of open adoption—that everyone can feel more secure, more confident, and more at peace with their past and their future if adoptive parents, birthparents, and their children all have open communication with each other. As I said earlier, I have no doubt that I am Tyler's mom, nor do I have any doubt that it is in Tyler's best interest—as well as that of all other family members—to have Christina to be a part of his life.

o

## IN THE BEST INTERESTS OF THE CHILD
### *Shelly Tenenbaum*

Dedicated to Monica Wolf.

o

By the time Glenn and I adopted our son, Samuel, we had worked with four different adoption agencies. Each time we changed agencies, we were assigned a new social worker, each with a very different personality, different opinions about how to best guide us through the adoption process, and different ideas about how to be a good parent. Had it not been for this exposure to their very different meanings of help, I would not be so keenly aware of how subjective these definitions are.

Prior to entering the adoption world, my only associations with social workers had been through friendships. I had never been assigned to work with a social worker before. It was a new experience, mandated by an agency and by the state: a person was there to provide help, but she also had a great deal of power over our ability to adopt a baby. First, she was the one who would make the decision about whether or not to approve our request to adopt. Later, she would play a critical role in connecting us with a child. At the end, she would represent the agency that possessed legal guardianship of our baby.

What we learned—among many other things—through this experience is that the power commanded by social workers, combined with the passionate desire and desperation of would-be parents, promotes a situation where many people end up acquiescing to conditions with which they may not be fully comfortable. While this power differential is ubiquitous, it is not acknowledged.

During our first meeting with our first social worker, Glenn's minor hearing loss was raised. The social worker asked Glenn if he had ever talked directly with Jonathan, our older son (who was then three years old), about his hearing. Glenn replied that Jonathan was fully aware that his dad did not hear well, but, no, we had never sat our son down and had a discussion of the issue. Glenn added that we were certainly not opposed to doing so. The social worker made her disapproval known immediately and informed Glenn that his lack of openness in dealing with his hearing loss made her suspicious about how open we would be in dealing with adoption. Later she told us that our homestudy would be approved only on the condition that we sought counseling regarding our lack of openness.

Glenn and I quickly realized that we could not continue with this social worker. Clearly she had very particular notions about the "right" way to parent, and these notions would be imposed on us. To make matters worse, we learned that she was married to the director of the agency, thereby limiting our ability to object to her positions. With clarity, but also with a great deal of emotional pain, we withdrew our application from that agency. The experience reminded us sadly of an earlier miscarriage—high hopes followed by great disappointment.

Since we were about to leave Massachusetts for a sabbatical year in California, we decided to have our homestudy done in our temporary new state. We located an agency and met with a social worker who used her authority more sensitively. At our first meeting she asked us if we had told Jonathan about our adoption plans, and we replied that we did not want to tell him this early in the process because he was so young and anticipating an event can be very difficult for a three-year-old. When I sensed that she might have a different opinion about this, I asked her what she thought, and in a respectful but direct tone, she explained that children overhear conversations and that if we were going to talk with family and friends about our decision, we should first talk with Jonathan. She further explained that she felt secrecy is damaging in that it implies shame. She added that since she would need to meet Jonathan, she preferred that we explain to him who she was. We appreciated this advice and used it.

After a year in California, we returned to Massachusetts and needed to have our homestudy updated with a local agency. We were assigned a social worker, someone I looked forward to meeting because she had been recommended to us after our debacle with the first agency. We had spoken by phone, and she had been very supportive to us.

During our first meeting with our new social worker, she asked us the usual questions about what age range of child we would accept, about whether or not we were willing to adopt a child with disabilities, and about our ethnic and racial preferences. When we explained that parenting a child of another race was not a challenge that we felt prepared for, she made it clear that we had given the wrong answer. She advised us to think about the issue further and to try to expand our ideas of who we could include in our family. I found her patronizing but did not feel that I could assert myself any more strongly than I already had, given the fact that I could not afford to antagonize her.

Our new agency required all applicants to attend a series of ten workshops on topics ranging from how to create a lifebook for a child to developmental issues to questions regarding open adoption. While the workshops were intended to help prospective adoptive parents, I was not sure that they were of help to me, since they required a nearly four-hour weekly time commitment that was difficult for a full-time working mother of a four-year-old. Certainly this was not a matter that I could raise with the agency, since it would likely be seen as a red flag of my lack of commitment to adoption. This reminded me of a *Boston Globe* article that I assign in the women's studies seminar I teach. The article is about Geraldine Churchwell, a mother of two children, who was kicked out of a homeless shelter because she refused to attend its required courses on child rearing, nutrition, and birth control. For Churchwell the program was coercive. She did not need classes on how to parent; she needed help finding a home. Similarly, sociologists studying battered women's shelters have found that shelter staff label clients as "good" when they demonstrate a commitment to seek help through the organization's counseling services. In contrast, women who refuse emotional counseling are regularly asked to leave.

I am troubled that there is often so little awareness on the part of social service providers regarding the control they are exercising when they force clients to seek *their* help. Clients are fully aware of the unspoken consequences of not playing the role of the good client. Among these consequences is the refusal of much-needed aid, including help in adopting a baby.

The social worker who updated our homestudy believed that open adoptions—adoptions where there is some interconnection between birthparents and adoptive parents—were in the best interest of children. One of her goals was to help adoptive parents become receptive to having ongoing relationships with their children's birthparents. In one of the ten required workshops, we were introduced to adoptive parents who maintained close relationships with the biological families, including birthgrandparents, of their children. That same month the agency newsletter featured a front-page article on one of these couples that had the tone of religious witnessing. The couple, as explained in the article, had initially been opposed to open adoption but had "seen the light" with the help of none other than the agency social worker. The parents reportedly were happily bringing up their child in the context of a close relationship with the birthparents. While I was not sure that I would want my family's life to be so enmeshed with the life of my child's birthparents, I was becoming a convert to open adoption.

Then our final social worker emerged on the scene. Through a constellation of fortuitous events, we received a call from this social worker while we were in Jerusalem visiting family. She is a woman whom I casually knew from work, who had tracked us down across the ocean to tell us about Sam. He had been born ten days earlier and was available for adoption. She made it clear from the outset that her agency opposed open adoption. By this time I had been so persuaded of the benefits of open adoption that I was very surprised by her opposition. I had assumed that everyone in the field agreed that an open process was in the best interest of the child. Now I realized that there are, indeed, varying views on what is in the best interest of children, that adoption agencies represent these often disparate views and that social work policies and stances are subjective.

With the support of our fourth and final social worker, Glenn and I had the luxury of being able to decide for ourselves what we believed was truly in the best interest of the child. No longer pressured to conform to an agency's perspective, we explored our feelings about open adoption in general and specifically about knowing Sam's birthparents. We realized that while we wanted to meet his birthparents so that we would be better able to answer his future questions, we did not want to predetermine any subsequent relationship. Rather, we wanted to wait and follow Sam's lead.

Although our final agency did not want us to even meet the birthparents, and Sam's birthparents had no interest in meeting us, our request to meet them was respected because *we* thought it was in the best interest of our child. The birthparents were comfortable with our suggestion that we always maintain a means to stay in contact, but that the actual decision to make contact again will ultimately rest with Sam. We are all committed to respecting and following Sam's decision in this matter.

If writing annual letters or getting together with the birthparents at some preset time interval had been a condition for our adoption, we probably would have agreed to those conditions. But this is not the decision that we made on our own. When our final social worker first told me that a reason she opposes open adoption is because it can be coercive to adoptive parents, I was confused and did not understand her concern. Now I do: if maintaining relationships with birthparents is a condition for adopting children, then it is very conceivable that prospective adoptive parents, yearning for children, will agree to conditions that they might not otherwise consider. From the perspective of some adoptive parents there is fear that voicing any hesitation about their willingness to comply with demands could jeopardize a potential placement.

I learned a lot along the complicated and often difficult road to Sam's adoption. Although the most important thing that I learned—or confirmed—is that adoption provides a wonderful opportunity to build or expand a family, I have also learned about the subjective—and often doctrinaire—nature of adoption social work practice. Sadly, I believe that the best interests of children—and of all their parents—sometimes get lost amid the fervent beliefs of social workers. They are there to help children find families, but sometimes their efforts are diminished by their certainty.

○

## A CHILD OF ONE'S OWN:
## SOME THOUGHTS ABOUT BIRTH AND ADOPTION
### *Ellen Sarasohn Glazer*

Several years ago, I was talking to a young boy about his family. When I asked him about siblings, he replied, "I have an older brother, Steven. We adopted him." In subsequent years, as my husband and I struggled to start a family of our own, I often thought about the boy's comment. I fantasized that I, too, would adopt a child and later become pregnant. I did not subscribe to the popular myth that adoption promoted fertility, but I felt that at some point after we adopted, some medical or magical intervention would cause me to conceive. I imagined that this would lead to the worst of circumstances: one child who was an outsider in our family and another who was truly our own. I expected that we would later regard the decision to adopt as a mistake.

I now have two daughters. Our older child, Elizabeth, came to us by adoption. Our younger child, Mollie, was born to us nearly three years later. I am now in the very predicament that I once feared. When I think back about the little boy and about my reaction to his comment, I cannot help but smile. I realize now that I understood so little at that time about attachments, about families, about the relationships that exist between parents and their children.

Elizabeth and Mollie are my children. I am well aware that they entered my life and our family in different ways. When they are old enough to know about these differences, they will certainly have feelings about them. However, what I did not know before I became their mother was that these differences would play a very small role in my perception of them and, at least at this point, in our ongoing experiences together. Moreover, I had no idea that the differences that do exist would add a valued dimension to our relationships.

When I have a quiet moment—and those are becoming increasingly scarce—I love to replay each of my daughter's arrivals. I try to rerun them in slow motion, giving myself a chance to enjoy moments that, at the time, went whizzing by. The deliveries, different in some ways, were each joyful experiences.

Elizabeth's arrival was announced by telephone. Don and I were sitting around one Sunday, planning our latest fertility strategy, when the phone rang. Don answered it and said, "Really, no shit!" Then he turned to me and said, "We have a daughter." I was startled. I thought for a moment about saying no, then suddenly found that I was ecstatic. I spent the next twenty-four hours in a frenzy, making scattered attempts to prepare for our daughter's arrival. I stayed up all night, and when she was finally delivered to us, I was too exhausted and too excited to look at her. I remember only a tiny bundle in yellow flowered bunting.

With Mollie, I stayed up all night, waiting for labor to begin. Having carried her for nine months, I had known that she was coming, but my years of infertility had made it difficult for me to believe that she was really on her way. Even that night, as I paced the house in the same kind of scattered state in which I had awaited Elizabeth, I did not have a clear sense that a baby would be born to us within twenty-four hours. When she was finally delivered after ten hours of hard labor, I was too exhausted and too excited to look at her. Mollie and I really met several hours later. I went into the nursery and realized that I had no idea which baby was Mollie. As with Elizabeth, others had to tell me which child was mine. Each time, once told, the attachment began.

The attachment, whether to a biological or an adopted child, feels the same; the pride feels different. I have been aware, since Mollie arrived, that I take a more private delight in her than I do in Elizabeth. With Elizabeth, I burst with pride. It is public. It is unlimited. It is never self-conscious. I don't hesitate to tell anyone that I think she is beautiful, that I suspect she is gifted, that I see her as the wittiest, most talented of children.

With Mollie, I *kvell* (a Yiddish expression meaning "burst with pride") silently. I see her as cute. I find her sweet, but I do not proclaim these thoughts publicly. Yesterday, I was changing her diaper with a friend and caught myself as I was about to say, "Oh, Mollie, you're so cute." Instead, I turned sheepishly to my friend and said, "I think that she is beginning to get cute."

The difference, as I see it, has to do with taking and giving credit. When I delight in Elizabeth, I never feel that I am bragging. I may know that I am, in part, responsible for who and what she is, but I don't feel it. When I admire her, it never feels as if I am admiring a part of myself. My public delight comes not only out of a sense of license, but also out of a feeling of commitment to her biological relatives. It is my effort, however futile, to include them, since they, too, would burst with pride if they could only know her. When I delight in Mollie it is very personal. I look at her fingers, her toes and cannot quite believe that they developed inside me. I am guarded about taking credit because I am staggered and humbled.

From day to day, I do not think of my daughters as different. When I am battling with Elizabeth to get her dressed in the morning or in for a nap, I do not think of her adoption. She is mine, for better or for worse. When I am feeding Mollie, I do not think of her as my firstborn. She is my younger child and will always remain so.

However, on occasions, particularly birthdays, there are differences—differences that I note and respect rather than regard as an intrusion. Mollie has not yet celebrated her first birthday. When she does, I expect it will be a happy occasion, one that will commemorate her arrival as well as celebrate her development at one year. I do not anticipate that it will be a very complicated occasion. Elizabeth's first birthday was a time of celebration, but it was also a bittersweet occasion. As it approached I realized that the day she was born, March 24, had little meaning for me; the day that I felt like celebrating was April 8, the day that she came to our home. Moreover, I knew that on March 24, there would be other people commemorating the day and that for them it would be a day without celebration. However, since her birth is for her and not for them or for us, March 24 has remained the day on which we rejoice.

Elizabeth's second and third birthdays have felt less complicated. April 8 has faded into the background, as have some of my concerns about her other parents. March 24 is her day, and I do all that I can to make it a special time for her. Nonetheless, the days between March 24 and April 8 remain a solemn time for me, an annual fifteen-day period in which I am very much aware that I was absent for my daughter's birth and early days. (Now these days take on additional meaning since they commemorate a time in which Mollie, too, was part of my life, but not yet known to me. Conceived on March 23, she announced her intentions by thermometer on April 8.)

Religious occasions, like birthdays, are a time at which I think about the differences in my daughters' origins. Mollie was born a Jew, will be raised as one, and will, I hope, find that her religion has something to offer. It is her birthright; there were no choices to be made. Elizabeth was born a Christian and was converted to Judaism when she was little over a month old. She had no say in the matter. We, as her parents, made a decision to take away one very rich heritage and to offer her another. Having made that decision, I feel it is my responsibility, as well as my pleasure, to offer her something in return. For Elizabeth, I hope that her religion will be special, that she will find it an enriching and satisfying part of her life. It is she to whom I sing in Hebrew, hoping that she will soon learn the words and the melodies.

When I was pregnant, I was very much aware that I was absent at Elizabeth's birth. I asked myself if I was sorry she wasn't my biological child, too. For her and for her future feelings, I wish that I could remove the fact of her adoption. For her other parents, excluded and undoubtedly in pain, I wish that they had not had to surrender their child. However, for myself, I do not wish that I had conceived, carried, and delivered her. What I missed prenatally and in those first fourteen days seems insignificant compared to the very special way in which she entered our family. Moreover, her delivery, so different from Mollie's and yet so similar, has added a special texture to the fabric of our lives.

o
_____

## LOVE THAT GROWS
### *Ellen Sarasohn Glazer*

We hear a lot these days about bonding. It is spoken of in hushed tones, with a reverence once reserved for natural childbirth and breast-feeding. Before I had children, I imagined bonding to be some sort of cosmic event, a few sacred moments on which a future relationship between parent and child was built.

I am the mother of two daughters, now nearly seven and four. They are the sources of my greatest pleasures as well as my worst fears. I cannot imagine life without them, and all separations—real and imagined—are difficult. We are clearly, inextricably bonded. Still, when I look back on our early days and weeks together, I recall no cosmic event, no magical, mystical moments of bonding. Instead I recall being tired, forgetful, ecstatic, and disoriented!

Elizabeth, my older daughter, came into my life suddenly, through adoption. She was two weeks old when she arrived home, a tiny five-pounder in yellow bunting. I was thirty-three and frantic, conditioned by years of infertility to childlessness. Each time Elizabeth cried, I said to her, "Don't worry, there's a mommy here." Looking back, I realize that I was talking more to myself than to her. I needed reassurance that this was for real—that I was not an imposter.

With Mollie, my younger daughter, I began with different assumptions. Because she was born to us, there was never a question of another mother. Because I had already been a mother for nearly three years, I no longer felt like a fake. Still, I remember her early days, like Elizabeth's, as a time of great chaos, with life spent in an ecstatic, sleep-deprived, bewildered daze.

Looking back, I have difficulty understanding how some see bonding as something that happens very early in a mother and child's experience together. Mollie was at my breast moments after birth. Elizabeth was in my arms at two weeks. I am sure that cosmic events can wait two weeks, but bonding, as best as I can tell, is something that happens over time.

My daughters and I bonded over tantrums in the supermarket and en route to the emergency room for stitches. We bonded making goody bags for birthday parties and costumes for Halloween. We bond anew each morning when I must hurry them out the door, threatening that Sesame Street will never, ever be on again if they don't brush their teeth and put their shoes on. Last week, our bonds grew deeper and stronger when they ruined the living room rug with nail polish. I screamed. They cried. I screamed again. Then Elizabeth said, "But Mom, you always told us that it is people and not things that matter." Anger and tears were put aside as, once again, we laughed together.

When my daughters were younger, I would often say to them, "I'm the luckiest mommy in the world because I have the two of you." I repeated it one day recently, and Elizabeth responded, "Not that again. Don't you think other mommies think that their children are the best?"

She's right. Of course most mothers adore their children and wouldn't trade them for anything. But that was not what I was talking about. I wasn't saying I was so lucky because my children are so wonderful; I meant that I was lucky to have become a mother at all, and I was especially lucky that it happened as it did. Infertility taught me to never take parenthood for granted. Adoption taught me to never take a family bond for granted. Together they taught me to cherish the children that I have and the bonds that we have built—and continue to build together.

## Update

My experience as Elizabeth and Mollie's mother has gone through several transformations since I wrote "A Child of One's Own" fourteen years ago. The babies that I cradled in my arms and sang to are now teenagers who dash in and out of the house just long enough to pick up their phone messages. The cute little girls, each with her blond pigtails, have acquired their own teen styles: Liz, clean cut, almost preppy and Mollie, moderate grunge. The years have gone by, as I knew—but never believed—they would, in a blur.

Looking back on my essay of fourteen years ago, I am struck by two things. One is the apparent freedom that I felt to write publicly about my daughters. Now that they are individuals, each in her own right, I no longer feel that freedom. The other thing that I notice in the original essay is the absence of any expectations, assumptions, hopes, or fears about their relationship as sisters. And so I will do what I just said I wasn't going to do and talk—very briefly—about Elizabeth and Mollie.

For me, one of the great surprises and immense joys of motherhood has been watching my daughters' relationship with each other. They are very different people, and perhaps it is this difference that enables them to be close, noncompetitive, and mutually respectful. I cannot remember the last time that they argued, but I can easily think of many times when I have been deeply touched by their concern for each other.

When the girls were young, people who knew they were not birth-siblings sometimes foolishly observed, "but they look just like sisters." The comment seemed odd to me at the time, and now it seems odder still. They are sisters.

○

## KATHERINE'S STORY
### *Rika Smith McNally*

After years of hoping for a baby—through first a miscarriage, then infertility treatments, later health problems—my husband, John, and I turned toward adoption. At times that turning felt like a gentle rotation toward a happier life; at other times it was a wrenching feeling. When were we ready to give up that monthly hope?

Our first foray into adoption, a domestic placement agency, was even worse than our infertility treatment—at least then we had the sense that the doctors, nurses, and counselors were on our side. An overly optimistic social worker combined with a birthmother counselor who didn't take to us (Was it our lack of participation in an organized religion? Our names? Did we remind her of someone? Were we too honest? Were we not playing the game correctly?) resulted in no matches. For over two years we were told that it could happen any time. I kept diapers and baby clothes in a closet, took them out, put them in the attic, and took them out again. I saw my baby as a small star in the heavens: one of those specks of light was meant for me, and I had to wait to learn which one.

We had thought of international adoption, but our desire to meet our child's birthmother—and indeed have a lifelong relationship with her—had delayed us from pursuing that path.

I don't remember when the idea of adopting from China first came to us. Early on, a couple in a support group we were in had agonized because the Chinese government had stopped international adoptions and had wondered if they should wait for that country to open up again. We wondered too. I saw a young Chinese baby being held by her father at an adoption conference; my throat blocked and tears came to my eyes. I wanted to go up to him and ask if I could hold her, smell her hair, cradle her head the way he did. I didn't, but I watched them together.

John and I began thinking more about adoption from China. We did not seek out the information; it just presented itself to us. An administrative assistant at the domestic agency where we were waiting told us about someone she knew who had adopted from China through a nearby agency. I don't know why this time we acted. It could have been fate; maybe we were finally truly ready. We called and met with Lillian, the director, later that day. Either out of relief or happiness, I cried at the meeting. It would be the first of many times that the director would see me in tears.

Although many families have told of the struggle as they waited for paperwork and waited for their child to be assigned to them, I was excited throughout the process. I liked the photocopying, the notarized documents, even the fingerprinting. The stars looked brighter and closer. I dreamed I was sitting on the peak of our roof at night and waiting for her to come to us. Our star, who would be Katherine.

Finally her picture arrived, and I went to the agency office to get it. She was so small! Her eyes were bright, and she held a little hand up in a wave. She had dark, thick hair, which went in all directions, and a rash on her forehead. Her face was a little thin, and there was some puffiness around one of her eyes. Mostly she looked worried.

Was she healthy? Was her reported weight correct? How could her weight be so low for her age? I would later show her picture to every doctor I knew, as if they could assess her well-being and predict lifelong health from a one-inch color print. I did this in part because I could tell that Lillian, the director of our agency, was worried as well. She told me that she was going to ask for special care for our baby and asked me to try not to worry. Of course, that only let me know that there were three of us worrying! I realized that Lillian was concerned that she would have to tell us that fate had chosen another child for us. We knew this sometimes happened— that a child was assigned to a couple, but then Lillian had the impossible job of telling them that a change needed to be made. I also knew that Lillian knew I was in love with *this* child even before I left her office.

Good fortune was with us, and the little baby in the photo was to become Katherine. I felt very calm when we traveled to China to get her. This was not entirely unexpected, as I do take comfort in travel and as I liked being with other parents waiting for their daughters. I had no doubts, no second thoughts.

The day after our arrival in Beijing, our group toured the Summer Palace and the Forbidden City. This tour was something that our agency had arranged so that we could get acclimated and so that there would be time to check on all the paperwork for our adoptions. While we were touring, I found myself in a mix of extreme emotions—a feeling of such joy that tears repeatedly came to my eyes, but also an anticipation of the pain that our daughter will probably (no, certainly) feel when she realizes the extreme loss she suffered so early in life and the anguish her birthmother must have felt at giving her up. We saw Chinese families with young babies, and as our small group approached, both sides would gesture and laugh. I quickly realized that the parents were acknowledging our delight in how beautiful their children were. I also found myself looking at the young women in the large tourist crowds, wondering if my daughter would look like one of them when she was older.

Our final tourist stop before flying to Wuhan in Hubei Province to get our children was the Great Wall of China. It was raining heavily when we were there, and we wore plastic bags in an attempt to protect our clothes while we climbed up to see the amazing view. The rain brought out the smell of damp stone and earth. Standing there, John and I made a commitment to bring our daughter back to visit China someday.

When our group finally arrived in Wuhan, I found myself becoming increasingly anxious. That anxiety reached its height the night before we were to go pick up our babies. The minutes and hours seemed to be crawling by. Then it was the day.

Our group awoke early, all eagerly awaiting the arrival of the babies. As it turned out, they did not arrive until two P.M.—it was a *long* morning! When I think back on it I can remember many details, yet it feels like a blur. I remember the nannies walking into the room, holding our children. John and I recognized Katherine immediately, but I was almost too nervous to look. We held our cold hands locked together, and then, as they placed her in my arms, I wept. Still, I can remember everything—her face, her eyes, her soft hair, her smell, her clothes, her little fingers that had beckoned from the photo. She was very small, but bigger and healthier than she had appeared in the photograph. She kept looking for my breast, and I wondered if a wet nurse had been found for her until we arrived. That night she did not make eye contact with us (she still does this when she meets a new person whom she's not sure of). That night she held my hand as she slept next to me (she still does this, too).

When we adopted Katherine in China, the officials held a small ceremony for us. There they gave Katherine three gifts—a red velvet bag with a small necklace with her birth year, a pair of Chinese slippers, and a packet of soil from her hometown of Yun Meng. Each of her gifts is very special to us and I'm sure will be so for her. The soil, in particular, is something we treasure.

Now we are a family transformed. At eighteen months old, Katherine shrieks with delight as she runs around the house after her bath each night.

The past year has been even better than I had imagined: I now know the joy and peace of having my child fall asleep in my arms, of knowing that she is happy.

Katherine is strong, beautiful, gentle, and funny. She brings me my glasses to get me out of bed in the morning, and she follows John around the yard. Her enthusiasm for singing and dancing is unbounded. She has preferences as to which of us read which books to her at bedtime, insists on helping me cook (she is in charge of wooden spoons and some spices), and loves to paint on huge pieces of paper on the kitchen floor. She is affectionate with her grandparents, and they adore her. She is so familiar to me now that I can barely remember our lives without her.

Yesterday Katherine called, "I love you" from her car seat, and gentle tears came to me again. Each night I point to the sky, and she calls out one of her favorite words. Not surprisingly, it is "star."

---
o

---

## LIFE'S JOURNEYS
### Katherine Thomas

My life has completely changed in the last twelve months. During that time I got divorced, decided to adopt as a single woman, and traveled to St. Petersburg, Russia, to pick up my now ten-month-old daughter, Aleksa. We have been together three months, and it is hard to believe that we were not always a family.

My path to adoption was easy in some ways and very difficult in others. The easy part, ironically enough, was the application to the adoption agency—the paperwork, the homestudy, the decision to enter their Russian program. Those aspects of adoption were straightforward, moving smoothly and pretty much uneventfully. The hard parts, for me, were the decision to adopt and, later, the waiting period between the time I received information about my daughter and the time I traveled to Russia. But first, the decision.

My decision to adopt came after much struggle in my fifteen-year marriage over the issue of having a child and after considerable efforts to conceive. Ultimately, neither pregnancy nor the marriage worked, and I decided to divorce and, at age forty-five, pursue motherhood as a single woman.

Looking back, I am somewhat amazed at my determination: I was very clear that I wanted to be a mother. It was not just something I thought I *might* want or *should* want. It was something I *knew* I wanted, despite the fact that I had had limited experience with babies. I was never one who did a lot of babysitting, nor did I reach out to hold the children of my friends and family. Rather, it had to do with motherhood: I wanted to be a mother. I suppose it could have been called an obsession, but I believe it is what they call following your heart.

As I mentioned earlier, the adoption process itself was straightforward. Once I had asked myself a million times whether I could do this at my age, whether I could bond with an adopted child, whether I wanted to be sixty-three years old at my daughter's high school graduation, and whether my family would totally flip out when I told them, I decided to move ahead and apply for adoption. Even after I did so, I continued to ask myself these and other troubling questions. I asked them, I struggled with them, but I remained steadfast in my resolve to adopt.

In general, I am a rather quiet person who has always prided myself on keeping feelings inside. Adopting as a single woman forced me to make a very dramatic change in this regard; it became an experience of reaching out to family and to friends, both old and new. Sometimes, I reached out to complete strangers. Although it was unfamiliar, this process felt very good. Wherever I turned, I was met with great support and encouragement.

Perhaps no one was as supportive or as helpful in the adoption process as my sister-in-law, Denise. I have always known her to be a spirited and spunky individual, and she certainly did not disappoint me in this adventure. As soon as I told her my plans, she responded, "I'm going. I'm going with you to Russia, and there will be no arguing about that." There wasn't!!

My widowed father and my stepmother, Grace, were also of great support to me. Because their first concern was for my well-being, they were cautious, but they let me know from the start that they supported my decision to adopt. That meant a great deal to me. I was especially moved to see that my father, whose style is to be reserved, was excited. He wouldn't say much, but he did talk about his Eastern European heritage and one day even said that he wished his father were alive to witness this adoption. That meant the world to me. Sometimes I would look at my father and see that he was trying to hold back a big smile. He saved that for our safe return!

Aleksa was born on May 1 and assigned to be my child soon after (Aleksa was the name I chose for her; it came to me early on as a name that sounded both Russian and American). The news came with a brief video of her, and I will never forget the experience of meeting her—on the screen—for the first time. Although the video lasted only a few seconds, I sat glued to it for hours. Playing it over and over again. Looking. Watching. Humbled. Curious. Frightened. Excited. Was she OK? Would she be mine? Would I love her? Would she love me? Would this all work out?

It did not take long at all for me to be sure that I wanted to become Aleksa's mother. Although I had the video evaluated by pediatricians at a local adoption clinic and anxiously awaited their findings, I was committed. I phoned physicians in Russia several times because there was a question regarding her vision, but even as I made the calls, I knew that I wanted to move forward. The little girl on the snippet of tape had somehow won my heart. Still, I was not free to go and bring her home. I had to wait for the Immigration and Naturalization Service forms to come through.

It was October when the INS papers finally came through and my agency was able to begin to make arrangements for a court date in Russia. I soon learned that I would be in Russia for eight days and that we would go to court on December 3. That meant that I would spend Thanksgiving with my father and stepmother, then leave for St. Petersburg with Denise, who never wavered on her decision to travel with me. Unfortunately, the plans did not go as smoothly as I'd hoped. There was a last-minute glitch with our visas, and they didn't arrive until the day before we were due to leave. Fortunately, I had developed a state of mind that allowed me to stay relatively calm even at the height of stress. I believed that the adoption would eventually happen, even if it was postponed along the way. However, I was concerned about Aleksa, who was waiting in the orphanage.

And then we were on our way. It was the most amazing experience of my life—to fly halfway around the world to bring a child home. Nothing that I had done in the past could ever have fully prepared me for this experience, and yet, in some ways, I suppose that everything did. There I was, somehow equipped for this adventure.

We arrived in St. Petersburg on a cold, snowy, dark Sunday afternoon. The days are very short in Russia at that time of year, and this added to what I would call an eerie feeling of being in a post–Cold War country that we did not know and where the language was completely unfamiliar. We were whisked off by facilitators and translators to the apartment that our agency had arranged for us. Although everything felt very strange, I began to feel relieved; we were clearly with people who knew what they were doing.

After an anxious, excited night in our hardly luxurious St. Petersburg apartment, we were taken to the orphanage. What an amazing experience that was! We met first with the orphanage doctor who told us, through a translator, about Aleksa's eating and sleeping habits. She also told us what she knew about the birthmother. Then, with no announcement, Aleksa was brought in!

Of the many moments in this journey that I will never forget, none is more vivid than that first moment of holding, seeing, meeting Aleksa. There was this little child—barely seven months old—with her eyes locked in a gaze at my face. Then she began to touch my face with her hands. She was quite a sight, wearing several layers of clothes, along with big, furry woolen booties and a tied-under-the-chin cap. I had heard that Russians dress their children very warmly, but this was even more than I had anticipated!

I remember every moment of those precious few minutes. After holding Aleksa for a short time, it was time to feed her, then change her clothes to some that I had brought for her. Not surprisingly, what I thought was more than adequate to keep her warm met with disapproval by the attendants, who clearly thought that the little child would be cold. Fortunately, I was prepared for this reaction and was able to pull out a fuzzy pink vest that met with their immediate approval.

Two busy and exciting days after we first met, Aleksa and I went to court (and so did Denise, of course!). During the proceedings the judge, who had all my paperwork in front of him, stated that Aleksa was available for international adoption because, as was translated for me, "no one had visited her in the orphanage, and no one had taken an interest in her life." I will never forget those words. They left an indelible mark. No one had taken an interest in her life, but now I had. I had taken an interest, and it would be a lasting one.

The judge left the room for a few moments of deliberation, then returned to announce that the adoption was approved. He stepped around his desk, handed me the paperwork, and congratulated me. The doctor from the orphanage gave me a big hug. I had wished I knew more Russian since the moment I had arrived in the country, but I felt it especially at this time. I wanted so much to talk with these people; it was one of the most important moments of my life, and I was so very far from home.

The remainder of our stay in St. Petersburg was filled with more official business—getting birth certificates, adoption forms, and so forth—and some unofficial business as well. We bought souvenirs, including some things from her homeland that I hope Aleksa will enjoy and treasure in the future. Despite the cold and our exhaustion, we even managed a visit to the famed Hermitage Museum. Aleksa went along with all of this in her usual good spirits. I had the sense that the more we did, the better she liked it.

Late on Thursday, the fifth day of our journey, we departed by overnight train for Moscow. We needed to make this trip in order to go to apply for Aleksa's visa at the U.S. embassy. Our agency had arranged for us to stay at the home of a very gracious Russian woman, who fed us well. Again we managed to squeeze in a little unofficial business—a tour of Red Square and a brief view of the Kremlin—but most of our time in Moscow was spent preparing for our return home. We were picked up at four in the morning for our flight to Frankfurt—and then to Boston.

Two weary, sleep-deprived travelers and one hearty, happy baby arrived at Logan Airport to be greeted by enthusiastic friends and family. My brother, the self-proclaimed "Mr. Mom" (he said he'd take over if something happened to both Denise and me), came with a red rose and a note for each of us.

Our reception in Boston was the beginning of several months of celebration. I have been thrilled and deeply touched by the support and the welcome that we have received from my colleagues, my friends, and, above all, my family. All have opened their hearts to Aleksa and have reinforced, again and again, the rightness of my decision.

For me, I don't think I could have anticipated the constancy of single parenting, although I was warned. It has to be experienced to know it, and I have had only three months with one child, at that. There is the constancy of caring for this little person who depends solely on you, and it leads to downright exhaustion sometimes. For me, it has brought new meaning to the term *time management*. I find myself feeling mildly triumphant when I manage to get out of the house on time.

In addition to the many challenges, there are innumerable joys. One is the developing, unfolding relationship with a child, one day at a time. It is an extra special pleasure to watch a little girl from a faraway country feel comfortable enough to splash and squeal happily in the bathtub, figure out a toy, or want to kiss the baby in the mirror.

In my years of infertility treatment and struggle, I never imagined that my road to parenthood would lead me to Russia and to this precious little girl who has taken over my home and won my heart. I think that my social worker described it well when she said that adoption is "about people who are meant to be together finding each other."

o

# FINDING THE SUGAR

## Mary Terhune

Many things have happened in my life that I did not anticipate or plan on. Among them is the fact that I now find myself intimately involved in the world of infertility. Years ago, I would never have dreamed that I would be a contributor to this book.

Let me say at the outset that I have not endured the pain of infertility. Nonetheless, I believe that my personal experience—as a woman who placed her firstborn for adoption—and my professional experiences—as a registered nurse and holistic health practitioner working with infertile women—have prepared me to talk about infertility. Doing so helps me continue to heal from my own loss as a birthmother years ago.

On July 24, 1964, I gave birth to a baby girl. At the time I was nineteen, single, and unable to see any path for myself—and my daughter—other than relinquishment. And so I did what was, for me, a desperate act, one that I would not easily recover from. I placed my daughter for adoption and attempted to move on. Instead, I went from that loss to an unsuccessful marriage, unhappy relationships, and a life that was filled with a sense of failure and regret.

Fast forward. It was October 1982. Steeped in depression and anxiety, fortified with tranquilizers, and aware that my life was slipping away from me, I decided to make a drastic change in my life. Looking back, I am not sure how much I understood about the connection between the loss of my daughter and my depression. I simply knew that I was deeply wounded and that I needed to heal. That awareness sent me on what evolved into a spiritual journey: it began with therapeutic massage, acupuncture, and Reiki (a Japanese form of hands-on healing) and expanded to meditation and the study of Eastern philosophy and ancient scriptures. Eventually I traveled to India—a spiritual journey that helped prepare me for the continuation of my adoption journey.

Fast forward again. It was August 24, 1994, and the telephone rang. I answered it, and the voice on the other end said, "Is this Mary Terhune?" When I said yes, she continued, "I am a social worker from New Jersey." That was all I needed to hear. I responded, "Is she looking for me?" She answered, "Yes, do you want to talk with her?" For an instant, I hesitated. This was a call that I had unconsciously awaited for thirty years, yet now, when it finally came, I was entirely unprepared for it. I knew then that saying yes would change my life. I wasn't sure whether I was ready for it, but somehow I found the courage to say yes. Twenty minutes later the phone rang again.

"Hello, Mary?"

"Yes."

"Mom?"

An amazing exchange. In those four short words, thirty years whizzed by. The baby that I remembered was now a woman who sounded almost identical to me. Although I had had the great pleasure of parenting my second daughter, I had never known anyone whose speech patterns, whose voice, whose thinking was so much like mine. "My God," I thought, "this is my daughter." What so many years of separation could not erase, in the end could only be acknowledged.

I need to pause for a moment now, because I know that some of the people reading this are adoptive parents and others are contemplating adoption. Having worked closely with women going through infertility and with some considering adoption, I know how frightened people can be of birthparents and of birth ties. Hence, I want to pause and say that nothing I am saying is intended to diminish the role of adoptive parents. There is a lasting mother-child bond between birthmothers and their offspring, and there is a lasting mother-child bond between adoptive mothers and their children. Both are real. Both are powerful. One does not diminish the other.

So back to my amazing phone call . . . and our physical reunion one month later. Cindy and I met at my mother's apartment in New Jersey. Although my mother, my younger daughter, Deborah (then twenty-three years old), and my brother and his wife were all anxious to meet Cindy, Cindy and I had both decided that it would be better if our first moments of reunion were left to just the two of us. My family agreed to wait at my brother's house for a call. We could then be free to feel whatever we needed to feel and not worry about taking care of the feelings of other family members.

The moment we first set eyes on each other was electrifying. I almost thought I'd have a heart attack! There she was at the end of the hall. "Mom, is that you?" I replied, "It's me." We fell into each other's arms sobbing. All the years of pain and separation fell away with each tear. We held each other like this for thirty minutes before we could even really look into each other's eyes. We just didn't want to let go to do it. Everything seemed astonishing. We looked so much alike, right down to our mannerisms. I felt compelled to look at her hands and feet to make sure she had all her digits. Isn't this what a mother does upon giving birth? I was later told this is quite natural; you pick up where you left off, and Cindy and I had left off the day she was born. I had never even had a chance to hold her.

We tried to make up for thirty years in eight hours; our respective families started calling to see if we were OK. I knew that Cindy and I would need a lot of time to process all the feelings. One thing was certain, though: we loved each other no matter what, and now there was an end to the separation. Later that day, my family met Cindy and took her in with great love. A month later I would meet Cindy's parents. We had a lot more in common than one would think. I realized that the pain of her mother's feelings of loss due to infertility echoed some of the pain I had experienced with the relinquishment of my baby.

These experiences put me more closely in touch with the depth of sorrow that I had felt for so many years and helped me to realize that there were two other things that I needed to do.

First, I discovered that I needed to meet with other birthmothers, adoptees, and adoptive parents. I joined a support group and found it immensely helpful to talk with others who were part of an adoption triad. Our experiences are very much shared experiences, and there is so much that we can give to and learn from each other. To my surprise—and relief—I found it healing simply to tell my story over and over again. Each time it was both the same and a little different. The facts didn't change with repeated tellings, but the feelings about them did.

The second thing that I needed to do—and this is where things come full circle—is that I needed to work with infertile women. This was not something that I realized consciously, as I had realized that I needed to join the support group, but it, too, was a truth in my life. It came to me when I was speaking at or attending meetings of triad members: I realized that many of the women were there because of infertility. I began to wonder if some of the tools that I had used to heal from my own adoption wounds might also help heal them from the wounds of their infertility. This led me to begin to study the endocrine system and to learn more about the ways in which the endocrine glands were connected to the main chakras (spiritual energy centers) of the body. Perhaps I could work on the chakras and have an impact on those endocrine glands that govern reproduction.

That is where I find myself today. Through massage, Reiki, meditation, and other forms of healing that I have studied, I work with infertile women. The work is immensely gratifying to me. I believe that the pleasure I feel comes not simply from helping people (because I have done that for a long time), but from the nature of the problem and the help. You see, in a very lovely way, each new pregnancy gives me a chance to revisit an old wound from a new perspective. Each new pregnancy reminds me that conception is, indeed, a miracle, and that each new birth is divine.

As I look back on my life, I can honestly say that I never planned for things to happen as they did. But when life gives you lemons, the best thing you can do is reach for the sugar and make lemonade. It took me thirty years to be able to find that sugar, but when I did, I knew that the search was worth it. Out of the loss and then the reunion with my daughter, so much was born, including myself.

○

## THE MOTHER OF MY CHILD
### *Judith Steinbergh*

For the birthmothers of my two adopted children.

○

*a baby fills my dream womb*
*like a full moon opened by tide*

*it is there*
*sudden as dawn*
*spinning toward me*

    the mother of my child
    is heaving tonight
    like a spring mountain
    winter is thawing
    from her insides
    she will give up the child

she will contract
into a young girl
wondering at this flood
wondering at this lost
territory

*a woman calls*
*official as a head of state*
*to declare*
*she is keeping her child*
*that is all*
*that is all*
*the phone withers*
*in my hand*
*sleep writhes*
*out of my skin*
*like a snake*
*I am new*
*to such night cold terror*
*the breaking of treaties*

the mother of my child
is a child
she whimpers
she can't remember
why
she has handed
the moon out of her sky
like a cookie

*I reach out*
*she is smiling*
*she hands me her motherhood*
*like a birthright*
*it is my child*
*golden as a canyon*
*for a moment guilt*
*slides away*
*like a sweet rain*

now the darkness
covers her with ivy
over her flat belly
over her knuckles
over her eyes
feeling
its persistent claw
she wills the slow wall
to blot her growing hollow

# 14

# HALF GENETICALLY OURS

*Donor insemination* is the attempt to conceive a child through sperm donated either anonymously or by a family member or friend.

*Ovum donation* is the attempt to conceive a child through an egg (or eggs) donated anonymously or by a family member or friend.

*Surrogacy* is the family-building option in which one woman conceives, carries, and delivers a child that will be adopted by another woman and reared by her and her partner, who is the genetic father.

FOR MOST COUPLES the decision to have a child together is accompanied by fantasies of a child who will be a combination of the two of them. These fantasies usually include physical traits and personality characteristics, as well as talents and intellectual capabilities. In their minds, most envision a child who represents the best of both of them. Although they know that their real child could be a mixture of their least favorite traits, it is fun to fantasize.

Definitive sterility in one partner, serious illness, or a genetic condition put some couples in the position of knowing that they are unable to have a child together. In light of this information, some decide to adopt or to live without children. These couples may feel that there is no reason to go to great lengths to create a child unless she or he comes from the two of them. Or they may have concluded that it would undermine their relationship or be unfair to the child if he or she were deliberately conceived to be genetically connected to only one of them.

Other couples have a different perspective. For these couples the option of having a child that is the genetic offspring of one but not both of them is indeed attractive. Such couples consider or pursue sperm donation, egg donation, or surrogacy because they are drawn to the opportunity to have some genetic and generational continuity. Many are also drawn to the opportunity to share a pregnancy together, an opportunity that comes with two of the three half-genetic options.

For some couples the attraction to a half-genetic option is predicated on the fact that a family member has offered to donate eggs or sperm to them or, much less commonly, to have a child through surrogacy for them. Many of these couples feel that it is not just a half-genetic experience: they will be the parents of a child who comes from both of their families; in the instance of sibling donations, the child actually comes from both sets of grandparents.

Unfortunately, some couples turn to half-genetic options more out of fear than desire. Some fear that they will be unable to adopt, either because of its high costs (donor insemination, the most common half-genetic option, can be very inexpensive) or because they believe, rightly or wrongly, that they will be turned down for adoption because of their age, a medical or emotional condition, or because of something else in their histories.

There are also couples who are frightened of adoption. Negative media attention has convinced them that adoption is a very risky venture, fraught with heartache and disappointment. Or they may fear that their families or others dear to them will not accept an adopted child. These couples may believe that they can have a half-genetic child and—with anonymous sperm or egg donation—keep the fact that they have "adopted" a gamete a secret.

Although the half-genetic options differ from each other in significant ways, they have much in common. Following are some of the central issues for couples considering half-genetic parenting: Is it necessary, or might we still be able to reproduce together? Will it work? Who should we tell about it? How will it affect family relationships? Is it in the best interests of the child?

## Is It Necessary?

Although there are some couples for whom sterility is definitive, others face some degree of ambiguity. Dramatic advances in reproductive medicine are certainly expanding treatment opportunities, making conception possible for people who were once told that they could never have children. For example, intracytoplasmic sperm injection (ICSI) has enabled many couples who were once told that their male infertility was definitive to have full genetically related children. In fact, among ICSI parents there are some couples whose first child came to them through donor insemination.

Hence, it is increasingly difficult to say "never." On the horizon is a new technology that involves the transfer of donor cytoplasm to aging eggs. Perhaps in a few years this technology will join ICSI in having widespread use and success. Couples seeking to avoid regret may wonder if they should wait just a little longer in order to avail themselves of this or yet another new technology designed to bring them a full genetically related child.

## Will It Work?

There are few guarantees in life, and although the half-genetic options frequently result in a successful pregnancy and live delivery, this is not always the case. Sometimes people go to great effort and expense only to meet with disappointment. In considering the half-genetic options, couples must ask themselves the question, What will we do if it doesn't work? and the attendant question, Are we prepared to deal with the emotional, financial, and time costs of a failed attempt?

The question of whether it will work is especially significant for couples who face some limitation—time, money, stamina. Those who are also considering adoption are in a difficult predicament, since they know that they will need to reserve some resources for this option.

## Privacy or Secrecy?

For many years the most common half-genetic option, donor insemination (DI), was shrouded in secrecy. People believed—and this belief was reinforced by their physicians and by society in general—that it was best for all involved to keep sperm donation secret. This was similar to the practice of closed adoption, in which adoptees, birthparents, and adoptive parents were all told to move on with their lives and forget events that had occurred.

In the early 1980s the adoption rights movement unfolded, and with it came vocal testimony to the destructive power of secrecy. Some DI offspring joined adoptees in voicing their need to know the truth about their origins and in arguing that even no information about a genetic parent is preferable to wrong information or deceit. Both DI offspring and adoptees made it clear that tightly guarded secrets erode both self-esteem and family relationships.

Many couples pursuing half-genetic options are now discouraged—by professionals and by changing societal norms—from keeping secrets from their children. Still, questions of whom, when, and how to tell the truth about the origins of a family remain challenging.

Privacy, however, is different from secrecy. The decision to tell one's child the truth about his or her conception does not mean that everyone must know. Some half-genetic options are more amenable to privacy than others. DI, because it often involves just a "simple" insemination, has the greatest potential for privacy. Surrogacy, by contrast, is a process that does not lend itself easily to privacy. Simply by virtue of the fact that the pregnant woman is not the intended mother of the child she is carrying, surrogacy is something that others will know about. The challenge for participants is, of course, to make determinations about whom to tell and what, when, and how to tell them. Ovum donation, though far from a simple procedure, can also be hidden and therefore kept private from those who have no personal stake in the process.

Regardless of which half-genetic option people participate in, privacy questions arise. Hence, it is important for parents to remember that they have an absolute right to privacy. At the same time, however, to one's child, disclosure (that is, the truth about his or her genetic history) is an entitlement, part of their birthright. It is therefore crucial that couples distinguish between privacy and secrecy before conception, during pregnancy, after birth, and throughout a child's early life.

## Effect on Family Relationships

"Half genetically ours" also means "half genetically not ours." What does this mean in the context of the family created in this way?

Again, there are distinct differences between the half-genetic options in the challenges that they present. A child born from a donor egg *does* have a biological connection to both of his or her parents (and in the case of intrafamily donation, a genetic connection as well). Perhaps the fact that her mother gestated her will minimize the child's feelings of rejection or disconnection. By contrast, a child born of surrogacy knows that he has another mother—a birthmother. Supporters of surrogacy believe that this knowledge will have minimal impact on the child's identity, because the child will always know who the surrogate is. Furthermore, the child will always know that it was never the surrogate's intent to parent him and therefore he was not rejected. Surrogacy critics fear that surrogacy offspring will always feel a profound sense of loss, knowing that they were conceived by arrangement for a prebirth adoption.

Perhaps the questions that arise with donor insemination are the most complicated because they are the least obvious. The child's mother is her mother, has always been and will always be. There is no ambiguity about this. By contrast, the child's father—like all fathers—did not carry the pregnancy and, unlike most other fathers, did not make a genetic contribution to the child. The significance of a genetic connection varies from one individual to another. Some may place little weight on genetic ties and long to be fathers for social and emotional reasons. Others feel a strong need to pass on their lineage, believing that is what determines fatherhood.

In half-genetic parenting, the donor (or surrogate) does not cease to exist once the child is conceived. What this means is that the child's genetic parent will always be an important part of who the child is, even if the child never meets the donor. The donor has an ongoing impact on the family. With an anonymous donor, this relationship exists primarily in fantasy. However, increased efforts on the part of sperm banks and egg donation programs to provide families with information about the donors (and the willingness of some donors to be identified) now help shape and define those fantasies.

When a couple has worked with a known donor or a surrogate, the relationship exists in reality, not in fantasy. What that reality will be is an evolving process that donors or surrogates and recipients must participate in over time. It is critical that everyone acknowledge this ahead of time. Furthermore, it is important that they have similar expectations for how their relationships will evolve and how much contact they will have. In the case of family members, they must conceptualize the role that the donor will have in the child's life and be able to balance dual realities (for example, the genetic mother may be the familial and social aunt). Will the donor or surrogate be a special aunt, uncle, or cousin? Might she or he be the child's guardian or godparent or have some other special designation in the child's life?

## The Best Interest of the Child

In considering a half-genetic parenting option, all participants must carefully consider the rights of unborn children. Each must ask himself or herself if it is ever in a child's best interest to be intentionally created from an unknown gamete and to be parented by a person other than his or her genetic parent. Some argue that the gift of life is enough to make gamete donation a positive undertaking, and they conclude that any child would—or should—be grateful to those responsible for his or her conception. Others argue that not everyone is grateful for the gift of life and that a child created in this way will suffer lifelong losses, perhaps concluding that he or she would have been better off never having been born.

Undoubtedly these are tough issues with which childless couples must grapple. They are especially difficult for those couples in which one or both partners oppose adoption: without pursuing a half-genetic option, these couples have no opportunity to be parents together. For compelling reasons such couples are tempted to put their concerns and their doubts aside and to hope that their child will be sustained by the knowledge that she or he was deeply wanted and is greatly loved.

Hence we see that the half-genetic paths to parenthood involve complex decision making both prior to conception and in the months, years, and decades that follow. In the following pages we hear from several people who have chosen alternative paths. In "Playing the Hand You're Dealt," Stephanie Brigham addresses both the pain of a definitive diagnosis of sterility and the joy that she and her husband experienced becoming parents through donor insemination. In "The Gift of Life" Michelle Parks tells of the fears and fantasies she experienced during her donor insemination pregnancy. Suzette Rizzo, in "Friends for Life," presents the moving story of her efforts to conceive a baby with the help of her lifelong friend. Marjorie Swift, mother of twins through ovum donation, celebrates her joyous outcome in "No More Doubts." Jane Sherman shares her incredible story of donor insemination, and finally, Dorothy Stewart tells of her journey to surrogate motherhood.

○

## PLAYING THE HAND YOU'RE DEALT
### *Stephanie Brigham*

It was unlikely that the sperm count was actually zero. Because the test was probably done incorrectly, we were advised to have another. It also reported zero, as did the one after that.

Our decision to proceed with donor insemination was an easy one to make; it was either that or adoption. The adoption process seemed endless and hopeless. We would only turn to it as a last resort. And at my age of thirty-eight, it was unclear whether an agency would accept us. Donor insemination would allow us to share the pregnancy and birth. Unlike couples with a low sperm count, we had no other hope and therefore did not have to agonize over other possibilities.

As we proceeded with the logistics of our decision—the doctors, nurses, therapists, and waiting lists—I felt hollow and empty, enthusiastic and hopeful. During the next year I became accustomed to feeling opposite emotions simultaneously. I had a long-term, constant, deep, and abiding sorrow that I would never bear my husband's biological child. I was surprised to learn that I had a picture in my mind's eye about what our child would look like, what features of his it would have, what characteristics of his it would inherit. All that was lost. For a time I couldn't look at him without breaking into tears. I would awake in the morning, see his profile beside me, and slip into sorrow.

At the same time, there were lots of positive actions to take. There was excellent news concerning my fertility, and we had every reason to expect success. But I still had erratic emotions. Taking my temperature every morning told me I was ovulating but also reminded me of our infertility: Up, down, Positive, negative, Happy, sad, Yin, yang.

My husband took the news much better than I. I experienced shock and regret, but he didn't have the ups and downs, didn't seem to experience the same bottomless sorrow. One day I asked him how he could simply accept the news and carry on with life in the new framework. His answer changed everything for me. First, he said one had to play with the hand one was dealt. Our hand was pretty good overall. How many tragedies had possible solutions, as ours did? Second, he thought of parenthood as two phases. The first was conception, which was an instantaneous roll of the dice. There followed a lifetime of love and influence in raising a child. All we had lost was the roll of the dice; we still had the lifetime. These words fostered a calm acceptance in my heart, yet made me ache anew that this fine man would not be the biological father of our child. Up, down. Happy, sad.

On the eighth try our daughter was conceived. She is lovely, she is an angel, she is ours. Ironically, she looks like my husband. She has his gray eyes and a cowlick in the same place. The roll of the dice seems a long time ago. Now we are living the lifetime. Sometimes I still cry. But mostly we all laugh and coo.

---

o

---

## THE GIFT OF LIFE
### *Michelle Parks*

When our son, Jeffrey, was a baby, the nurse in our pediatrician's office always commented on how much he looked like his dad. My husband and I would turn to each other and smile. I'm sure that when she saw us smiling, the nurse had no idea why her comment brought us such delight. She had no way of knowing that Jeffrey was conceived by donor insemination.

Looking back on our journey to parenthood, the decision to use donor insemination seems, in many ways, like the easiest part. If I concentrate, I can remember struggling with it and grieving the loss of our ability to have a child together. But with our diagnosis of azoospermia and our strong wish to be parents, DI seemed like a good option—and opportunity.

Making the decision to try DI was easy; becoming pregnant by it proved very difficult. First, we learned that I did not ovulate. Then, with various combinations of Parlodol, Clomid, and HCG, I was able to achieve a "normal" cycle. We tried fertility drugs together with DI and eventually achieved pregnancy, only to lose it at eight weeks.

The miscarriage was extremely painful for us. A pregnancy that had been so hard to come by was lost. It felt as if there would never be another. Also, the process of becoming pregnant was exhausting to us. We had to drive three hours each day from our home in rural Vermont to our doctor's office in Boston. These trips were scheduled only a day or so in advance, so it became very difficult for us to be reliable at work. And the treatments themselves were unpleasant: a cold speculum, a plastic cervical cup, then a half hour on my back after the insemination. I remember lying there on the table and wondering if there would ever be any light at the end of this cold, dark tunnel.

Then the light came. I was pregnant again, and this time things went well. I remember being very anxious during the first trimester but then relaxing once a heartbeat was confirmed. Once the pregnancy became real to us, my husband and I were able to share some of our thoughts and fears about its outcome. Would we have a child that looked nothing like us? Would we be able to love the child? Would something be wrong with the baby? How might he or she interfere with our marriage? We had a vague sense that some of our concerns were shared by all first-time parents, but we wondered what was just a result of donor insemination.

We were awakened from our fears and fantasies about our baby by the reality of a very hard labor and delivery. I had medical problems and complications of anesthesia that resulted in a difficult and alarming high-tech birth. What a strange irony that I had equal trouble getting pregnant and unpregnant.

When Jeffrey was a baby, my thoughts turned, at times, to his conception. I remember a recurring dream in which the donor appeared with a daughter named Susan. In reality, I knew little about him and had felt comforted by the fact that we lived far apart. I knew only that he was a physician, married, and a father. I guess that his appearance in my dreams with his child, Susan, was my effort to make him real, to make sure that his life was complete, and perhaps to differentiate him and his family from our own.

I have heard that couples considering DI worry that the father will not be involved with the child. I was not particularly concerned about that, and it has never been a problem. If anything, I think that our infertility and DI experience has made both of us more involved and enthusiastic parents. My husband takes great delight in his son, and Jeffrey, who worships his dad, has already picked up most of his expressions and mannerisms.

Jeffrey will turn four next month. This birthday, like those that came before it, will be a big occasion. We'll have a party for Jeffrey and his friends and then another for our families. At the family gathering, Jeffrey's grandmother will undoubtedly comment on how he has inherited her love of music; his uncle will talk about how Jeffrey is as curious as he is; Grandpa will reluctantly admit that "the boy is as stubborn as I am"; and all will agree that he got the best of his dad and me.

In the midst of it all, I will probably take a moment to say a silent thank-you to a man whom I will never know. Though he must remain ever nameless and faceless, he is not forgotten. He gave Jeffrey the gift of life, and he made all of us a family.

○

## FRIENDS FOR LIFE
### Suzette Rizzo

In some ways our infertility story is similar to that of many other couples. My husband, Michael, and I met and married in our early thirties and assumed that we would soon have children together. Instead, we went on to six years of infertility treatments, including several IUIs and two IVFs. During that time we nurtured hope and encountered repeated disappointments. This past Christmas we suffered a devastating miscarriage. That is the very short version of our story and the part that probably sounds familiar. I would like to turn now to the rest of it.

When I reflect on what we have been through so far, I realize that our infertility story is as much about relationships—and one relationship in particular—as it is about the disappointments and losses we have experienced. I want to write about the relationships because I hope that others will see that infertility is not simply a dark cloud.

When my second IVF cycle failed or, more accurately, was canceled because I didn't produce enough eggs, my doctors brought up the subject of egg donation. At first I thought it was a weird idea. It was just too foreign; at least, that was what I thought at the time. I was already a parent, having had my daughter, Holly, when I was twenty, and I had pretty much raised her as a single parent. Now I wanted to have a child *with* Michael and to share both biological and parenting bonds.

Although we had been going through infertility for quite some time, Michael and I had told very few people about our problem and about our efforts. We felt that it was a personal matter and that others didn't need to know. But feeling as devastated as I did, I had to tell someone. Rose, who has been my best friend for over twenty years, was the person I most wanted and needed to talk with.

Before I begin to talk about my present relationship with Rose and what she has done for me and meant to me in recent months, I need to go back a bit. You see, Rose and I met on our first day of high school (we were riding the bus home together) and have been pretty much inseparable ever since.

As I said, Rose and I were buddies in high school. We are different in many ways, but we were close from the start. We were at a Catholic high school where each of us started off not knowing anyone else. We discovered that—and the fact that our dads knew each other—on that first bus ride, and I guess you could say that we bonded.

We bonded in high school, and we bonded even more immediately after. It was then that I gave birth to Holly and found myself a young, single mother. Actually, this is all very ironic: at that time I had a baby when other friends chose to have abortions. Many could not understand my decision and actually stopped being my friend. They were busy partying, and I was pretty much home with Holly. What I will never, ever forget—nor cease to deeply appreciate—was the way Rose acted. Although she wasn't particularly into babies herself, she would spend every Friday night with Holly and me. Rose had a routine, and looking back on it, I am even more amazed and more touched than I was at the time.

Since neither of us drove, and we lived about a twenty-minute walk from each other, every Friday night Rose would walk over to my house. Regardless of whether it was cold and icy or hot and steaming, she would arrive with two things—some wonderful chocolate goody that she'd baked and a hot pizza from Papa Gino's. The two of us would eat and watch TV and play with Holly. But as I said, Rose was not particularly a "baby" person; I always felt that she was there to see me and not Holly. She was there for Holly when we needed her, but mostly Rose was there for me.

Over the years, as Holly grew, Rose remained an important part of our lives. Holly has always experienced her as a kind of special aunt. I think that this background is what made me react as I did when Rose offered to donate eggs to me. Yes, my friend of twenty years reacted to the news that my eggs were no longer good by unhesitatingly offering to donate her eggs to me. And I, who would never have thought that I would accept such an offer, did so. But it is not that simple. This is how it happened.

Rose and I went out to lunch one day. Michael and I were in the midst of one of the worst times of our infertility. The second IVF cycle had been canceled, and I was beginning to face the fact that our dream of having a baby together would probably not happen. I was feeling really down, and although we had chosen to be pretty private about our infertility until this point, I decided that I needed to talk with Rose about it. She listened and, as I said, offered immediately. I said thank you and thought about it.

In the many months since Rose's first offer and through all that has happened, I have thought a lot about our conversation and about the way she offered and stayed with that offer. Some people might make an offer like this and then hope that it will be turned down. That is not what happened to us: Michael and I were actually fortunate enough to have two other people make what I believe were genuine offers. We turned them down because in each instance, it didn't feel like the right thing to do. For example, one person who offered had five young children at the time, and I felt that taking the medications and going through the procedures would simply be too difficult for her. So it didn't feel right.

Although I filed it away and by no means accepted it immediately, Rose's offer *did* feel right. Looking back on the ways in which she had been there for me and for Holly, this felt like a natural continuation of the relationship we already had. She has always been my parenting fairy godmother—there when I need her most. But I'm jumping ahead again.

Our story actually continues a few months after Rose's offer. It was one of those awful days when I was really suffering with my infertility. I was tearful, and when Michael saw my distress, we talked about all that had happened. I had not previously told him about Rose's offer, but at this point, I found myself beginning to think about it more seriously. To my surprise, he responded as Rose had—without hesitation. "Let's do it," was all he said.

I remember being very relieved by Michael's response. For the first time in months I felt optimistic, and I called Rose immediately. On that call I began to tell her all that was involved. Although I know her to be a person who can always be counted on, I also knew that we were asking a lot, and I wanted her to feel free to withdraw the offer at any point. She had just met a man who lives in Dallas, Texas (we live in Massachusetts), and was thinking of moving there. For that reason alone, she might want to withdraw the offer.

Just as Rose could be counted on on Friday nights many years ago, she could be counted on in the weeks and months following our acceptance of her offer. Although her life was in tremendous flux, since she was not only moving to Texas but also thinking seriously of moving to Australia (which was where Steve, her boyfriend, was from), Rose stayed the course. It quickly became clear that she was willing to move heaven and earth in order to follow through with her offer to us. And so we began the process.

Egg donation is not a simple, everyday activity. Rose, Michael, and I found ourselves involved in what seemed like an endless series of tests and appointments. In addition to exams —for each of us—with the physicians, there were meetings with a social worker and with a lawyer. They were all telling us—and we were realizing all the more—that this was a very big undertaking. To us, yes, it was big, but definitely, definitely worth it.

Rose began taking her fertility drugs, and I began taking the medications that I would need to support a pregnancy. Thankfully, she responded really well, which was not something we had counted on, because she was thirty-nine at the time and we had been told that donors should be under age thirty-five. Meanwhile, she was making plans for her move, giving notice at her work, and giving up her apartment. Still, she was able to focus on her donation with hope and optimism. As always, she amazed us.

On the day of the egg retrieval, Rose, Michael, and I went together. He gave his specimen, but then he left because he thought we would both be more comfortable without him. I think he was right. Although he and I were trying to make a baby together, at this point in the process it was really Rose and I who were working together. I was very worried about how the retrieval would be for her, since I had found the retrieval I'd gone through quite painful.

When they brought Rose into the IVF suite, I stayed close to her side. We held each other's hands and squeezed each other at each puncture. I fought back tears throughout the procedure because I knew that if I let go at all, there would be a flood. I was amazed both by how many eggs they were retrieving and by the fact that I could watch them come out. But I was even more awestruck to think that she was doing this for me. It was truly the most selfless act that I have ever, ever seen.

There were thirty eggs! Yes, my thirty-nine-year-old friend produced thirty beautiful eggs, and we were all thrilled. We went back two days later and learned that fifteen had fertilized but three didn't divide beyond two cells and two didn't look healthy. So we had ten to work with. We decided to transfer four embryos because we wanted so much for this to work. The other six we froze. Then we went home, and I began the long, slow wait to learn if I was pregnant. Meanwhile, Rose went off to Australia to see Steve, who was, we all now realized, the love of her life.

Needless to say, the hours passed very slowly during the twelve-day wait. During that time I spoke often with Rose, and we both tried hard not to talk about it, but to remain positive. The day before I was going to have the test I began to feel like I was getting my period, and I tried not to panic. I didn't think I could survive hearing that the test was negative—not after all that we had been through.

To my great surprise and joy, we got good news. Great news. The test was positive. I called my husband first and then my mother. I couldn't call Rose, because she was en route back from Australia. Instead, I made a big sign that said, "It's a yes!" and brought it with me to the airport when I went to pick her up. When she came from the gate, I held up the sign, and the two of us hugged and cried in the middle of the terminal. It had happened!!

Two weeks after the blood test, Michael and I went for the ultrasound (Rose was off to Texas at the time). I kept thinking beforehand that if I could actually see something on the screen, it would make it all the more real for me. With Michael by my side, we both saw for the first time a little sack with a heart beating in it. This was our baby. I looked up at my husband and saw tears in his eyes. I had known that he had had his doubts about whether this would ever work, but now he really believed it. We had gone to extreme measures and they had paid off. We were truly the lucky ones. Lucky to have Rose. Lucky to have insurance that let us do this. Lucky to have doctors to do it. Lucky to have our baby. Lucky.

Michael and I returned home with the ultrasound picture. It was time to tell Holly the news. Up to this point we had kept a lot from her because we didn't want her to become excited and then disappointed. Also, we didn't know how she would react to becoming a big sister at age seventeen. When we told her, she was quiet at first. Later we were very touched to discover our ultrasound picture in a frame on her dresser!

While we were enjoying the excitement of our developing pregnancy, Rose was off on her own adventure. She was someone who had never married, and she had begun to think that she would remain single. Now Steve had come along and it was becoming rapidly apparent to all of us that he was "the one." But the geography of it all was getting very complicated! It became even more so when he took a trip to Toronto and was detained there when it was time for him to return to the States. After a long, complicated to-do about his visa, he was sent to Australia. Rose soon followed, and they both began efforts to straighten things out so that he could return to his home—and his job—in Texas.

Then everything changed.

Fortunately—and unfortunately—Rose was away when our great joy turned to sorrow. I say unfortunately, because it was very difficult to have to tell her sad news when she returned. I say fortunately, because she had given us so much and was experiencing so much joy herself. It would have been even harder for me if I had felt that I was burdening her with my sorrow, especially at such a happy time in her life.

So what went wrong? Of course we will never know, but what we learned—on a routine ultrasound—was that the fetus had stopped growing, probably soon after the first ultrasound. It was a dreadful experience. I had gone there alone because I assumed everything was fine. Even when the technician was taking pictures I assumed that all was normal. In fact, I even asked her for another picture for my daughter. It was only when she took me into the doctor's office and he reconfirmed my dates (when you have an embryo transfer your dates are never wrong!) that I learned of the loss. "I'm sorry, I believe there was a fetal demise about two weeks ago." That was all he said. That was all he had to say. I felt like someone had punched me in the chest and I could not breathe. This wasn't happening! It felt like a bad, bad dream.

My doctor told me to go home and rest, and he predicted that in a day or so I would have what appeared to be a heavy period. I don't even know how I managed to get myself home, and I certainly don't know how I was able to tell Michael. But I did; I phoned him and he was home in ten minutes.

I think that it would have been easier had I started to bleed as the doctor had predicted. I didn't. Instead, I waited for four long days. It was torture. I felt like I was losing my mind. Then I received a call from my doctor. He wanted to see how I was doing, and when he learned that I had not started to bleed, he suggested scheduling a D&C for the following day. I was relieved to hear this, because the wait had become unbearable.

The time before, immediately after, and the three weeks following the D&C were the worst time that I have ever known. I cannot begin to describe the grief that I felt. Grief that our baby was gone. Grief for Michael, who had been so excited. Grief for Rose, who had given so much. Grief for Holly, who had shown such joy and who had offered us so much support. Grief for myself, who had been blessed with so much kindness and love from so many, but who had ultimately lost someone very precious.

Now as I see the spring ahead, I find myself beginning to feel some renewed hope. Each day I think of our six frozen embryos and look forward to the time when I will be able to give each of them a chance at life. In the meantime, I am able to celebrate—albeit long-distance—with my friend Rose. At forty, she is about to marry for the first time. She and Steve are now talking about having children together. I hope and pray that it will happen for them.

So as I said earlier, my story is about relationships as much as it is about infertility. This awful ordeal has taught me a lot. Through it I have gained a much greater appreciation for my husband and my daughter and for others in my life as well—my parents, other friends and family. But above all, beyond all else, there is Rose. She has taught me the true meaning of friendship. It is beyond words.

○

## NO MORE DOUBTS
### *Marjorie Swift*

Lately my husband and I spend a lot of time simply watching our seventeen-month-old twins and wondering how we ever got so lucky. It's hard to believe that three years ago, after several years of high-tech treatment and one failed pregnancy, we were in the depths of infertility despair. For me, much of that despair had to do with the realization that I would not be able to have a child who was genetically mine. My grief over this loss was compounded by my fear that I wouldn't be able to bond with a nongenetic child. Now, as I wrap my arms around Jake and Hannah, our donor-egg miracles, that grief and fear seems a distant bad dream; it is impossible to imagine my life without these two particular children and impossible to imagine loving any child more than I love them.

I was forty when Sam and I married, so we knew we might have trouble conceiving. But I was active and healthy, and my sister had conceived easily at forty-two, so we didn't worry too much. After a year of trying on our own we began the standard infertility workup, escalating over the

---

All names in this story, including the author's, are fictitious.

next year from IUI to IVF and GIFT. After losing a GIFT pregnancy at three months due to a chromosomal abnormality and stimulating poorly during several subsequent cycles, it was clear that my eggs were compromised. I remember feeling somewhat relieved to have a definitive diagnosis; now we could let go and move on to the next stage, whatever that might be. Our clinic had a twelve- to fifteen-month waiting list for anonymous donor eggs, and we put our names on it; we also began to explore adoption, thinking we would go with whichever happened first.

At this point, already demoralized by three years of infertility, I grew increasingly anxious and depressed. As I struggled to let go of the dream of having a biological child, I realized how much of my grief had to do with having lost my mother at sixteen; a biological child, I was convinced, would bring her back and perpetuate her memory in a way that a non-genetic child could not. In part because of this conviction, I was sure I could never really bond with a child who wasn't genetically mine, whether adopted or conceived through a donor egg. Wouldn't I continually find fault with a nongenetic child and imagine that a genetic child would have been smarter, prettier, happier, more well-behaved, and so on? (How I flattered myself!) And even if the child turned out to be terrific, would I ever feel like I was his or her real mother without that genetic connection?

The prospect of donor eggs raised one huge question that adoption did not: Could I accept the imbalance inherent in having a child who was genetically my husband's but not mine? It was very hard to be grappling with this question at a time when Sam and I had become so polarized by our infertility experience that we weren't even sure we wanted to stay together. Sam found it hard to sympathize with my prolonged grief over the loss of the biological connection and my inability to move on to other possibilities; he was much more pragmatic and procedural, eager to forge ahead and do whatever it took to make a family. He wanted me to stop obsessing about what might go wrong and take a leap of faith; I thought his attitude was cold and simplistic. We both felt we had lost the person we married: to him, I had become negative, withdrawn, and boringly fixated on our infertility; to me, he had become shallow, uncaring, and maddeningly immersed in his work. Did I want to have a child at all with this man, let alone a child who was genetically his but not mine? I could imagine transferring all the tension, anger, and resentment I felt toward Sam onto a donor-egg child. If we went ahead, would I end up thinking it was the biggest mistake of my life?

Our fourteen-month wait for a donor gave me plenty of time to wrestle with these fears and worries. It also gave me and Sam a much-needed respite from infertility treatment and a chance to rediscover what we loved about each other; with the help of a good couples counselor, we began to feel newly committed. Some of the adoption literature helped me to work through my grief over the loss of the biological connection and to be more open to the prospect of loving and parenting a nongenetic child. By the time the clinic called to say they had a donor for us, I felt ready to take that leap of faith. Not all my worries had vanished, but I had reached a point where I felt positive enough about egg donation that I could trust we'd find ways to deal with problems if they arose.

We were fortunate to conceive on our first try. From the day of the pregnancy test my remaining fears began to fade, eclipsed by the miracle of creating and harboring new life. Seeing Jake and Hannah on the ultrasound monitor and, later, feeling every kick and hiccup, I felt profoundly that these were *my* kids. Carrying, nourishing, birthing, and nursing the babies made me feel like a full partner in our venture.

When Jake and Hannah were about six months old, I had a revelation that has helped me to let go of any lingering regrets about not having a genetic child. By then it was clear that each of them had a wonderfully unique, inborn sense of style, humor, and personality. It struck me that they—and *all* children—are so uniquely themselves, so individual and unfathomable, and I realized that my own genetic children would have been equally unique, equally full of surprises—in short, equally different from me.

During the first year I did sometimes look at Jake and Hannah and feel wistful, knowing that I would never see myself in their physical features. But when I mentioned this to Sam he was taken aback, because to him they seem so much like me. When he sees me down on the floor, he said, tumbling around and giggling with them, he's struck by how much I've imparted my own sense of fun to them; when he sees them sitting quietly in a corner, studying their little board books, he thinks how much like the scholarly side of me they are. It was comforting to realize how little it figures in Sam's consciousness that Jake and Hannah aren't genetically mine and to be reminded how much of myself I *am* passing on to them, day by day.

As for wanting to perpetuate my mother's memory, I am also passing on an appreciation of all the things I loved in her, and that is far more important than knowing that my children carry her genes. In my more cynical moments, I even feel somewhat relieved to know I'm not perpetuating my own family's less desirable genes. I also sometimes wonder (is it wishful thinking?) if it might be easier to parent children who don't share my genetic makeup; perhaps I won't be as apt to see things in them that remind me of myself or my family and to pigeonhole them accordingly; perhaps my expectations of them will be more tempered and open-ended; perhaps I'll be less likely to revert to old, unproductive family dynamics in raising them.

My biggest remaining concerns are how to tell Jake and Hannah about their origins and how they will feel about them. We have already begun to talk to them about the donor's role, and I intend to tell them as much as they want to know at each stage of their development. But I worry about finding the right words and the right balance: How do we explain the fact of donor eggs early and often enough for it to be woven into their sense of who they are, but without confusing or burdening them and without putting undue emphasis on it? I also wonder how they will feel about the donor and whether they will want to meet her. Will I feel threatened if they do, or if in a fit of adolescent pique they tell me I'm not their real mother? In dealing with these issues, it's been helpful to read some of the literature on donor insemination (*Helping the Stork* by Vercollone, Moss, and Moss is especially good) and donor egg (see Carole Lieber-Wilkins's pamphlet, *Talking to Children About Their Conception: It's Easier Than You Think*). Our family is also fortunate to know a number of other donor-egg children and their parents, and I'm sure we'll draw on one another's experiences as we face these issues in the years ahead.

Looking back, I can see that all my fears about egg donation served a purpose—that working through them got me to a place where I felt ready to go ahead. At the same time, I can also see that I was so focused on potential problems that I couldn't begin to anticipate how powerful the pull of love would be, and how transcendent. Today, marveling at Jake and Hannah, I can barely remember how anxious and negative I once felt. Though I'm not a very spiritual person, I truly feel that all the infertility heartaches we went through happened for a reason: they led us to these particular children. I have never looked at Jake and Hannah and wished they were genetically connected to me; for if they were, they wouldn't be the marvelous little individuals that I know and love so dearly.

○

# AS THE SPERM TURNS
## *Jane Sherman*

There must be a law that women undergoing donor insemination will ovulate on weekends. Inseminations must be carefully timed to coincide with the release of the woman's egg, but doctor's offices are often closed on the crucial days of the month.

I was in this predicament one month, so I prepared a small ice bucket on a Friday morning, brought it to work, and called my doctor's office to arrange to pick up the semen. I was using frozen semen rather than a "live" donor. I knew that it had to be kept frozen until I was ready to use it, or the sperm would begin to die.

I had done this before. Once I got the semen home, I would put it in the freezer. On the proper day, my husband would inject the semen into my cervix, using a speculum and syringe provided by the nurse. This was anything but romantic, although it provided a real hands-on anatomy lesson for Charlie. But I digress.

Upon calling the nurse, I learned that the doctor had decided to allow me to take home the cylinder in which the semen had been shipped from Michigan, to ensure that the semen would not defrost. The nurse cautioned me that the cylinder was heavy, but I figured that I could manage to carry it for the fifteen minutes it would take to walk to my car.

Imagine, if you will, a rounded silver milk can, two feet high, with a handle at the top, and weighing approximately twenty-five pounds. Inside the silver metal exterior is a white plastic inner seal, containing incredibly cold liquid nitrogen and three tiny semen samples in clear plastic capsules, clamped in a metal bracket.

As I lifted the cylinder in the doctor's office, I knew I was in trouble. I'm short, with a slim build. Gritting my teeth, I dragged the damned thing out of the building, resting every few feet. By the time I hit the street, I was sweating.

I was in downtown Boston, in the financial district near my office building. As I staggered along the street with my unusual burden, I prayed that I wouldn't run into anyone I knew. Charlie, upon learning that I would be in this predicament, had asked me how I would explain what I was doing should the need arise. Obviously, I couldn't just say that I was carrying the father of my children. I had assured Charlie that I would come up with some false but logical explanation when the time came, but I still hadn't thought of a good story.

Then it happened. "Janie! What's that?" It was Mary, a woman I hadn't seen in months, and she was staring at the cylinder with fascination. Oh, shit.

"Hello there!" I chirped. "How have you been?"

"I'm fine," she replied, doggedly adding, "but what's that?"

Desperately, I offered the only explanation that came to mind. "It's something I picked up from a laboratory for a scientist friend of mine. He lives near me, and he asked me to do him a favor."

This story had more holes than Swiss cheese. There are no laboratories in the financial district, and the "scientist friend" theory sounded pretty lame. Nevertheless, I was committed to it now.

Predictably, Mary persisted, "But what's inside of that thing?"

Uh-oh. Now what should I say? "I don't know," I blurted. "He didn't tell me." Mary clearly thought I was dim-witted, but after a few more questions she gave up, and we parted.

Two blocks and twenty sweaty minutes later, three voices chorused in unison. "Janie! What's that?" Oh, great! Three coworkers were returning from their lunch hour. They were all examining the cylinder with interest, and one even started to lift it up and down.

Once again I offered the cockamamy scientist friend story. This time I even complained that my friend hadn't told me that the cylinder was so heavy, adding, with feeling, that when I saw him I was going to kill him. My friends were amused by my professed ignorance as to the contents of the cylinder and started to speculate about what could be inside. One guessed that I was carrying a germ warfare experiment. Nuclear waste was also suggested. After a few more yucks at my expense, one of the three insisted on carrying the by-now-loathsome article to my car.

Oh, Lord. The car wasn't there. Charlie had taken it to pick up his relatives at the airport. When he returned with them, I would have to satisfy their curiosity too. In the meantime, I had to stash the cylinder somewhere, and I sure didn't intend to lug it into my office just to endure another inquisition. Thanking my friend for his help, I dragged the thing into the nearest bar. The bartender agreed to let me put it behind the bar counter for a few hours. I begged him to keep an eye on it, as it contained a "valuable scientific experiment." I was beginning to believe this myself.

I could tell you about finally getting home, and trying to find a time to do the insemination without tipping off the relatives who were visiting. This was complicated by a bedroom door without a lock. When, on Saturday afternoon, Charlie and I sheepishly said that we were going upstairs for a short nap, they probably thought we were planning a "quickie." We were—a quickie in a tube.

I wish I could end this story by telling you that a baby resulted from all the craziness. Instead, I must report that I have nothing to show for over one year of insemination attempts. Still, I have a loving husband as well as my health. For those I am grateful and, for the moment, they will have to suffice.

○

# PERSEVERANCE
## *Dorothy Stewart*

When I was very little, I used to say that I wanted 119 children. Later, when I was "older and wiser," I thought that two or maybe three children would be great. And much later, when it became clear that it was not going to be an easy process for us, I thought that one child would be wonderful. What didn't change—at least for many years—was the assumption that I would have a family.

Married in my twenties, I used birth control and believed that we were waiting for the right time to have children. When that time never came because my husband did not want children, I left the marriage. Then, as a single woman, I considered having a child on my own but decided to postpone that decision in the hope that I might still find the right partner. Then I met the right man and married him. He was older, childless, and ambivalent about having children. But he was willing to try, and we began a brief but all-out effort to create a child.

Like so many other women of my generation, I came to learn that my biological clock had already stopped ticking. That was not immediately clear, since I still menstruated like clockwork, but after several failed attempts at pregnancy, our physician advised us to move on. He explained that all eggs are not good eggs, and that mine were simply too old. We could consider an egg donor, or we could adopt. We paused.

Although I had wanted children all of my life, there followed a substantial time in our marriage when it seemed that we would live out our lives without children. Happily. My husband and I both believe in working hard and playing hard, and we did. We traveled extensively and spent a lot of time together and with friends. We created a wonderful, child-free life, and for a time we believed it would work for us.

Although we were very happy together and our personal and professional lives were very full, I never let go of the desire to have a child. Even in the face of a loving relationship, someone very dear to me was missing. When I realized this and told it to my husband, we began to talk again about the possibility of pursuing some other way of becoming parents. Maybe we had not given egg donation fair consideration? And what about adoption? For various reasons, neither was right for us. Then we suddenly found ourselves exploring an option that we never thought we'd consider: surrogacy.

It was one of those "one thing led to another" situations. A friend and colleague recommended we consider surrogacy; I did some initial research, then talked with several families and a lot with my husband. We did some serious soul-searching, asking ourselves challenging questions about whether surrogacy was right for us. We also talked to friends and family to get their reactions. To our surprise, we began to feel confident that surrogacy was the path we needed to follow.

That is not to say that we did not have concerns. Although we liked the idea that we would know our baby's birthmother and that we would be involved during her pregnancy, we were also concerned about what an "out of body" pregnancy would be like. Would we worry excessively about the baby? And what of the birthmother's health and well-being? Would she let us know how she was feeling and what she was experiencing, both physically and emotionally? Would we feel left out?

Despite our fears, we were excited about working with a surrogate and decided to move ahead, becoming involved with a large agency. What we did not know at the time was that we were in for another roller-coaster ride, not dissimilar to the one we had briefly ridden through the world of infertility treatments. Although we would ultimately have success and be blessed with a wonderful son, we would first have to go through disappointments with three surrogates.

Because our perseverance ultimately paid off, I think it is worth saying something at this point about our disappointments. I include them now because I want others to know that the roller coaster can be incredibly jolting at times, but that it can pay off to hold on tight. It did in our case, and I hope that it will for others as well.

Surrogate Mother Number One was a nice woman whom we visited in a distant state and moved forward with optimistically. To our great surprise—and hers—she never ovulated. After waiting several months simply to be able to attempt conception, we decided to move on.

Surrogate Mother Number Two suffered an ectopic pregnancy and two miscarriages. These losses were extremely difficult for all of us, since each of us was dealing with both a personal sense of loss and with empathy for the others. After the third loss, all of us decided that it was time to let go.

Surrogate Mother Number Three did become pregnant, and we rejoiced, believing that our time of disappointment and loss was behind us. Our delight, however, turned to puzzlement when we learned at a sixteen-week ultrasound that the gestational age did not match the date of the insemination. This puzzlement turned to shock and outrage when we further learned that the surrogate and her husband had violated the contract and had conceived *their* baby while letting us believe that it was ours.

Enter our fourth and, really, our only surrogate mother. We actually met her during the time that we thought that the third surrogate's baby was ours. It was one of those "let's cover all our bases" things, and we are certainly glad that we did. Not only is she the birthmother of our beloved child, but had we not had her waiting in the wings, we would surely have given up after the devastating blow of the "not ours" pregnancy.

As it all turned out, we could not have asked for a more wonderful birthmother, whom I'll call Lisa for the purposes of this story. She is a kind and compassionate woman who was able to understand that we were shell-shocked after our other experiences. With Lisa we were able to establish a trusting and supportive relationship that worked well for all of us. But I'm jumping ahead of myself.

Lisa conceived easily and encouraged us to participate in her pregnancy from the start. I held her hand during the amniocentesis and remember immediately bonding with our son when he waved at the end of the procedure. It was as if he were saying, "Hi, I'm OK. I'll see you soon." I was thrilled but also frightened. So much had gone wrong in our other experiences that it was hard not to expect the other shoe to drop.

It didn't. Lisa's pregnancy went well and proceeded fairly uneventfully. There were worries along the way, but ultimately we all made it through the long, slow nine months. Then, as the due date approached, my husband and I traveled to where Lisa lives so we could be with her when she went into labor and, certainly, when she gave birth.

I have heard about situations where things go wrong. Expectant parents don't make it to the birth. Hospital personnel are confused or even rude when they hear about the situation. Worse still, there are problems that arise in childbirth. Thankfully, none of this happened to us. It seems that our rough roller-coaster ride ended with the earlier surrogates, and we were blessed with a smooth, comfortable course with Lisa. Her labor and delivery went well, my husband cut the umbilical cord, and the baby was handed to me. I brought him to Lisa to hold. Then a nurse taught me how to bathe and diaper him. It could not have been a more shared experience.

Our shared experience continued for the next five days. We stayed in a hotel near Lisa and visited with her, her partner, and her partner's parents. We also visited a pediatrician to make sure that it was safe for our baby to fly. Then, with many mixed emotions, we said good-bye to Lisa—a temporary good-bye, as all of us will stay in touch for the rest of our lives.

So that is the story of our happy outcome after perseverance. I realize, as I look back on our experiences, that there were several points in the journey where we could have stopped, given up, walked away from parenthood, and tried to reclaim the child-free life that we had established earlier. We could have done that, but somehow we had the ability—or the stubbornness—to keep our eyes on the prize. I think that we did it because we knew, all along, how very dear the prize would be.

15

# GESTATIONAL CARE

---

*Gestational care* is the process by which one woman—the gestational
carrier—agrees to have the embryo or embryos of another couple
transferred to her uterus and, if a pregnancy occurs, to carry and
deliver that child (or children) for the couple. A gestational carrier may
be an unpaid volunteer—usually a relative of the prospective parents—
or she may be paid through a contractual arrangement.

PERHAPS MORE THAN ANY OTHER reproductive option, gestational care
is the product of modern medicine. Prior to the advent of in vitro fertilization in 1978, it was impossible for a woman to carry and deliver a
baby that was not her biogenetic child. Fertilization outside the human
body changed that construct, paving the way for women to carry babies
for other women. Among those who can benefit from gestational care are
women who were born without a uterus or who have had partial hys-
terectomies, as well as those who have malformations of the uterus or
malfunctions in the uterine lining. Women who have medical conditions
that make pregnancy unwise can also benefit from gestational care.

Gestational care is an often-misunderstood reproductive option, frequently equated with surrogacy, since both options involve a woman carrying a baby that she does not intend to parent. In fact, it is often referred
to as gestational surrogacy or host-uterus surrogacy, yet there are profound differences between the two. With gestational care the child will be
raised by his or her genetic parents; with surrogacy the child is conceived
by one woman for the purpose of being parented by another woman and
her partner, who is the genetic father.

Because parenthood through gestational care does not involve a genetic
disconnection, it poses different ethical and psychological questions from

other third party paths to parenthood. For one thing, it is difficult to argue that this option is not in the best interest of a child, since he or she will be planned, wanted, and, presumably, loved and parented by his or her genetic parents. A child born of gestational care is not expected to suffer the questions of identity that often puzzle adopted children or children produced by donor insemination (and that can be assumed to affect children produced by surrogacy and anonymous ovum donation), since there will be no questions of genetic origins or generational ties.

Instead, the ethical considerations that arise with gestational care have to do primarily with the carrier, who undertakes the risks of pregnancy without anticipating the rewards of parenthood. When the carrier is a family member or friend of the biological mother, questions may arise as to whether she felt pressured into carrying a child for a loved one in need. This pressure seldom comes in the form of overt pressure from family members but rather stems from the seriousness of the need and the poignancy of the loss that the infertile family member or friend has experienced.

With a "commercial carrier"—a woman paid to carry a child for people she does not know—other ethical issues arise. These involve the possibility that women will rent their wombs, that poor women will be exploited by rich women, or that women will enter into arrangements without an understanding of what it will mean for them both in the short term and in the years to come. It can be difficult to achieve informed consent with a woman who is determined to be a gestational carrier but who may not appreciate the potential physical and emotional risks involved. (There may, of course, also be unanticipated rewards.)

Occasionally, ethical questions involve the intended mother. Although some ethicists have argued that women will use gestational carriers to avoid the rigors of pregnancy, there is no evidence that this is happening. However, there are women who probably should not become mothers through gestational care. These are women who are too ill to parent, sometimes so ill that they probably will not be alive when their child is born. Such situations arise when a woman has had embryos cryopreserved prior to developing or being treated for a lethal disease.

Gestational care is an expensive (usually $30,000 to $40,000 if only one IVF is necessary) and time-consuming procedure that offers no guarantee of success. In addition to the substantial medical costs, there are fees for psychological screening of the intended parents as well as the carrier and for the legal work necessary to establish a contract and to ensure that the parental rights of the biological parents are established and preserved. In addition, those couples who do not have a volunteer carrier face the costs associated with both finding and contracting with a commercial carrier, who usually receives about $15,000 for a successful delivery (and significantly smaller sums for failed attempts or pregnancy loss). In light of the fact that the process may not work—the carrier may not become pregnant or she may have a miscarriage—most couples with limited finances are reluctant to spend money on this undertaking or to use money that they may have saved for an adoption.

Even those couples who are fortunate enough to have a volunteer carrier, saving them the costs of a contractual arrangement, or to have the resources to afford one or more cycles face many hurdles in pursuing parenthood through gestational care. Following extensive medical and psychological evaluation (of both themselves and their carrier), they enter a complex treatment process that requires the synchronization of two women's cycles.

Some couples turn to gestational care because they have embryos that were cryopreserved prior to chemotherapy or surgery. Although these situations do not require the synchronization of the two women's cycles, they involve additional emotional stress, since such couples have only a finite number of embryos. Given the last-chance nature of these efforts, it is likely that would-be parents and their carriers will all be more anxious about the outcome.

The challenges of gestational care do not end with the establishment of a pregnancy. Understandably, a gestational care pregnancy can be fraught with anxiety, since a couple has entrusted their unborn child or children to the prebirth care of another, and since a woman—sometimes a close and beloved relative and other times a complete stranger—has subjected her body to the rigors and risks of pregnancy. How all participants share the process without burdening each other with their feelings and concerns is undoubtedly complicated, making even an "uneventful" gestational care pregnancy eventful.

Some gestational care pregnancies are truly eventful. In the worst cases, they may end in early miscarriage or ectopic pregnancy. Or there may be multiple gestations, thereby raising the question of either selective reduction or putting the offspring at risk (especially if there are more than two) and limiting the activity and basic comforts of the pregnant woman. Even when all have prepared for this eventuality, it is difficult to face.

On a much more positive note, gestational care brings children into the world who were, as one carrier put it, "needing to be born," but whose mothers were unable to carry them. When these babies are born there is genuine cause for rejoicing. Their arrival cannot erase all the losses that have occurred, but for those who have faced emergency surgery or life-threatening illnesses, the birth of a child who was created from their genes can be profoundly healing for the couple.

Gestational care can be a very positive experience for the carrier as well as for the parents and child. Many carriers observe that it gave them the chance to do something truly significant—to make a real difference in people's lives. For some, this difference can be for people who previously were strangers; for others, gestational care is something they would do only for someone very near and dear to them.

In the pages that follow, we hear from Monica Vachon and her sister, Helen McLaughlin. Theirs is the immensely moving story of one woman's desire and drive to carry a child for her sister. We see here how the human spirit can successfully partner with assisted reproductive medicine. Together they provide the gift of life—the gift of a lifetime.

○

## TWICE IN A LIFETIME

*Monica Vachon*
*Helen McLaughlin*

Our journey to become parents was long and difficult. In some ways it began many years ago, when I was twelve years old and diagnosed with a very rare form of childhood cancer. Consultations with experts determined that I would need to have a hysterectomy in order to survive. And so, at age twelve—as a foster child whose alcoholic parents were unable to care for their children—I underwent the surgery. It was my understanding then, and for many years to come, that I would be unable to have children of my own.

I met my husband, Steve, in 1982 and faced the difficult task of telling him that I could not give him biological children. This was especially painful for me because I had just lost my own father to a massive heart attack at age fifty. This loss came shortly after he and I had been reunited following his success in achieving sobriety. So I lost him at a very important time in our relationship, and I feared I would lose Steve as well once I told him of my condition. To my great relief and delight, he asked me to marry him anyway.

My story then jumps ahead to 1991 and to a conversation that occurred on a beach in Maine with my sister, Helen. Helen told me that she had read about a new medical procedure that would make it possible for her to carry a baby for Steve and me. She explained that it was a form of in vitro fertilization: the egg would come from me, the sperm would come from Steve, and they would be united in an embryo that would be placed in Helen's uterus. Helen, who was nineteen at the time of my surgery and remembered more of the medical details than I did, said that she was almost certain that the doctors had left one of my ovaries when they did the hysterectomy. Before letting my hopes fly, I contacted the hospital where my surgery had been done and obtained the records. Sure enough, I had an ovary. That piece of good news was step one on our journey to be parents.

Step two was a visit to an IVF clinic—and that was not an easy step. For one thing, it took several phone calls to locate a clinic that would meet with Helen, Steve, and me to discuss our situation and our goals. For another, it was very scary to feel at the mercy of doctors and nurses. I had already "been there and done that" years earlier when I first faced surgery, so it was wasn't great to be back in that position. I wondered if the consultation would again bring bad news.

Fortunately, things went well at the initial IVF meeting and at those which followed. The staff was kind and supportive of our desire to have a child and felt that it could happen, with Helen's help. They explained that all of us would have to undergo testing, as well as counseling, before we could begin the IVF cycle. But they also said that they would move the process along and that we would not face unnecessary delays. In fact, it was just a few months later that I began medication and underwent an egg retrieval. I was thrilled that my one ovary produced eleven eggs and that nine of them became embryos. If there was a step three, this was it. We'd taken a giant step forward.

All of us were very excited! When I say "all of us" I include the staff at our IVF program as well as, of course, my family and friends. Although the doctors, nurses, psychologists, and others in our IVF program were very busy, they always took the time to be there for us, with words of encouragement, with their good wishes, with a genuine sense that they were involved and that they cared.

Since I was twenty-eight at the time and therefore potentially very fertile (not exactly a way I'd describe myself!), we had three embryos transferred. The doctors advised us that this was a number that had a good chance of achieving a pregnancy, with a low probability of a multiple birth. This sounded wise to us, since we didn't want to put Helen through the difficult experience of a multiple birth. Also, we knew that we could have the other embryos cryopreserved and, if this worked, be able to use them in the future.

Then came the anxiety, the worry, the hopes, and the prayers. The days between the embryo transfer and the scheduled pregnancy test passed very slowly, but eventually the day that we both longed for and feared finally arrived. In the morning I went with Helen for the pregnancy test. Then we went back to my house for the call. Although it came early—at 12:30—it felt like forever. But the news was good: the test was positive! The nurse who phoned told me that everyone at the program was very excited. Now we'd all taken another giant step forward!

During Helen's pregnancy—our pregnancy—we felt like the luckiest people in the world. The odds had been against us, and we'd beaten them. We were pleased and tickled, and each day felt like a precious gift. Helen shared all of her feelings with us. Perhaps the biggest thrill came when the baby began to kick and Helen placed my hand on her abdomen.

Our joy did not last long enough. Instead, it turned quickly to great sorrow. We received a call from Helen saying that her water had broken. She was only twenty-three weeks along, so we knew that this could mean a real problem for us and our baby. The doctors explained that we had to wait; there was still a chance that Helen would not go into labor. We would know this within twenty-four hours; if labor did not begin, our baby would have a chance.

But as I said, things had turned bad for us. Helen began labor, and two days later our daughter, Natalie Marie, was born. She was too small to survive and died soon after. The pain of her death is indescribable, but there was one thing that brought us comfort: Helen offered to have another baby for us. I was deeply moved by her selflessness and remain so.

Following Natalie's death, I felt pain, anger, rage, and hopelessness. I felt angry at God for putting us through this and found that it was difficult to maintain my faith. I wondered how God could have given us this extraordinary gift and then have taken her away. Why had I had to live my whole life believing I would never have a biological child, then be given that miraculous gift, only to lose her? Perhaps the worse part of all of this was that people tried to console me by saying that there is a reason for everything. What reason?

It took me some time, but I did return to church. I remember asking God to give us a sign as to whether this was His will. Then one day I was driving in my car, and an incredible thing happened. The sky was cloudy, but when I looked ahead, I saw a hole in the clouds. It was not just any hole; it was formed in the shape of a cross, and it had sunlight steaming through it. I asked my nephew, Ryan, who was with me, if he saw it, and he said that he did. It was my sign. I felt better.

Despite the excruciating pain we all felt following Natalie's death, we did begin to heal. After about three months, we realized we were ready to try again—just once. I could not bear to put Helen through more than one more attempt, so if this didn't work, we'd have to move on. To make things even more difficult, we knew that the odds were really against it working, as we would be using frozen embryos.

The embryo transfer was an especially difficult time for all of us. What I hadn't been fully prepared for was how much it would bring back memories of our first cycle. Instead of the joy and expectation that we had felt then, we now felt sadness, loss, defeat. I was standing there crying when I looked over and saw that the embryologist was also crying; she had been there when we did our first cycle.

When we learned that only two of our embryos had survived the thaw process, I experienced a shift in my feelings. Much of the sadness and sense of defeat was miraculously replaced by hope and optimism. Suddenly, I had a positive outlook. I decided that God would not make this possible for us twice and still leave us without a child.

If the wait for the pregnancy test during the first cycle had been difficult, this time it was unbearable. Each day passed so slowly, making it feel like an eternity until the pregnancy test. But of course the slowest, most torturous day was yet to come—the day of the test. I remember spending that day pacing the floor, waiting for the phone to ring. When it did, it was truly the call we had been waiting for. Positive again. Our luck had turned around.

Because of Helen's history of premature labor, we were advised to go to a high-risk obstetrician this time around. We did so and met with a doctor who told us that she would try to determine whether Helen had an incompetent cervix. If so, she would need to have a cerclage, a stitch on the cervix. That stitch would hold her cervix closed, hopefully enabling her to carry the baby to term or near term.

Unfortunately, the cerclage was not all that Helen would need in order to successfully carry the baby. Early in the pregnancy, she was told to leave work and was restricted to bed rest, with only "bathroom privileges." I, who had already been totally blown away by all the sacrifices that Helen was willing to make for us, was now all the more awed by her selflessness. I could not believe all that she was willing to do for us, and with such kindness. My wonder at her generosity reached a new high when we learned that she was suffering from gestational diabetes. What else could possibly happen, and how much more would she have to go through in order to do this for us?

Because of the diabetes, the baby grew rapidly. It was decided that at thirty-seven weeks, the doctors would check the baby's lungs by amniocentesis and determine if they were developed enough to induce labor. Indeed, the test results said that everything looked good, and we all decided to go ahead and have labor induced. Several hours later, our second daughter, Amy Marie, was born. She emerged into the world strong and healthy.

And that is the story of how we came to be parents. I am amazed by it, even as I retell it. It remains hard to fathom how much Helen was willing to sacrifice for us—and for her then-unborn niece. It is also hard to believe that so much could go so wrong and so much could go so right.

I have emerged from this with an ever stronger faith in God and in other people. Although it was Helen who, from the very start, made this all possible, others played a big role as well—the doctors, the nurses, our counselor, the embryologist with tears in her eyes. Each one played an enormously important role in Amy's creation and ultimately in her safe arrival.

Today Amy is a beautiful, smiling, happy two-and-a-half-year-old. Because she is so precious to us, it is a real challenge for me not to be overprotective of her. I have to frequently remind myself to keep some of my feelings to myself, lest I cause her to feel that she is different. Having known so many losses, it is hard not to fear another one, and it is hard not to react out of that fear. What helps me most, in addition to my faith, is the fact that I have known so much sadness and pain. These experiences have left their mark on me and granted me the ability to truly enjoy what I have.

*And a few words from Helen:* I was touched by Monica's chronicle of our joint efforts to bring Amy into the world and certainly by her comments on my role. Perhaps it goes without saying that others have told me I was selfless, incredibly generous, and so forth. I know that is how others see what I did, but I want to say that what I did for Monica and Steve I did for myself as well. Although it was a struggle to bring Amy into the world, it was also a great joy. I was able to fulfill a promise that I made to my sister. More important, I was able to help her to be whole again—to restore at least a part of what I saw her lose when she was twelve years old.

There are not many times in life when a person gets to do something that really makes a difference in someone else's life. I had the opportunity to do something that made an enormous difference in three people's lives. No, it was actually many more than three lives; Amy will grow up and most likely marry and have children of her own. Was I a saint, or was I the lucky one? How many times in life does someone have the chance to make a real difference?

## 16

# RESOLVING WITHOUT CHILDREN

WHEN THEY ARE IN THE MIDST of infertility diagnosis and treatment, most couples experience their childlessness as an acute pain. Someone is missing from their lives, and they wonder how they will ever survive continued loss. Most endure their infertility by holding on to the belief that sooner or later treatment will work and they will be blessed with a child. Some soften their pain further by identifying an alternative light at the end of the tunnel of infertility. Usually this alternative light identifies another path to parenthood; sometimes it locates a satisfying life without children.

Once identified as "child-free living," the decision not to have children after infertility is now referred to as "resolving without children." The terminology was changed because the old term *child-free* sounded too much like *carefree,* perhaps too glib for the very serious decision that people had struggled to make. The more sober *resolving without children* accurately captures the experience of those who move on to a resolution that does not include parenting.

In fact, the decision to resolve without children does not mean that people's lives will be without children. Many who choose this path do so with confidence that their relationships with nieces and nephews and friends' children will be very important and satisfying to them. Some "resolvers without children" are already actively involved with children on a regular basis, perhaps leading a youth group or coaching a sports team.

Needless to say, the decision to resolve without children does not come easily to couples who have actively pursued infertility treatment. Most went to considerable lengths to conceive a child, only to meet with devastating disappointments. Had they not had some belief that treatment would work, none would have put themselves through such demanding physical, emotional, and financial tasks. To leave the process without a child is exceedingly difficult and is inevitably followed by a period of grieving. Not only must they mourn the loss of all their potential children, but couples must also say good-bye to the idea of parenting together. This leave-taking means giving up rich fantasies that may have been with them for many years, both as individuals and as a couple.

Why does a couple decide to resolve without children rather than to seek an alternative path to parenthood such as adoption or gamete donation? Most couples who make this decision do so because they feel that for them parenthood requires a full biogenetic connection. Such couples are usually quick to say that they are happy for their friends who adopt or who have a child through gamete donation and that they see how much these parents love and cherish their children. However, they make a distinction between these friends and themselves and emphasize that *for them* the alternative paths to parenthood would not work.

Unfortunately, there are some couples who face a stalemate over adoption or another parenting option: one member wants to pursue that option, and the other opposes it. Because parenthood is a lifelong commitment, the partner who wants to resolve without children must prevail (assuming that he or she is sure that he or she can never adopt). Such couples face a challenging road ahead, since one may have given up a central life goal for the other. Their challenge may be further complicated by the specifics of their infertility diagnosis: if the partner who wants to adopt is also the designated patient, he or she may feel obliged to defer to the presumably fertile partner. These couples must make sure they talk openly and honestly together, since they are engaged in what may well be the most difficult decision of their lives. Without open, honest conversation, their marriages are vulnerable to erosion by resentment, hurt, and misunderstanding.

There are also second marriages in which the partners decide to resolve without children. These include instances in which both partners have children from earlier marriages but the couple was unable to have children together, as well as situations in which one partner entered the marriage with children and the other did not. Couples in this latter group face the challenges of stepparenting, challenges made more complex by the fact that it is the childless partner who is also in the often-difficult position of stepparent. Some of these couples find that their situation eases over time, as the children or stepchildren get older and begin families of their own. Ironically, some people suffer the losses of infertility, take steps to accept childlessness, and then find their lives filled with grandchildren. In some instances the grandchild is born to a young, single parent and raised by the grandparents.

Finally, there are a small number of people who decide to resolve without children by default. They are people who decided on adoption or possibly on gamete donation or surrogacy but met with disappointment. Fortunately it is rare, but there are instances in which a couple is so thrown by an event—an adoption that falls through or a pregnancy loss after gamete donation—that their quest to have a child is derailed. Some conclude that they are better off getting on with their lives without children rather than leaving themselves vulnerable to yet further losses.

One of the most challenging aspects of deciding to resolve without children comes to the fore when people present their decision to others. Many are unprepared for the lack of social acceptance of their decision. Even family members and friends who are trying hard to be understanding and compassionate may prove hurtful when they say such things as, "Did you try to adopt?" or "Maybe if you give up you will *finally* get pregnant."

In addition to the challenges of telling family and friends about their decision, couples who decide to resolve without children face the even more formidable challenge of telling their infertile friends. These individuals usually will choose—or have already chosen—adoption as a second option. Although their friends explain to them that their decision to resolve without children is not a generalized rejection of adoption but, rather, a personal decision, it may still be hard for them to hear and understand this. Feeling vulnerable about their own decision, they often look to others who seem to be endorsing it. This reaction, though understandable, may promote feelings of isolation and disconnection in those who decide to move on without becoming parents.

There are also some couples who have not told those close to them about their infertility and who therefore encounter misunderstandings following their decision to resolve without children. Others may unwittingly ask what they are waiting for or make other comments based on their assumption that the couple has not yet tried to have children. Unfortunately, these innocent comments serve to prolong the resolution of the couple's infertility; it is hard to move away from the goal of becoming parents when they are frequently being reminded of it.

Once a couple has decided—or concluded—that they will resolve without children, they can begin to move forward with a sense of optimism. Many express a sense of relief as they find that without doctor's appointments and treatment protocols, they have more time to pursue other activities and interests. Some of these pursuits are undertaken as individuals or as "a couple family." Others are activities that they can do with nieces and nephews, stepchildren and grandchildren, or other children in their lives.

In addition to confirming that they are not isolated from children, couples who resolve without children are relieved to find that they are not separated from their friends with children. In fact, most are pleased to discover how much they and their friends have in common. Although many new parents gravitate to others with very young children, this changes over time. Couples who have resolved without children often pursue or renew relationships with couples who have older children and who are no longer absorbed in the time- and energy-consuming care of very young children.

Unfortunately, the process of moving forward does not go smoothly for all couples who conclude that they will not be parents. In addition to those in which one member still wants to pursue adoption or another parenting option, there are couples in which both partners agree to resolve without children, but neither knows how to make this resolution happen. They find themselves floundering, often disconnected from family and friends, and sometimes even revisiting their decision. This floundering, though deeply unsettling when it occurs, is often a necessary phase in the resolution of infertility without children. Nonetheless, because it is so painful and potentially divisive, it is often helpful for couples to seek counseling or therapy during this time.

In the pages that follow, Martha A. Maxfield talks about life as a "couple family" in her 1987 essay, then provides us with an update, written eleven years later. Next, in "Life Goes On," Debby Ferrer tells of her efforts, together with her husband, to build their couple family and to move on to a satisfying life.

o

## A COUPLE FAMILY:
## THE DECISION TO LIVE CHILD-FREE
### Martha A. Maxfield

It has been nine years since we decided to remain a child-free family. There have been major changes in our expectations for the future. During our seven years of trying to conceive, we had occasionally discussed the possibility of not having children. It was part of coping with month after month of nonpregnancy.

Like most women raised in the fifties and sixties, I had the usual expectations of marriage, children, a home of our own, a part-time job. My career in nursing fulfilled the future part-time job; I met and married a wonderful man; and we decided to wait two years before starting our family. On our second anniversary, we stopped using birth control and started discussing names for our soon-to-be child. Five and a half years later, after on-and-off infertility testing, we decided to give it one last attempt and devote one full year to concentrated testing. By the end of that year, I was emotionally spent, working closely with coworkers who were pregnant, and still not pregnant myself. I was sick of being in limbo and of answering "we're trying," when asked about starting our family. After all the years, that statement was wearing thin.

Our first contact with other infertile couples was through an ad for a six-week workshop sponsored by a community center. It was a great help to be able to talk with others going through the same tests and feeling the same stresses that we were. We were finally able to talk with others about our anger and frustrations, and they understood. It was during this time that we reached our decision to remain child-free.

We did not reach that decision overnight, nor was it easy—nor did it immediately resolve all our emotional stress. It had begun to evolve over the years of nonpregnancy. I've occasionally been accused of not having wanted a child very much in the first place. Not true! I wanted Bill's child so badly I ached for it. I wanted to go through a pregnancy with a child conceived and born of our love. Making the decision to give up trying was not easy.

There were many factors involved. Emotionally, I couldn't take much more testing and treatment that might or might not work. Our age was also becoming a concern to us. I think almost every couple has a target age for becoming parents beyond which they prefer not to go. My first one had been twenty-five, and I was already several years beyond that. I did not want to be an "older parent." We wanted to be able to visualize a time of financial freedom occurring when we would be young enough to enjoy it. We had heavy financial responsibilities for the first ten to twelve years of our marriage, and we wanted to be able to see an end to that.

When we finally sat down to seriously consider remaining child-free, we made two lists: why we wanted children, why we might wish to remain child-free. The child-free side outweighed the other. The most important reason then and now is that our relationship does not need a child to complete it or fulfill it; we are very happy as a couple. We talked about it over and over for several days; we kept asking ourselves if we were making the right decision.

We never considered adoption. There is no real reason why; it is just something neither of us wished to pursue. For myself, the child I wanted was Bill's child—to go through a pregnancy and birth together. This is Bill's second marriage; he has two children from his first. He had the financial support of them but few of the pleasures of fatherhood. My feelings for his children are the same as I have for my nieces and nephews. I love them dearly, but they are not our biological children—the product of our love. Both of us felt the pain of not being able to have a child of our own.

The decision to remain child-free ushered in the worst period of my life. My unborn child, whom I had named and who was the object of my fantasies, was dead. My whole future had been planned around motherhood, and now it was a blank. I was grieving for my loss, but no one could understand. Unfortunately, it was two to three months before the local RESOLVE chapter was started and a support group was available to us.

We had to go through the grieving process, which included feeling angry and lashing out at others, until we finally came to truly accept our decision. For years, our lives had revolved around temperature charts, doctor's visits, and timing; now there was nothing but us. Like any major loss, it took several months to heal. And, as difficult as it was, I never considered reversing the decision and continuing the infertility testing. Things did get easier when we got into a support group with others who could understand our loss. For even though the people in our group did not elect to remain child-free, they were very supportive and understanding.

Several months after our decision, we made plans to finalize it. Since I had had difficult menstrual periods, I decided to undergo a hysterectomy. The surgeon discovered that I had endometriosis, so we had an answer of sorts about why I couldn't get pregnant. I was not depressed after surgery; if anything, I was happy. Since we had never been given a diagnosis for our infertility, there had always been the possibility I might conceive. After going through the pain of grieving, and finally healing, I did not want to find myself pregnant in my late thirties. The hysterectomy freed me of this possibility.

Many positive changes accompanied being child-free. One change is financial security. We have only ourselves to support. We don't have to plan for child care or clothing or college tuition. Being child-free has given me the freedom to step back and make career decisions. I work part-time as a nurse, part-time as a craftsperson, and do volunteer work. Another positive change is that we recovered our sexual spontaneity. Years of temperature charts and sex on demand had taken its toll on our sex life. It was wonderful to recapture that intimacy.

What hasn't changed is us. We started out as a couple, and we remain a couple. Our relationship has only gotten better over the years. We present ourselves as a couple family. Although we have no children, we're still a solid family.

My regrets are fleeting and infrequent. The feelings of loss for my unborn child are similar to the ones I have for my grandmother and other
important people who have died. There are happenings—a song, a sun-
set, for example, that remind me of them, and I feel a pang that they are
not here to share life with me. My infertility has had a big influence on
my life and will always be with me, but it does not rule my life. I can go to
baby showers and outings with children and enjoy myself very much.
When things get noisy, as they inevitably do, I know that I can return to
the quiet of my house.

I decided many years ago that I was not going to live my life with regrets and "if only's." Trying to undo the past would leave me no time to
enjoy the present. I am busy, content, and feel very fulfilled. There are,
however, many things I would like to do for which I just do not have time.
Perhaps I will in the future.

Our marriage has weathered sixteen years, and everything we have
gone through has made our relationship stronger. Being a child-free family is not for everyone, but it has been the right choice for us.

## Update

When thinking about updating my essay, the question I thought about is
whether we are still happy with our decision. The answer is a resounding
yes. We remain very happily married (twenty-seven years) and still consider ourselves to be a family of two. While we are aging (no alternative!),
we are not growing "old." Our infertility is part of our past and does not
affect our present life other than giving us more freedom of choice than
couples with children.

While remaining child-free is not an option many couples choose, it can
lead to a happy and fulfilling life with as much or as little contact with
children as one wishes.

○

# LIFE GOES ON
## Debby Ferrer

"Why don't you just adopt?"

"My friend's neighbor recently adopted a little girl, and they are so
happy."

"I heard about a great adoption agency. How about it if I get the number for you?"

These are the comments and questions that we heard a lot of in the first year—the first year of our life after infertility. Now, in the midst of our second year, the chorus of advisers is beginning to quiet down, and the comments and questions are fewer and farther between. Still, we get the sense that most of the people we know don't know what to make of our decision to end our infertility efforts and not adopt.

It's not that we are against adoption. I know that for many people, adoption can be a great way to have a family. In fact, I was in a support group and saw two of my friends there go through adoption. They both had wonderful experiences, and now they are happy mothers. It's easy to see that adoption was the right thing for them. It's just that it's not right for us.

I feel lucky that Jim and I are on the same page about this. It would be awful if we disagreed, but fortunately we don't. We both come from big families, have many nieces and nephews, and therefore have lots of opportunities to spend time with kids. We don't need to adopt a baby in order to have children be part of our lives. Perhaps it would be different if we both came from small families and did not have ties to so many children.

That is really all I can explain about our decision; it wasn't a rejection of adoption, just a statement that we felt no need to adopt. In addition to lots of kids in our lives, we also have careers we enjoy. It's true that I never set out to be a career woman, but I've got a busy and interesting job. Jim does as well, and we enjoy our time together. So the decision came pretty clearly and easily to us. It's the aftermath that has been surprisingly difficult.

There are no instructions on how to lead a life without children after infertility. My friends who got pregnant had lots of baby care and childbirth instruction. My friends who adopted had lots of help as well. I could see that all of them appreciated the company of others in the same boat. That is something we have deeply missed: it seems that there is no one in our boat.

The first place where I realized the significance of this was in my support group. Some of the women became pregnant, and others adopted. Although some of them seemed to be encouraging me to adopt, they did seem to get it when I explained that adoption was not for us. They got it, and they didn't push me, but I found that we had less to say to each other. I could ask them about their adoptions, but what could they ask me about our life after infertility without children? That was what I began to find everywhere: people didn't seem to know what to say. As a result, some said some stupid things and some just avoided us. The latter was worse than the former.

Our local RESOLVE chapter offered an evening workshop called Resolving Without Children. I went alone, figuring that if it was uncomfortable, I'd rather not go through it with Jim. As it turned out, I was glad I made that decision. There were only five people there, and all of them were women. The group facilitator told us that she is someone who has resolved without children, and she presented herself as pretty content with her decision. But the other women seemed far less content. In fact, I would venture to say that they seemed downright unhappy. I realize that I could be projecting my feelings onto them, but I don't think that I am. To me they really seemed unhappy—and angry. It was *not* what I needed.

What I feel I need is some guidance. I need a mentor—not someone to tell me how to live my life, but someone who can show me how she is living hers. I'd like to meet someone who made this decision five or so years ago and who feels like it is working out for her. One of the upsetting things about the meeting I went to was that two of the women said that they were actually rethinking the adoption question. One spoke of a couple she knows who had decided not to adopt, but then someone offered them a baby. They said yes, and now they are reportedly as happy as can be. This story upset me. Sure I'm happy when someone is happy about an adoption, but it bothered me that the happy new parents are people who had decided not to adopt.

So I am floundering. I think that Jim is doing better than I am, and that makes it easier for me. Each weekend he makes a point of trying to do something special with me. The things we do are not exotic or elaborate— just fun things that we can do as a couple and that don't surround us with a lot of children. I hope that we will soon feel more comfortable taking our nieces and nephews out, but so far it has been difficult. I think we are both afraid that people will think we are the kids' parents, will say something to that effect and upset us. I think that we will need a bit more distance from our infertility experience before we are ready to be around a lot of parents of young children.

Although we are finding ourselves alone on a difficult road, I think that ultimately it will feel like the right one for us. We have a strong faith in God and this offers us comfort, if not always guidance. I believe that as the years go on it will become easier. In the meantime, we will continue to try to figure out ways to establish a full life that doesn't include parenthood. Maybe someday I can be a mentor for someone else.

# 17

# CANCER AND INFERTILITY

"BE THANKFUL—at least you don't have cancer." Infertility patients sometimes receive this admonition from their well-meaning friends and family. Other times, they may say it to themselves, trying to gain a hold over the pain of infertility. Although the words sting, they represent an attempt to gain a new perspective on infertility.

In fact, a growing number of infertility patients already have a perspective on the pain of cancer and the pain of infertility: they have experienced both. Advances in oncology—and especially in the treatment of testicular cancer and Hodgkin's disease and in the detection of cervical cancer—have meant that there are many people of reproductive age surviving cancer. Although some remain fertile after treatment, many become infertile as a result of surgery, chemotherapy, or radiation. These men and women are now turning to reproductive medicine, either to maximize their chances of a successful pregnancy with a finite number of cryopreserved sperm or cryopreserved embryos, or to make use of alternative paths to parenthood such as gamete donation or gestational care.

Although their experiences vary, depending on the type of cancer they have had and their age and marital status at the time of diagnosis, people who survive cancer at the expense—or partial expense—of their fertility tend to share common feelings:

- A sense that infertility perpetuates the impact of cancer, even after they feel the disease is behind them, and questions about whether they—or their physicians—could have done more to preserve their fertility

- A sense that others fail to understand the impact of this dual diagnosis

- A sense that infertility treatment and third party decision making is another complex medical maze that brings up feelings about their cancer diagnosis and treatment
- A fear that if they are turned down for treatment or adoption, it will be an ominous sign that others do not believe in their future

*A sense that infertility perpetuates the impact of cancer, and questions about whether they—or their physicians—could have done more to preserve their fertility.* Those who believe they are cured—and who feel that their cancer is behind them—can be startled by the impact of infertility. Some say that it feels like the cancer still has a hold on them. More than surgical scars, infertility reminds them that cancer has taken a cruel toll on their bodies. These feelings can be very difficult to acknowledge, even to oneself, because survivors are the lucky ones. Indeed, it is hard to complain when you have survived a disease that many others have not survived.

Infertility prompts cancer survivors to revisit their cancer experience from a new perspective. Some find themselves unexpectedly angry at the very physicians and caregivers who saved their life. Why didn't the doctor send me down the hall to bank sperm? Why didn't anyone warn me that the chemotherapy would destroy my eggs? Why didn't anyone acknowledge what a price I would be paying for a cure? These and other questions haunt those survivors who look back and wonder whether more could have been done to preserve their fertility.

Other cancer survivors think about their previous caregivers with unanticipated gratitude. Some remember their physicians taking a strong and active stance about fertility, urging them, in the midst of a devastating crisis, to cryopreserve sperm or to consider an IVF cycle prior to treatment. These survivors are comforted by the efforts that were made on behalf of their reproductive capacities, regardless of whether these efforts led to the birth of a child. Some recall feeling puzzled by their physician's focus on future fertility when their focus was on survival but now realize that addressing fertility issues at the time of diagnosis served two essential purposes: it alerted them to fertility-preserving options (or "reserving," in the case of cryopreservation before surgery or chemotherapy), and it confirmed that their physician believed in their ability to survive the illness.

*A sense that others fail to understand the impact of this dual diagnosis.* As they move into the world of infertility, cancer survivors express feelings of isolation not only from the fertile world but also from other cancer survivors who are not struggling with infertility and from other infertility patients. They report that family members, friends, and physicians expect them to be grateful to be alive and fail to appreciate the significance of reproduction. Similarly, they find that other infertile people are also in a different place: infertility may well be the first life crisis they have experienced, and even those infertile people who have survived other life crises are unlikely to have endured such a serious and life-threatening illness. This isolation may be sadly reminiscent of the isolation they felt when they were first diagnosed with cancer and realized that some of the important people in their lives did not know what to do to comfort or support them.

*A sense that infertility treatment and third party decision making is another medical maze that brings back memories of their cancer diagnosis and treatment.* Cancer survivors are veterans of demanding medical treatments; many of them had to sort through complicated information in order to make informed decisions about treatment regimens. Yet they may still feel daunted by the options that they must sort through in the world of reproductive medicine. For example, a man who cryopreserved sperm prior to chemotherapy must decide—together with his wife—how aggressive to be with treatment. While some elect to begin with intrauterine insemination (often in conjunction with fertility medications), others, especially those whose sperm supply is not plentiful, will want to maximize their chances of pregnancy by undergoing in vitro fertilization.

Options involving third party reproduction offer different kinds of challenges to infertile cancer survivors. Some survive their cancer with only part of their reproductive capacity intact: some women may lose their ovaries, but are still able to carry a pregnancy, while others are in the reverse situation, with intact ovaries but a compromised uterus (or none at all). Thus they may be toying with decisions about using donated eggs or seeking a gestational carrier. These decisions become all the more complex when family members or close friends offer—or do not offer—to help out. For example, one woman may fear that her sister feels obliged to donate eggs to her, while another may resent the fact that her sister has not offered, even after all she has endured.

The enormous expense of infertility treatment adds insult to injury for some cancer survivors. How cruel that their cancer robbed them of their fertility and now the high costs of medical care may preclude treatment. Other survivors may not be limited so much by finances as by access to treatment: they may live in a remote area where it is difficult for them to access high-tech treatment for infertility. Ironically, such people may have already had to travel a great distance—at social, emotional, and financial expense—to secure effective treatment for their cancer.

*A fear that if they are turned down for treatment or adoption it will be a sign that others do not believe in their future survival.* Another concern of cancer survivors is how they will be received in the world of reproductive medicine and, possibly, of adoption. Will others actively support their efforts to build a family, or will they be received with caution, even skepticism? Some feel very vulnerable in this regard, worrying that they will perceive any delay or denial of treatment as a sign that others do not believe in their future. This is especially true with regard to adoption, since there are some adoption agencies that will not accept a cancer survivor until a prescribed period of time has passed since the diagnosis and end of active treatment.

Some cancer survivors actually postpone seeking treatment or adoption because they fear that their request will be turned down. This rejection would, for them, have a double meaning: it would represent the loss of a desired option, and it would indicate pessimism about their future. If the denial were to come from a physician, this would be especially devastating, perhaps prompting the patient to wonder if the doctor knows something that he or she doesn't know.

Although they approach fertility treatment and alternative paths to parenthood with understandable fears and trepidation, I have known many people who have successfully built or expanded their families after cancer treatment. These include people who have undergone assisted reproductive technology, those who have used donor gametes, and many who have adopted. What all groups appear to have in common is a sense that the arrival of a child goes a long way toward helping them move on from their cancer with hope and with confidence in their future.

In the pages that follow we hear the compelling stories of two successful battles with cancer and of the encounters with reproductive medicine that followed. First, in "Battles Won, Battles Fought," Deborah Shea tells of her successful battle with ovarian cancer in her early twenties and of her ongoing struggle with fertility. Then, in "You Can Take That to the Bank: A True Story of Cancer and Fertility," Alex Sagan tells of his feelings about fertility both at the time of his Hodgkin's disease diagnosis and in the years that followed.

○

## BATTLES WON, BATTLES FOUGHT
### *Deborah Shea*

When I was twenty-three years old, I was diagnosed with ovarian cancer. Because I was so young, the doctors had assumed that it was just a cyst. I had surgery, left the hospital, and then was called back to see my doctor.

I will never forget the moment when I was sitting in his office and he told me that I had ovarian cancer. I did not know at that time that ovarian cancer is most often a lethal disease, nor did I know that mine was a rare tumor, one that responded well to treatment. I only knew that I was young and that the doctor was telling me I had cancer.

The next few months of my life were very intense. The intensity began with my tearful question, "Am I going to live?" and continued through the explanations of the chemotherapy and surgery protocols. As awful as the initial diagnosis was, what followed brought me hope. My first doctor was able to refer me to a specialist who had had good success in treating my form of cancer. He was able to answer my question, "Am I going to live?" affirmatively. He thought I would. I knew I would.

I fought cancer like a trooper. The chemotherapy was an ordeal—so much so that I had to be hospitalized and anesthetized in order to take it. Nonetheless, I withstood it. Losing my hair was very difficult—I would wake up in the morning and find hair on my pillow—but that, too, was something I managed. Even after I finished the initial rounds of chemotherapy, I faced additional surgery because I had what turned out to be a benign cyst.

As difficult as cancer was, I can honestly say that it never "got to me." I believed I would survive, and I appreciated the enormous support I received from my family, who took care of me throughout the ordeal, and from the wonderful man who would later become my husband. It was a tough battle, but I fought it and I won, and I moved on with my life. In fact, I not only moved on, I thrived. Cancer gave me the courage to return to school and then to graduate school and to fulfill my dream of being a social worker.

And so it is hard to admit that I am now fighting another battle that is so much more difficult for me: infertility. I know that that comes as a surprise to some people, who assume that cancer is much worse than infertility, but for me, infertility is much worse than cancer. Cancer you can fight, and you can triumph over it. With infertility, it is hard to know what you are fighting—and how to fight it.

My infertility story began nine years after my cancer. I was relieved to be cancer-free, and the doctors told me that I had a normal life expectancy. At that time I asked them the question that I had asked them over and over again through the years: Did I still have an ovary, and if so, could I have children? The answer was always yes to both questions. Encouraged by that news, my husband, John, and I tried to have children. We assumed that it might take somewhat longer because I had only one ovary, but we trusted that it would happen. The doctors had been right about curing my cancer, so of course they would be right about my fertility.

They were not. Although I do have an ovary, I also have a damaged fallopian tube and scar tissue. This news was devastating to me. I felt an enormous sense of loss, and I also felt guilt that I was denying John a baby. In addition, I felt responsible for having had so many follow-up surgeries on benign cysts. I also felt shame, despair, and sadness as never before. I was furious. Hadn't I paid my dues by having cancer? Wasn't that enough? Over and over again I complained to John that it wasn't fair. All he ever said was, "No, it isn't."

I have been dealing with infertility for three years and have gone through many stages. I have begun to accept my situation, but it has been a slow process. In the beginning I was incredibly angry, but I was also convinced that a mistake had been made. This simply couldn't be happening. I had elaborate daydreams that I was pregnant. They would begin with my imagining a positive home pregnancy test, followed by visits to the doctors and then the great joy of telling John—and, later, my family—the good news. Then came my favorite part of the daydream: I would go back to the doctors and show them how wrong they were about my infertility.

In the past year, my daydreams have changed. Now they are about pregnancy after an in vitro cycle. I imagine getting a call from my doctor's office sixteen days after the embryo transfer. This daydream isn't quite as wonderful as my former one, but it, too, will do. If only it were true. If only. If only.

Perhaps someday soon I will begin to have daydreams about getting pregnant with a donor egg. Or maybe I will have a daydream about adoption? I can feel myself beginning to let go of the dream of having a biological child, but that is so painful and so difficult for me. I have come to realize that I had hoped to have, counted on having a baby that looked like me. I wanted John's baby, but I also wanted a baby that had something from my side of the family. Maybe my blue eyes? Or my ears? Or my knees? Something passed on from me.

Cancer has robbed me of my ability to have a child, and infertility feels like an extension of my disease. Once I thought that I was the luckiest person in the world to have had cancer and beaten it, but infertility has changed my mind. When I think of these life-altering situations and the impact they have had on me, it's my infertility that haunts me with despair and hopelessness. My cancer was a triumphant victory that was recognized and respected by my family, friends, physicians, and even strangers. Everyone hailed me as courageous and strong.

My infertility has been so different. It has been a shameful, lonely battle that no one seems to really understand or appreciate. People rarely bring it up, and those close to me try to avoid the subject because they know that it makes me so sad. My cancer is gone, yet it keeps its hold on me. I wasn't prepared for this.

## Update

Deborah had a successful IVF cycle shortly after this was written.

○

# YOU CAN TAKE THAT TO THE BANK: A TRUE STORY OF CANCER AND FERTILITY

## Alex Sagan

I am a survivor of Hodgkin's disease and of the chemotherapy and radiation that saved my life. The chemotherapy left me sterile, without the ability to produce even a single new sperm cell. Fortunately—very fortunately—my cancer doctors told me that this might happen, and I banked sperm before starting chemo. That was ten years ago. Today my wife is pregnant.

My oncologists included me in the decisions concerning my treatment. In the case of Hodgkin's disease, a lymphatic cancer with a high cure rate, there were actually choices to be made, and my doctors fully informed me of the trade-offs involved in each of the possible treatments. So I was told that some treatments would make me sterile, that others would not, and that the effect of some drugs on fertility was not yet fully known. Sterility was not the only risk, of course, and I avoided a real but unmeasured potential for heart and lung tissue changes by opting for a chemo cocktail that could compromise sperm production. Coupled with radiation, this mixture of poisons was supposed to kill my cancer and leave the rest of me intact.

The tumor in my chest was so big that the doctors had to zap it with radiation the day of my biopsy and on the following two days. The tumor, which had been constricting my breathing and blood flow, shrank noticeably. This got me out of immediate danger and provided a brief window during which we decided on my course of treatment. These first blasts of radiation, aimed only at the chest, also allowed me the time I needed to bank sperm before starting chemotherapy.

The doctors said that the initial radiation made it safe to wait a few days to start chemo. Saving my life was foremost, of course, but they also understood that banking sperm could be important to my future quality of life. A couple of weeks, they said, could safely be used for sperm banking. Suddenly, the most fruitless pubescent pastime was an urgently needed skill.

My college roommate had had testicular cancer the year we graduated, and his description of the degradation of visiting the sperm bank prepared me for the worst. My experience was better than his, and I did my best to look past what might be depressing or demeaning aspects of producing a vial of sperm for a lab tech to examine. For me, it really wasn't that bad.

Luckily, my fertility had not been precipitously affected by my illness, and my specimens were very good. Counts and motility were both very high (that is, I had lots of active sperm). This actually helped me feel good about my body, even my virility, at the same time that my illness was making it harder to maintain any sort of positive self-image of myself as a healthy young man. The ejaculates—that's what they called them—were subdivided into vials and frozen in liquid nitrogen. I paid my storage fees at the sperm bank and turned my attention to the ordeal of treatment.

I underwent chemotherapy, then a full course of radiotherapy. I tolerated the treatments pretty well, and scans indicated that the cancer in my body was in remission. A nervous period of follow-up exams found no recurrence of Hodgkin's. This was, of course, great news, and life slowly returned to normal, though I was greatly changed by the whole experience.

As my body healed from the disease and the destructive nature of the treatments, I wondered what the effect on my fertility had been. Tests were not encouraging, showing no sperm production at all. There were no low counts that might slowly improve. Nothing. Nada. Zilch. Except for all those vials frozen in liquid nitrogen.

So there I was, sort of pseudo-sterile. I knew this mattered to me, though I was still single, and I wasn't happy about it. I was in a sort of limbo, neither clearly sterile nor fully fertile. This was sad news, but at least I had been told at the outset that this might happen.

Thinking about all the issues involved, I briefly joined a support group dealing with cancer and infertility. We were all struggling with infertility, but the difficulties were much increased for those individuals who had never been warned that cancer treatment could cause sterility. It was clear that their doctors did them a disservice by never even discussing this issue during or after treatment.

There I was, in my late twenties, single, and dating. It was not easy to decide when in the course of a relationship to mention my paternity issues. In one lucky instance this problem was solved for me. I met a woman whose older brother was sterile from two bouts with Hodgkin's. She knew all about his case. His doctors actually forgot to suggest banking sperm before beginning treatment, even though he was going to receive chemotherapy that always wipes out sperm production. Once they remembered, some time after starting chemo, tests revealed that it was too late. I did not know about her brother when I mentioned my past illness. She made the connection immediately and assumed I would be sterile, too. I suppose her empathy for her brother helped her to sympathize with me. For Julie, cancer-related sterility was not grounds for reevaluating our month-old relationship.

We dated for seven years and often discussed the full range of options available to a couple in our situation: in vitro fertilization with frozen sperm, donor sperm (anonymous or from a relative), adoption, and so on. The issues raised in these conversations were painful and worrisome. Using my frozen sperm was technically daunting and might not work. Other options were more emotionally complex and, for us, less ideal. I suppose it was always clear that we would first try to use my frozen sperm. Failing that, we resolved to build a family in some other way (though which way was never determined). We decided to get married, knowing that we would immediately start trying to have children.

My oncologist referred me to an infertility specialist for advice on how to proceed. This doctor suggested in vitro fertilization (IVF) because it had the best chance of working. The other option was intrauterine insemination (IUI), but the doctor said she didn't want to waste my limited supply of sperm on less successful methods. She estimated that one cycle of IVF had a one-in-three or one-in-four chance of success, while the odds with IUI were one in five or one in six. We realized that months or even years of trying might be necessary to get pregnant.

IVF required lots of drugs to stimulate Julie's ovaries, then a procedure to extract her eggs for fertilization, and more drugs along with a second procedure to implant the embryos in her uterus. Julie was willing to do all this in order to have children with me, but I wondered if it was absolutely necessary. Was it possible that IUI, which would be less arduous for her, could work for us?

The quantity of sperm I had banked was crucial in this deliberation. I had made thirteen "deposits," which were divided up and frozen in eighty-four individual vials. Many men in similar circumstances have less than ten vials, so I was in a very good position for someone otherwise rendered sterile by cancer treatment. This meant, I figured, that we could risk a few vials on IUI (though the idea made me pretty uneasy). Julie, who was concerned about the injections and medical procedures involved in IVF, also thought this made sense. We decided to try IUI just once before going on to IVF. Our doctor agreed.

After a few days of injections to regulate ovulation, Julie would be inseminated with my ten-year-old sperm. Giving the shots was an adventure in itself. Every day at the same time, I prepared the syringe and Julie stuck herself. Daily ultrasounds tracked the ripening of Julie's eggs. In a week she was ready.

We sat in the fertility lab's waiting room while three of my best vials, delivered from the sperm bank, were thawed and prepared for insemination (seminal fluid and dead sperm were washed away). Our long-standing questions about how those specimens had weathered their ten-year hibernation were about to be answered. Julie wondered if there would be any live sperm after so much time in the deep freeze. The lab technician emerged with a tube and a page of test results. Though not as vigorous as they once were, the sperm were still fairly active. Just as important, the thawed vials yielded about twenty million moving sperm, which our doctors considered the requisite amount for IUI. We checked the original vials to be sure they were mine(!) Then I took the prepared tube from the technician and, as instructed, tucked it under my arm to keep it warm on the way to the doctor's office down the hall. It was a very strange experience to carry my own living sperm after years as a sterile man.

The doctor kept us waiting, which was a bit unnerving, but the insemination went fine. She used a syringe with a tube on the end, going past the cervix and depositing my sperm directly in the uterus. I held Julie's hand and tried to make sure everything was done carefully and correctly, though I suppose my most essential work had been done a decade earlier.

We returned the next day for another insemination, spending another three vials to improve the odds of a pregnancy. Julie took it very easy, though the doctors said it probably wouldn't affect the outcome.

Then we waited. We were warned that no matter what, Julie would feel pregnant from the shots. She didn't. We were also warned that home pregnancy tests would indicate a pregnancy regardless. The fertility clinic would give Julie a blood test in sixteen days.

So we waited. On the sixteenth day, they asked us to wait over the weekend; the nurse admitted that this was because Julie might get her period during the weekend, revealing she wasn't pregnant without a blood test. Every slight abdominal twinge seemed to be the beginning of another menstrual cycle, but by Monday morning we still had no clear answer. Julie went for a blood test, and again we waited.

Julie was home when the nurse called. The news was good. It could not have been better. I called Julie, and she said, "Hello, dad." I rode home, overcome with emotion, and found Julie standing in the doorway. We embraced and shared joyful tears.

For us, this pregnancy is nothing short of miraculous, a blessing born of science. Something I feared might never happen, and which we wanted very much, has happened, and without the months of trying that we anticipated. Amazingly, we got pregnant on the first attempt.

The first weeks of pregnancy, however, were trying. An episode of extremely heavy, abnormal bleeding looked like a miscarriage. I was already resigning myself to resuming fertility treatments when the ultrasound showed the beating heart of an apparently unaffected fetus. We have had a scare or two since then, too, but the further along we get, the less we worry and the more excited we are. Last week we began to feel the baby kicking. Our dream of a large family may yet come true.

None of this would have been possible if my cancer doctors had ignored the fertility-related side effects of chemotherapy and radiation. In the years since I was ill, I have met many men who were not even warned before receiving cancer treatment that left them sterile. These men, and their partners, suffer not only the sadness of infertility, but also the shock of discovering their situation willy-nilly, often in ways that deepen the unhappiness that being sterile can engender. Whenever possible, fertility issues should be considered in the counseling of patients and in the selection and timing of treatment. Not every man with cancer will be able to bank healthy sperm, but opportunities to do so should not be missed. With cure rates rising for many cancers, doctors and patients have a chance to think about life after treatment. For more and more of us, this can be a life enriched by the pleasures and challenges of parenthood.

# 18

# SECONDARY INFERTILITY

*Secondary infertility* is the inability to conceive or carry to term a second (or third or more) pregnancy after a woman has already given birth to one or more children.

SECONDARY INFERTILITY, with its own brand of loneliness and anguish, is often an invisible or misunderstood problem. To the fertile world, couples with secondary infertility are people who simply have not yet gotten around to having a second child, or they are people who have decided to stop with one child, presumably because they are "too selfish" or "too involved in their careers" or "too involved with their child." In the infertile world, couples with secondary infertility are often envied and resented. Childless couples see them with their child or children and feel that they have nothing to complain about.

For some couples with secondary infertility, the world of reproductive medicine is familiar terrain: they have been there before. As veterans of primary infertility, they have developed skills in navigating through the maze of treatment possibilities. Moreover, they return to treatment with firsthand knowledge that it can work for them. This knowledge is comforting to them as they prepare themselves to once again enter treatment and make the commitment of time, energy, and financial resources that it involves. Nonetheless, the return to treatment can be difficult; no one relishes the prospect of needles and ultrasounds, or even of timed intercourse and ovulation kits. Being back on the cyclical roller-coaster ride of infertility feels dreadful.

Couples whose journey through primary infertility was long and arduous often decide to return to treatment as soon as possible. Some want to fortify themselves for another long bout, and others want to move ahead before some treatment option is closed to them by virtue of a change in insurance coverage or a change in their physical condition. Older women in particular do not want to delay their efforts at having a second child.

Although an early return to treatment can allay some anxieties, couples find that there are several potential problems with renewing treatment efforts when they have a baby or toddler at home. First, they may easily feel cheated of time with their first child. This will occur if they again encounter a long, difficult course of treatment that depletes them of time and energy, and it will surely occur if they become pregnant early on and have their children very close together. If they are pursuing high-tech treatment, they are also facing the possibility of multiple births, a prospect that can be both exciting and frightening.

From a practical standpoint, too, it is difficult returning to treatment when a couple has a young child. Having experienced the anguish of primary infertility, couples with secondary infertility are acutely aware of how painful it is for other patients in their physician's waiting room to see them with a child. Some go to great lengths to make sure that they don't have to take their child with them to medical appointments, but even then there are times when a babysitter cancels or when for other reasons they must undergo the awkward and unpleasant experience of bringing their child with them to a test or appointment.

Many couples come to secondary infertility with a very different history: they conceived their first child easily. For them, the world of reproductive medicine is entirely unfamiliar terrain. Most attempted a second pregnancy assuming that it would occur swiftly and proceed uneventfully. For them, secondary infertility has been a startling experience and the entry into treatment unsettling. Most find themselves in a place where they never expected to be.

There are also couples who had no difficulty having a first child but subsequently encountered a medical or surgical problem that rendered them infertile. These couples are not surprised to find themselves in the world of secondary infertility, but the treatment process is unfamiliar. Although they may have tried to prepare themselves for what is involved, it is still difficult to learn about the medications and procedures that are available to them. Those who have undergone a very demanding treatment regimen, such as chemotherapy, or who have experienced major surgery and a prolonged recovery, may feel understandably reluctant to undertake yet another rigorous course of treatment.

There are many couples coming to infertility in which one person has secondary infertility and the other has primary. This often occurs when a man has children in his first marriage, then divorces and marries a younger, childless woman. Many of these men have had a vasectomy, which is the primary cause of the couple's infertility. Sometimes the situation is reversed, and it is the woman who has had a tubal ligation. There are also couples in which the partner who is a parent did not have an elective sterilization but now finds himself or herself in an infertile second marriage. Finally, there are couples in which each partner had a child or children in a first marriage, but they encounter infertility together in their second marriage. What all of these couples have in common are feelings of regret, confusion, and isolation: theirs is truly a hybrid problem that combines some of the elements of primary infertility and some of secondary infertility. The course of treatment is unfamiliar to them.

One of the most difficult aspects of secondary infertility involves the parents' relationships with their existing child or children. Some who suffer from secondary infertility get angry at themselves for focusing so much energy on the child who is missing and "so little" on the child they have. They fear that they may be giving the child that they love and cherish the message that he or she is not enough. Many parents struggling with secondary infertility also dwell on the issue of spacing, fearing that even if they are successful in having a second child, the siblings will be too far apart to be close. People often torment themselves each month with a new tally on the spacing of their children. It usually goes something like this: "If I don't conceive this month, then they will be X years and X months apart and that means they won't be able to X and Y and Z together."

Another way in which couples with secondary infertility may torment themselves (as do many couples with primary infertility) is by believing that God must have a plan for them to only have one child. Others may fear that the plan came about because they have not been good enough parents to the child they have or do not appreciate him or her enough. When friends and family say things such as, "Maybe it wasn't meant to be," or "You should be happy with what you have," they reinforce the couple's fears of being undeserving.

Regardless of their history, couples with secondary infertility face decision-making challenges. Unlike many couples with primary infertility, who move on to adoption with relative ease, knowing that their goal is to be parents together, most couples with secondary infertility are more hesitant to consider adoption. They grapple with fears that they could never love a child they adopted as much as the child they conceived together. Similarly, decisions about gamete donation are usually more difficult for couples who have had the opportunity to have a child who is the combination of both of them.

Some couples with secondary infertility, however, react in a different way to second-choice decision making. Having been blessed with a child born to the two of them, these couples (who usually struggled long and hard to have him or her) feel confident that they can now approach parenting with goals that go beyond reproduction. Such couples embrace adoption—often international adoption—and feel that it offers them an opportunity to build their family in a different a way. Others may turn to gamete donation, feeling that they want to share another pregnancy and that the combined genetic connection is not as important the second time around.

Some couples consider alternative paths to parenthood and decide against them. For a variety of reasons, they may conclude that the best option for them is to remain with one child. Closing the door on the possibility of a larger family is very painful, but it also offers them an opportunity to regroup and regard the family they have as a complete one. As they begin to do this, parents can begin to focus on some of the real advantages of having one child and can direct their energies toward enjoying these advantages. For example, parents with one child may become very active in their child's school or sports team. Others develop and pursue a special hobby or interest—often a very time-consuming one—with their child.

Couples who have two or more children and face subsequent infertility—with or without a history of earlier infertility—are in an especially lonely position. Even others with secondary infertility may fail to understand their dilemma. It can be difficult to appreciate that when the number of children is less than what the parents dreamed of or planned, it feels incomplete, as if someone is missing.

In the pages that follow we hear from Lucy Marcus, whose spirited essay "Only" touches on many of the concerns of parents experiencing secondary infertility. Then Theresa Gleason Grady presents "Thank God You Have Evan," the story of a woman advised not to become pregnant again for medical reasons.

---

o

---

## ONLY

### *Lucy Marcus*

"Is she your *only* one?"

If I've heard it once, I've heard it five thousand times. And if it sounded awful the first time, it's gotten worse. I'm sick of hearing it. Sick of the questions. Tired of having to feel bad for wanting another child. Tired of feeling bad.

Sometimes I feel that *nobody* gets it. My mother had five children, but she still manages to say, "Why do you want another? Isn't Anna enough?" My sister has a big corporate job and says she doesn't want any children, so she can hardly understand why I'd want Anna, let alone another. My doctor says that I shouldn't worry: "If it happened before, it will happen again. A history of pregnancy is the best prediction of future fertility." So if it is going to happen, why hasn't it happened yet?

There are so many ways in which this is hard for me—for us, I should say, but especially for me. John, my husband, is very happy to have Anna. He says that he would like another, but he seems to feel that his life is going well the way things are. He loves his work (he does something-or-other with computers, I can't really say what it is) and he loves spending time with Anna. She is six now and starting to be able to do lots of things with him. They ride bikes. He helps her practice her soccer kicks. He is planning to teach her to ski next winter. So John wants another child, but he is happy now.

Me, I'm different. I wish that I could say I am happy, but I always feel that something—*someone*—is missing. Take Anna's soccer team, for instance. John loves to go to the games and cheer for her team. I'll be the first to say that it would be fun if only . . .

If only I didn't have to see pregnant mothers on the sidelines. If only people weren't there with their babies. If only some of the people didn't have three and four and even five children. It is a terrible thing to be living in a world of "if only's."

I feel guilty. After all, who am I to complain? I was lucky enough to get pregnant with Anna when I was thirty-four, with only four months of trying. I know lots of people who had a lot of trouble having their first. I also meet women in the waiting room of my fertility doctor's office who would give everything to have one child. They look at me with such envy when I admit that I have Anna. That's what I have to do there— "admit" it. I don't want to mislead anyone, but it is also very hard to tell them.

So I find myself living in this strange world of anger and guilt, of awkwardness, sadness, and envy. I know that I am blessed, and I do what I can to never lose sight of my good fortune. Nonetheless, I am hurting. I look at Anna and can just about taste another child. Yes, I know that a second child might not be as wonderful as Anna, but I do not really believe it. In my heart, I feel that our second child would be different from Anna, but equally wonderful.

I am turning forty this summer and that is not helping things any. My doctor doesn't mean to upset me, but it is part of his job to acknowledge that age is a factor in my case. He checks my FSH every few months and although it is still OK, I am always a wreck waiting for the test results. I would never have believed that a simple number could mean so much. But it does. I worry each month that the test will come back high, and everything will be over.

And what if it is? What if I am never able to have another baby? I try to force myself to consider that possibility and to practice living with it—not easy! Sometimes I force myself to make a list of all the advantages of having one child, but that always bombs out. What are the advantages? More money. Who cares? More time with Anna? So what? She'd rather have a sibling. More time to myself and with John? Not much fun when someone is missing.

I try not to blame myself, but I do. I was thirty when John and I married and did not have to wait almost four years to try to have a baby. We were both finished with school and had good jobs and good incomes. We could have had a baby when I was thirty-one or thirty-two and been ready to try for another before I was 35. Instead, we took the time to be together and figured it would happen. Then, when it did, we took some time with Anna. She was over two years old before we began trying again. Now I look back and it all feels like hubris. Who did we think we were? What biological time clock did I feel I had dominion over?

It was very bad when Anna began school in the fall. I tried my best to hide my feelings so that I would not ruin kindergarten for her. Still, it was awful. I felt like my baby was leaving me, and it made me miss having another baby all the more. It seemed like all the other mothers were pregnant and that many were having their third. I felt like Anna was the odd kid out and that it was my fault for doing this to her. There was one particularly awful day when she came home with a family picture that she had drawn. In it there were the three of us and there was a baby. I tried to stay cool and calmly pointed to the crib, asking who the baby was. Anna didn't seem the least unsettled by my question. She simply responded, "My future, imaginary, hope-he-comes-soon brother." I later learned at a parent-teacher conference that Anna had left out the imaginary part when she showed the class her picture.

Often it feels like there is no place that I fit in and no place that we fit in as a family. Last summer, we took Anna to a family resort. It was a wonderful place with all sorts of activities for kids as well as adults. But everything was designed for families of four or more—the rooms, the rates, the dinner tables, and many of the activities. Fortunately there were a few other families there with just one child, so that helped.

When I see a family with one child, I am immediately curious about their situation. I've learned from some painful experiences that sometimes I am wrong: sometimes it appears that there is just one, but the family has another child or more not present. Other times, I am correct: they do have just one child, but what then? I always want to find out whether it is one child by choice. I am always looking for others with secondary infertility.

There have been times along the way when I have found others who are in the same boat. But even then it is hard. First, I begin with a comparison: How old is their child, and how old is Anna? If they have a young child, I feel bad, assuming that they will succeed at having another before it is too late. (I have several explanations for "too late," including too much space between the children and becoming parents again at too old an age.) My next comparison usually involves the infertility diagnosis and the mother's age: Is she younger than I am? She usually is, and this, too, bends me out of shape. If she's younger, of course she'll become pregnant. I could go on and on, but the point is clear: I feel alone, even with other people trying desperately to have another child.

When and how will this end? Sometimes I almost wish that my FSH *would* rise or that something else would happen that would define things. In some ways it would be easier to have no hope; then we'd have to figure out a way to move on. Maybe we would think about adoption, but I suspect we'd find a way to live contentedly with our one child, whom we love so deeply.

Without a definitive "no go," it is very difficult to give up. I look at Anna and say to myself, "Persist. Keeping trying. It may just happen again, and if it does, it's worth it." Yes, if it happens, it will be worth everything.

○

## THANK GOD YOU HAVE EVAN
### *Theresa Gleason Grady*

I thank God every day for my now nearly three-year-old son, Evan. He is a wonderful child, and my husband, David, and I are surely blessed to have him. This is not something we forget. It is also not something we like being reminded of. And we get reminders aplenty:

"Thank God you have Evan."

"Many people are trying hard to have a child. You are so lucky."

"People are choosing to have just one child. You guys should think about the advantages."

And so forth and so on, ad nauseam. Why don't they simply say, "I'm sorry" or "it stinks"?

As I said at the start, we are deeply grateful to have Evan, but it is very painful for us when people remind us of our good fortune. Shortly after his birth, we learned that although blessed, we had also encountered a major misfortune—one that prevents us from having another child. I have cardiomyopathy, a weakening of the heart muscle.

My diagnosis of cardiomyopathy came as a complete surprise. I was a healthy thirty-year-old at the time of Evan's birth. I eat right, exercise regularly, don't smoke, hardly drink, and I felt fine throughout my pregnancy. In fact, I felt fine postpartum. Had a nurse not been sent to my house by the insurance company to see how Evan and I were doing, I might never known of this potentially life-threatening condition. Sometimes I wonder about that. Could I have gone on to have a second, even third child without ever knowing? Or would I have died during pregnancy or in childbirth? I will never know the answer to either of these questions, because I was diagnosed, and that diagnosis changed the course of our family life.

The visiting nurse let me know that she was concerned and urged me to see my doctor. To be honest, neither her concern nor her recommendation really registered with me. What was registering for me was that I adored Evan, loved being a new mother, felt great, and had returned to work and to aerobics. Life was great, and there was no way that I was going to get worked up over something a nurse thought she heard. My sisters have heart murmurs, and I simply assumed that I did as well.

When I went in for my six-week postpartum visit, my doctor did an office EKG and recommended that I see a cardiologist the next day. Looking back, I suppose I should have been alerted by this, but I didn't give it much thought. In fact, I was so casual about it that I went alone to the appointment. This proved to be a big mistake, since the visit turned out to be devastating. The doctor did an echocardiogram, asked me many questions, and looked at me with a terrible look of alarm in his face. This all perplexed me, since I not only felt fine, but I could honestly answer "no" to such questions as, "Are you breathless after walking up stairs?" I was sure this was all a big mistake, but the puzzled, grave look on his face told me otherwise.

"You have cardiomyopathy," he said. "Probably postpartum. It's a serious condition."

"Can I have another baby?" That was all that was on my mind.

"It's too early to discuss that. We'll have to see how you are doing in a year. One-third of the people with your condition do improve somewhat. One-third remain the same. Another third have progressive disease that can lead to death."

Great news! There I was happily six weeks postpartum, feeling well, and I was being told that I might have a life-threatening condition. Worse still, I was alone. I needed David with me, yet no one had warned me. No one had had the common sense to tell me to bring my husband. I was alone and terrified.

I will never forget that awful train ride home and the tremendous sadness that I had when I saw David holding Evan. My friend's sister had just died of breast cancer, leaving two very young children. So I knew this could happen. Mothers could die before they had a chance to raise their children. Although I had been stoic until this point, I broke down in a flood of tears when I saw them.

What followed was a terrible time. I couldn't sleep for fear that I would not wake. I couldn't eat. I couldn't work. All that I could do was continually focus on my breath. Was I breathing OK? Was there shortness? Was I having chest pains?

Afraid to tell my mother, I turned to my sister, Clare, who is a cardiac intensive care nurse. I expected that she would be able to offer me some reassurance, but instead it was the opposite. Clare had only bleak things to say about my condition, so much so that when she did a paper chase at work and found more bad news, she refused to show it to me. From talking to Clare I got the sense that I was doomed.

By some miracle, I managed to cope with the stress of my situation for the next three months, then returned for more tests. To my surprise and enormous relief, the tests revealed substantial improvement. I was relieved, and that relief grew when later tests revealed even more recovery. By the end of the year I had reached 80 percent recovery, which I was told was sufficient to live a full life span.

So after a year of torture, life pretty much returned to normal. Eventually I was taken off all restrictions save limiting caffeine and alcohol, neither of which represented much of a loss for me. I was instructed to remain on medications, but that didn't really bother me either. The only thing that troubled me—enormously—was that I was told not to become pregnant again. I don't think that anybody but David could understand how devastating this was for me.

I have learned, throughout this experience, that if you can't offer someone helpful advice, it is best not to offer any. There are times in life when the best thing to say is simply, "I'm sorry" or "I wish it were different for you." Unfortunately, some of those closest to me had not heard this sage advice, and they said things to me that really hurt. I know that they did not intend to hurt me, but my mother and one of my sisters said things that were painful to hear. My mother, who had eight children, managed to say, "Thank God you have Evan" more times than I could have imagined. And my sister, who also meant well, reminded me of all the people who were *choosing* to have one child. Had I had more strength at the time, I would have explained to her that choosing is different from having a choice taken from you.

Because it was so hard to believe that I was being restricted from pregnancy, I consulted other physicians, including a high-risk pregnancy cardiologist. All gave me the same response: my condition was simply too serious to risk another pregnancy. In time, I came to believe them, and in time, David and I began to feel comfortable setting out on another path: adoption.

As I write this we are still in the process of adopting. It has not been an easy experience for us, but we are hanging in there and have faith that we will have a second child in the coming months. What was more painful than the original diagnosis, however, was something that occurred this past fall, at the time of my thirty-third birthday.

Each year my dad takes my sister and me out for a combined birthday dinner. This year we went to a really nice restaurant, and my dad asked me to choose the wine. When he did, I realized that I didn't want wine—not because of my cardiomyopathy, but because I felt nauseous. In fact, I realized that I had been feeling nauseous for the past week. Talk about denial—it took the nausea to remind me that my period was late! There in the middle of my lovely birthday dinner, I knew the worst: I was pregnant. I have never before experienced such a collision of emotions: wanting something desperately and not wanting it at all.

My pregnancy was confirmed the following day, and David and I faced the most difficult decision of our lives. Although the doctors could not be certain that I would have a problem, they were quite clear that to proceed with the pregnancy would be to risk heart failure and death. As much as the thought of an abortion horrified me, I knew that I could not knowingly take the risk that I would leave Evan without a mother and David without a wife.

And so I had an abortion. It was a horrible experience then and remains so. I managed to get through it only by reminding myself that I had no choice, that I was making the responsible decision for my husband and child, and that I would be able to parent another child through adoption.

And had we been able to adopt soon after the abortion, it would have eased my pain. Unfortunately that was not in the cards for us. Our loss was followed by other losses, including the death of a baby and the death of our adoption social worker. There have been times when I have wondered why all this is happening to us, but I try to keep faith.

Evan helps me. As I write this, he is tap dancing around the house. I watch him and smile and thank God for him. Every day.

## 19

# PARENTING AFTER INFERTILITY

MOST PEOPLE—both fertile and infertile—assume that infertility is a time-limited experience. They believe that the pain it brings vanishes with the birth of a child or with an adoption. Hence, it is a surprise to infertile couples to discover that even when their prayers have been answered, infertility leaves a lasting legacy. This legacy sometimes takes the form of recalling old pain, but there is also a silver lining within its cloud. This silver lining is the deep and abiding appreciation that parents feel for their children and for the opportunity to parent them.

One of the first ways in which a history of infertility affects new parents involves the question of if and when to try to have—or adopt—a second child. Although some know they will not attempt another pregnancy or adoption, many are determined to expand their families. And although they would like to enjoy their long-sought first child without having to focus on high-tech treatment or on an adoption process, they are all too keenly aware of how difficult it may be to have another. Hence, many parents embark on efforts to add to their families before they truly feel ready to do so. As a result, some infertile parents end up spending a good portion of their early parenting time pursuing treatment or adoption. Some even find that their second child arrives a whole lot faster than their first. In fact, some couples have or adopt one child, return to assisted reproductive technology and find that they are expecting twins or triplets. It is not at all uncommon for infertile parents to have more children than they planned—and sooner than they are prepared to parent them.

Another difficulty for many parents after infertility involves their relationships with other new parents. Perhaps not surprisingly, infertile parents don't quite feel that they are "members of the club." Amid constant talk of pregnancy, labor and delivery, and nursing, they feel like outsiders. Even those who gave birth to their children find that their concerns are different from those of their fertile friends. For example, it is difficult to complain about a fifteen- or twenty-hour labor, when they labored five or ten years to have their baby. Similarly, it is hard for an adoptive mother to listen to endless discussions about nursing. To their relief, infertile parents discover that the upsetting conversations of other new parents vanish by the time the children are a year or so old and that as their children move into toddlerhood and beyond, the sense of being outside the club diminishes.

A third area of concern for parents after infertility involves promises and bargains. Many new parents look back on their years of infertility treatment and remember that they made many vows along the way: If I am able to have a child, I promise to never, ever complain. If I am able to have a child, I promise to be eternally grateful. If I am able to have a child, I promise to never take him or her for granted. And on it goes.

When earnest bargainers become parents, they begin to have different feelings about promises made. Like their fertile friends, they feel tired, stressed out, even occasionally resentful of the children they cherish. However, unlike their fertile friends, who can more easily reconcile conflicting feelings and chalk it up to normal ambivalence, infertile parents feel guilty. After all, they are the lucky ones—the ones whose prayers were answered. Some become frightened that they will be punished for promises broken.

Fears of loss seem to arise more readily for parents after infertility than for other parents. Part of this seems to be their fear of retribution—that they will be punished if they forget to be grateful for even a moment. Another aspect of this fear seems to be that their years of childlessness have left an imprint on them: they can so easily and so painfully remember their childlessness that it is difficult to feel safe in its shadow. Some become overprotective or overindulgent in their efforts to keep their children near them and to create an illusion of safety.

In addition to the fear of losing their child, parents after infertility must also confront their real losses, of which there are several. There is lost time. The time that it took to build their family is gone, and some look back on those years as a blur. Although many couples are able to successfully keep their lives moving forward, others look back on their years of infertility treatment and feel sad about the passage of time. Career advancement, a return to school, or a move may have been put on hold while the couple directed their energy toward fertility.

Another loss is grandparenting time. Parents look on their aging parents—or worse, grieve the recent death of a parent—and realize that infertility cheated all of them out of years of grandparenting. Even those grandparents who know their grandchildren and enjoy time spent with them have been robbed of grandparenting years that they otherwise would have had, years in which they were probably stronger and healthier.

There is also lost money. Even those couples who are fortunate enough to have much of their infertility treatment covered by insurance suffer some financial consequences. Lost wages and payments for treatment or adoption add up, and some new parents look with envy at their friends buying new homes or enjoying more luxurious lifestyles. Those parents who had to pay in full for treatment or for adoption are certainly in a more difficult position, since their financial resources may have been significantly depleted.

Finally, there is the loss of pride or confidence in one's body that is frequently the residue of infertility. Month after month and year after year of failed conception usually leaves its mark. It is hard to take pride in one's body or to feel a strong sense of femininity or masculinity when one's body is unable to do what it was presumably designed for.

Having said all of that, it is important to turn to what I believe to be the central features of parenting after infertility: joy, celebration, and wonder. True, the years of childlessness take their toll, but they also leave parents with an indelible sense of awe and gratitude. These feelings enable them to notice and appreciate all the little miracles of childhood and give them a helpful perspective on many of the tiny trials and tribulations of parenthood. A couple who has cried together after numerous failed cycles does not particularly mind waking up to a baby's cries in the middle of the night. Parents who spent many a lonely weekend waiting for test results or undergoing a procedure are unlikely to mind giving up a Saturday evening out because the babysitter cancels. And perhaps even more important, couples who have survived the crisis of infertility feel stronger, both as individuals and as a couple.

In short, a history of infertility is both a burden and a blessing. Once parents are alerted to the ways in which their infertility continues to keep a grip on them, that grip begins to lessen. In its place comes a powerful, inspiring sense of wonder. Unable to ever take their children—or their own status as parents—for granted, parents after infertility approach each developmental milestone with curiosity, excitement, and awe. Their journey through infertility has prepared them for life's highs and lows and for the unexpected bumps in the road. It has prepared them well for the unfolding, ever-changing adventure of parenthood.

In the pages that follow, we hear from several parents after infertility. First, Amy Schoenbrun confesses some of the frustrations she feels in "And Be Ye Eternally Grateful." Then, in "Predictions and Unexpected Blessings," Wendy Evans describes her high-tech/low-tech experiences. Dorothy Allen, in "The Hardest Job I've Ever Done," describes the ambivalence as well as the joy that she feels as a mother. Carol M. Schraft's "Looking Back" is her reflection on many years as a parent after infertility. Finally, Stacy M. Ellender presents her powerful story "Enduring Losses."

○

# AND BE YE ETERNALLY GRATEFUL
## *Amy Schoenbrun*

When my daughters were ages two-and-a-half years and two-and-a-half weeks, we spent one memorable morning in the dentist's chair together. I had unwittingly scheduled my older daughter Emily's first dental exam to occur just after her sister Sally's arrival. Worse still, I had made the appointment for 8:00 A.M., having no idea that it is one thing to get an adult to an early appointment and entirely another to manage it with a toddler and an infant.

Emily, Sally, and I made a crash landing at Dr. S's office. Since Emily is a very independent little girl, and since she was particularly proud— or so it seemed—to be a big sister, I had not anticipated a problem with the exam. Hence, it was a surprise for me when Emily let out a blood-curdling shriek and tried to run out the front door.

I won't go into the details of how we arranged seating, but it turned out that the only way Dr. S could get Emily into the chair was to have her on my lap, which of course meant having her next to Sally, who was always on my lap in those days. Nor will I go into the record number of diaper changes that Sally needed during that eternal forty-five minutes. I will mention, however, that Emily vomited all over Sally's Snugli and Dr. S's shoes.

My fertile friends would surely regard this episode as a nightmare. For me, after years of infertility, it was a mild inconvenience, in some ways even enjoyable. I remember looking up at Dr. S's puzzled face and thinking, "He should only know what I went through to become a mother. He should only know what these children mean to me."

Several years have passed, and my daughters are now nearly seven and five. As I look back on this incident and on the several hundred less dramatic ones that have occurred throughout these years, I am aware of the impact that my infertility has had on my experiences as a mother. It has given me a valuable perspective, one that enables me to accept— even embrace—dreadful moments like the one when Emily's vomit landed on Dr. S's shoes. At the same time, however, infertility has also left me with certain burdens that make motherhood more complicated and more difficult.

"Be ye eternally grateful," my infertility tells me. "Remember how much you wanted these children. Cherish them. Do not take them for granted. Remember never to complain," and on it goes. My infertility limits my ability to express frustration and disappointment and, at times, it has kept me locked into a system of magical thinking. Sometimes I feel that I've signed an imaginary contract that commits me to gratitude. Should I ease up on my side of the bargain, I face that most feared of punishments: the loss of my children.

I did ease up once recently, and the experience was an unsettling but necessary one. The girls and I were in the Orlando airport, returning home from a week at Disney World. They were playing happily but noisily as we waited for our plane, now two hours late. As they hopped, skipped, jumped, and danced about, vying for my attention, I found myself growing increasingly impatient with them. Worse yet, I was intolerant of my own intolerance. They were just being kids—good kids, in fact—and I was being an ungrateful mother. A man sitting nearby said, "Mom, I can tell you've had it."

I responded, "I sure have. I can't wait until they go back to school." The words slipped out. When I heard them I felt jolted. I had broken the contract—I had gone public with my ingratitude. There was a moment of fear, but it was followed by a sense of relief.

Here, at the seven-year mark, I think I am beginning to make a truce with my infertility. I am starting to acknowledge, however hesitantly, that motherhood is not exactly the promised land. I adore my daughters, and they are a source of great joy and satisfaction. Still, being their mother can be frustrating and exhausting. It is a job well worth doing, but not always a dream come true.

## Update

Two teenaged girls. A houseful of lipstick and nail polish. A telephone— two, in fact—never free. Loud, dreadful music blaring. Late-night worries and lots of accusations that I'm a dork, or worse. Yet still I am eternally grateful. And that is a blessing.

○

## PREDICTIONS AND UNEXPECTED BLESSINGS
### *Wendy Evans*

Do you believe in prophecy? Our experience with infertility has taught us that there are some things we think we can accurately predict and there are others that come as complete surprises. That is how I would describe the arrival of each of our two children. Liza, our older, came as predicted, after years of effort, frustrations, and disappointments. Luke, our younger, came as a complete surprise. In fact, his actual entry into the world was such a surprise that it made the local newspapers: he was born at home, delivered by the local fire department!

First, the expected. I always knew I would have problems conceiving a child. It was something that I anticipated for years before it actually happened. In fact, I was so sure of this that I had actually had my hormones tested long before we were even trying to have a baby. Being sure made it difficult to go along with my husband's wishes to postpone having children for a few years after we were married. We were in our late twenties, many of our friends were having children, and Roy felt we needed to wait. Worried and resentful, I reluctantly agreed to wait. When we then encountered problems, it made it harder for me to accept them.

Looking back on our actual infertility treatment experience, it was not terribly complicated or prolonged; it just felt that way. Because I was burdened by my prophecy and by the regret I felt for waiting, I found myself envious of my friends who because pregnant so easily, resentful of Roy for having us wait, and angry at myself for knowing something for so long and not doing anything about it.

What I did do was take action quickly once it was clear that there was some problem. After eight months of trying, I was in a doctor's office, and after initial tests were done, I was pushing for aggressive treatment. When no definitive problem was found and efforts with less high-tech treatments didn't work, I pushed for IVF. The more active I became in the process, the better I felt. In fact, at one point I was so much more at ease that I began getting phone calls from other infertile people needing help. It turns out that Roy had designated me an infertility counselor and was readily giving our phone number out when he encountered others in similar straits!

What helped? A few things. One was that early on I found a therapist who helped me cope with my anxiety and specifically with my fear that we would never be parents. She helped me to see that since we were both willing to adopt, this situation would ultimately be resolved: either we'd succeed in having a pregnancy or we would adopt. She also confirmed that my many feelings—envy of pregnant friends, difficulty waiting for procedures and for news, the sense that I was on a roller coaster—were all normal.

Another thing that helped was that treatment went very well for us. To my relief, the egg retrieval produced twenty-two eggs, and eleven of them fertilized. We did have a setback in that we had to wait a cycle to implant them, because my hormone levels were high and my doctor was afraid of hyperstimulation. As someone who felt like she'd already waited too long, this delay was difficult. Still, in retrospect, it passed quickly, and to our delight, we had a successful transfer the following month and the news that we were expecting twins.

Then more upset. That first pregnancy, so long in coming, ended very early. I had three days of great happiness and then bleeding began. Needless to say, I was devastated. My grief only worsened as one person after another tried to console me by saying, "It happened once; it will happen again." How could they know? How could they pretend that they did?

The miscarriage was devastating. It perpetuated my sense of prophecy and left me feeling that maybe I had been right after all; maybe pregnancy would never happen. At the same time, however, I was encouraged. Two embryos—two embryos that had been frozen—had "taken." Even in my anguish, that seemed like some good news.

Once I had recovered physically from the miscarriage, we were able to do a second transfer, and this resulted in a healthy pregnancy and the birth of Liza nine months later. She came out crying and never stopped. I didn't care that she was high-strung, as I was so thrilled to be her mother. Her birth and the time that followed were a very happy period for us, in which our friends and family joined us in celebration.

When Liza was a year or so old, thoughts of infertility returned to us in an active and troubling way. Because she was such a noisy, challenging baby, Roy and I were not sure that we wanted to have another. We were especially concerned that if we returned to IVF, we might have twins. Three Lizas would be more than we could handle! What to do? Should we remain a one-child family or risk the abundant blessings of IVF? To our surprise, this decision became a difficult and troubling one. Ultimately we decided that we would not return to IVF.

Then our surprise. Luke was conceived at home and, as I said, delivered there. But that is jumping ahead. The pregnancy itself came as a big surprise and taught me a lot about what I can and cannot predict in life! Then the home delivery. The last thing I ever expected was to have the local fireman quoted in the paper saying, "He was born in the same bed he was conceived in." Surely, no one could have ever, ever said that about Liza!

There were more surprises after Luke was born. I found that I had a difficult time postpartum. Luke, like his sister, was a challenging baby. In his case, he wanted to eat—all the time. It took him forty minutes to feed, and sometimes I felt like I was going crazy. I had many sleepless nights and ultimately sought therapy and medication to get me through it.

And here we are—a family. It was a complicated road leading through the territory of both the expected and the total surprise, and parenthood continues in that vein. I have found that the pain of infertility is almost all gone for me personally, but that I continue to feel empathy for those who are still struggling to have their family.

Life has been good to us. I praise God every day.

◦

## THE HARDEST JOB I'VE EVER DONE
### *Dorothy Allen*

During the long period of my infertility, I never once thought about being a mother. What I thought about constantly was having a baby. Somehow this baby never grew up; in fact, she never did a lot of things—like whine or talk back or refuse to listen to me. The point is that I had no idea what the job of parenthood really entailed. I had no idea what the emotional commitment was all about. I assumed the task would be easy. The only entrance exam required was fertility, and I believed if I could get beyond that I would have it made. After all, I reasoned, I was approaching thirty, had a few years of psychotherapy behind me, a decent marriage, a master's degree, a good job, and had done some traveling. In short, I felt ready to relax and enjoy the blissful experience of motherhood, which I believed consisted of the sweet smell of talcum and a happy, gurgling baby. My children are now eleven and seven, and those smells and sounds are a distant memory.

Motherhood has been an ambivalent state for me during these eleven years. I have experienced moments of bliss—like when my daughter crept silently behind me the other day, planted a kiss on my cheek, and told me she loved me. And I have experienced moments of utter misery—like when she told me I was the meanest mommy in the whole world and she wanted me to get a divorce so she could live with daddy. Both my children have strong personalities, which is to say they are independent, stubborn, direct, articulate, bossy, self-confident, and curious. I love these attributes, and I hate them. I loved that my son felt ready this past summer to go to overnight camp, and I love it that he wants to go on the scary amusement park rides with me. But I hate it when he won't read directions to a new game because he's convinced he can figure it out by looking at the board or when he tries to get me to change my mind after I've already said "no" four times.

There are only two facts, seemingly paradoxical, about which I am very certain. One is that if either one of my children died or was taken away from me, I would never get out of bed again. I know that I could not go on living. Surely, I would never smile any more. The second fact is that if I had known twelve years ago what I know today, I might have decided not to have children. Certainly the lists, pro and con, would be about equal in length.

When I was infertile it did not occur to me that I would have babies who would grow up into children, who would grow up into teenagers. And it did not occur to me that they might also develop—by virtue of heredity or upbringing, I have not yet decided which—some of my own most disliked traits. If I weren't so independent, stubborn, direct, articulate, bossy, self-confident, and curious, we would rarely clash. And some of the most painful realizations I have experienced as a mother are the ways in which I am like my own parents. It is their negative characteristics, not the positive ones, that wave before my eyes like flags on a windy day.

In watching my children grow up, and in being an active participant in that process, I have discovered, to my dismay, that I am not the nice person I thought I was. Nor would I qualify in any way for the Mentally Healthy Person of the Year Award. Among my unfortunate discoveries is an unrelenting tenacity that I didn't know existed. I lack patience much of the time, I scream a lot, and at least a handful of times I have been mildly physically abusive. I have often felt emotionally out of control. When I remember my infertility experience I sometimes feel ashamed, believing it was a sign from God that I would be an unfit mother. When I can get some distance from my negative perceptions, I sometimes play a game with my children. I tell them, "Just before your next life, when you're up in heaven, tell God you want a mother with much more patience than the last one." Or "Tell God you want a mother who will let you stay up as late as you want at night."

My image of myself as a mother is not all terrible. I do some things quite well. For example, I make up clever bedtime stories that have just the right moral for that day's mishap. I'm good at comforting my children when their feelings have been hurt. I am open about my own experiences and feelings, can easily talk to them about love and sex, and am physically affectionate. When I'm feeling good about my interactions with my children, it all seems worth it. At those times I tell them, "When you're up in heaven, just before your next life, tell God you want a mommy who is as great a storyteller as this one." Or, "Tell God you want a mommy who bakes chocolate cake as well as I do."

Actually, motherhood is teaching me a lesson similar to the one that infertility taught me. It's about control. I can't always be what I want, and I can't always have what I want. Although I don't like some things about myself as a mother, I am learning to accept myself while trying to do better. My children are not always who I would want them to be, but I am doing my best to accept them for who they are. Loving them, of course, has never been an issue.

Mothering is the hardest job I've ever done—more difficult than writing my doctoral thesis, more difficult even than learning statistics. I have encountered the best and the worst of myself. At times I have regretted the job immensely and experienced great sadness, like last week when my son in his anger said, "In my next life I hope I have a mom who understands kids." At other times, the job is delightful and my children make me laugh, like tonight, when my daughter, glum-faced, looked up from her broccoli and said, "In my next life, I'm going to ask God for a mother who won't make me eat my vegetables." Motherhood has indeed been an ambivalent state.

---

# LOOKING BACK
### Carol M. Schraft

The story of our infertility is so much like the others. There were several years of tests, drugs, temperature charts, surgery, more tests, new drugs. It was a long, anxious, often embarrassing, unhappy time. Yet, as I write about those events now, nearly twenty years later, it is hard to recapture them. I can see the temperature charts, roughly drawn with an odd collection of ballpoint pens; I can describe the hospital room that was, as requested, on the surgical rather than the OB-Gyn floor. I can tell you about the hours passed with outdated magazines in the waiting room of Yale–New Haven Hospital Infertility Clinic. But the experience itself is complete, finished, a historical event devoid of life, safe in the archives.

The story of our children is, as I am frequently told, much like the stories of others like my husband and me: that is, we adopted a child; within a few weeks I became pregnant and, after the birth of that child, unexpectedly pregnant again. So, we went quickly from years of longing for a single peaceful child to a noisy, somewhat chaotic household strewn with cartons of Pampers and what seemed like the complete line of Fisher-Price toys.

For fifteen years, the Pavlovian response to the story of how our family came to be has been, "that's what happens all the time," followed by an account of a second cousin or a friend of a friend who adopted a child and immediately found themselves pregnant. While I have come to believe this bit of conventional wisdom, much the way I believe that a stitch in time saves nine, I have never actually met or even talked on the phone to a person who adopted a child and soon after gave birth to another. I do think this last bit unusual, given the fact that I was first a social worker and am now an elementary school principal and that in nearly a quarter century of working life I have met what by now must number thousands of parents.

I doubt that my experience of pregnancy after adoption happens with the frequency imagined. I would guess that it occurs with the same frequency as does pregnancy after many years of infertility. I suspect, however, that the myth is popular as a way, albeit well-intentioned, of trivializing infertility or making it a psychological problem that clears up as soon as you just calm down and relax. This is a point of view that helps no one, least of all a woman unable to conceive. The arena of infertility is filled with beliefs and "mother wit" that cloud an already miserable condition. In fostering the point of view that the most common occurrence after adoption is conception, one fosters the belief that infertility is primarily in the head.

Other common beliefs about infertility have to do with genetics. In trying to overcome infertility, one is making a statement about the importance of genetics; in choosing adoption, one is making a statement about the importance of upbringing. Either way, we, as potential parents, are central to an unfolding drama as either biological or social engineer. With that disclaimer, impressions of my own experience follow.

I remember the period of my own infertility, so long ago, in an intellectual way, but empty of feeling. Often I have talked about it, in what I hope has been a helpful manner, to others struggling with childlessness.

As with all struggles, however, I believe that it is transitory. No matter how many years, how many pills and injections and surgical procedures, how many cycles counted day by unending day, infertility must eventually be resolved either by bearing a biological child, adopting, or remaining child-free. My own resolution, though, was not nearly as important to me as the realization preceding it that my life could not continue forever in an obsessive concern with reproduction. I finally had to let go, move on, and allow infertility to take its rightful place in my memory, no longer draining energy from day-to-day life.

Our particular resolution to infertility was adoption—an event recalled from the heart. I can remember no happier time than when we adopted our daughter, our first child. Although I have never been a religious person, a friend recently told me that I described her as "a gift from heaven." That sense of complete love and exhilaration, of overflowing joy is what, I believe, the literature has come to call *bonding*. To me it felt like a spiritual transformation. I am well aware, though, that the counterweight to our happiness was probably sadness beyond any that I can even imagine for our daughter's biological mother.

Shortly after adoption I ovulated. Whether my job in being a mother had some impact on my hypothalamus or whether it was some fluke of nature does not matter. What is important in the history of our family is that one son, then another, was born. During all those years of waiting, fantasies about what it would be like to have children had had ample time and a fertile imagination in which to grow. Interestingly, my imaginary children never grew to be more than two or, at most, three years old. They were very attractive, cheerful, well dressed, well behaved. They never cried, fought with one another, had tantrums, or had fevers of 105 at 3:20 in the morning. These longed-for fantasy children were not, in fact, real children at all, but rather loving and complimentary extensions of my husband and me.

Our real children—all three—though similar in cosmetic ways, have turned into people with unalterable traits that "just are." One is outgoing, one is shy, and the other cautious. Two are excellent students; another dislikes school. One is almost compulsively neat, the others slovenly. One is a superb athlete, another average, and the other can barely catch a ball. Two have gourmet palates; another eats strictly burgers and fries. One loves basketball, another Shakespeare, and the third loves tennis. Learning to live with these traits that "just are" is, in my experience, at the heart of parenthood. Sometimes it has been delightful, sometimes it has been maddening, sometimes it has caused nights without sleep. But the essence of parenting has been raising people different from me and learning to live with the inability to control or alter the way they "just are."

Having been a parent for nearly sixteen years, I now see how little I understood about it when this all began. Yes, the wish to leave one's mark on the world is very powerful. But it is also easy to forget that as parents, our darkest sides get recreated right along with our best, or that an adopted child comes from a place we probably will never know. Even when our children are biologically ours, they are still strangers when they arrive.

In the end, it doesn't matter so much how the children got there. It doesn't really matter whether you take them for swimming lessons or take them to the playground, whether you let them watch cartoons or restrict them to Mister Rogers. What does matter is your ability to love and accept them, whatever they look like, however they are.

○

## ENDURING LOSSES
### *Stacy M. Ellender*

I have a three-year-old daughter. At least we think that she is three; her birth date is unrecorded. In a safe in my basement, I have a document that says that she was "forsaken on the street" in Hunan Province, China. Once found, she was brought to an orphanage, and it was from there, nearly a year later, that she was adopted by my husband and me. Because she was malnourished, attempts to determine her bone age were inconclusive, and professional estimates vary by up to eight months. All we had was the date provided by her Chinese caregivers, her official date of birth. But we did not trust it.

When the day arrived that was supposed to be her first birthday, she weighed eleven pounds, she was still learning to suck from a bottle, and she couldn't push herself up off her bed because her arms were too weak. But she had a smile that was luminous and a way of looking right at you that was startling. Her first birthday came and went without our noting it, as we decided we would figure out how to deal with it later.

I laugh at that now, mostly because that attitude, for all that is good about it and for all that is bad about it, was a coping strategy I developed while I was an infertility patient. And I was a very good patient. I learned how to go through daily invasive procedures and follow complex, unpleasant instructions, all while keeping my eye not on the rigors of each cycle but on the hoped-for outcome. I stopped living in a daily world and started counting time by monthly cycles, then treatment cycles, then trimesters. My life as an infertility patient was focused on the attainment of a prize whose winning I could not control, a prize that was not granted on the basis of my proficiency, training, endurance, or skill, although I needed all of those. I have never figured out what most guarantees having a child through high-tech reproductive treatments, although I have read many books on the subject and even spent three years working in a teaching hospital's reproductive science center. What I know is that these clinics have a pervasive culture that is unique to them, and that patients can be shaped by these cultures as much as the treatments and their outcomes.

I became an infertility patient at the age of thirty-two, when it was my partner who had the diagnosis of infertility, not me. When that was later resolved, I went on, over seven years, to have more failed treatment cycles than I can count and, ultimately, four GIFT miscarriages. Twice we stopped treatment for significant periods of time, to reflect and to reprioritize. We became foster parents; we thought about adoption. But we stayed invested in treatment, and, in the end, came back to it twice.

The miscarriages were indescribably painful. Each pregnancy lasted longer, each was worse than the last, each one diminished me more. I felt like Alice; I grew smaller every cycle. Since no one could tell us what was wrong, we kept hoping that the next time treatment would work. But each cycle brought more complications, more difficult decisions. To others, our course of treatment began to seem confusing, chaotic, and, worst of all, bedeviled.

Once I was asked at a dinner party, "Why do you keep doing this to yourself?" I understood the point but found the choice of words stunningly insensitive. Of course I was making choices that were hard to explain, even if I had wanted to, to someone who had not stood in my place. And I resented the hint of condemnation. But on the other hand, it was becoming increasingly obvious that I should be thinking about when it would be time to stop treatment should our efforts continue to be fruitless. This is, I think, one of the most difficult aspects of infertility care; to expend one's energies developing a game plan for terminating treatment (prior to "aging out" of the program), one must first admit that there is a strong possibility that a birth may not occur. To do that, one must sustain a dichotomy of perspective that is in nearly total conflict: one perspective that says, "do everything you can to have a baby," and one that says, "protect yourself; make a limited investment; the procedures still fail three-fourths of the time." Going nearly every day to receive treatment, it is easy to soak up the hopeful tenor of the clinic. You are like the quarterback in a high-stakes football game; everyone is working toward getting the ball in your hands so you can score. All their efforts are aimed at you, at *you* completing the play. Are you really going to be able to say, "I think we all need to think about the fact that I may not be able to do this"? I don't think you would stay on the team long with such a negative attitude. So you check your doubts at the door, getting increasingly invested with each attempt.

But outside the clinic, particularly in the company of other women, the larger picture *is* talked about, and everybody has an opinion (informed or otherwise). In time, there is an aching dissonance between what we fearfully regard as our realistic chances of having a baby and the positive attitude with which the clinic seems most comfortable. And this dissonance takes a toll on our already depleted energy, as well as our sense of competence in dealing with the world. It is hard to stay levelheaded in a room that is built off kilter. And more than that, it is hard to stay tethered to the outer world if that world has no grasp of the complexity of the pressures bearing down on you.

And so it was that in my third year of treatment, I began distancing myself from those who could not understand our choices or our pain, and I began to live in the world differently. I became more tentative, more guarded. While never gregarious, I had been friendly and had easily connected with people. Now I felt bruised and vulnerable. Despair hung on me, and I could feel the aversion that others had to it and, eventually, to me. In time, I packed the fetal ultrasound pictures with the books on morning sickness and amniocentesis into the attic. I learned how to protect myself. I stopped going to movies unless I was certain that childbirth was not part of the story; I limited my time at family-friendly places; and I separated myself from other women for whom childbearing was easy or, worse yet, had been achieved after only a brief period of infertility treatment. I told myself that this period of estrangement from others would pass, that the sharpness of my grief would ease. While I never expected to get over it, I did expect to get on with my life despite it. I expected forgetting to take over. But that is not what happened.

Instead, remarkably, I have found that the reality of my infertility is still a significant piece of my life. I moved heaven and earth to have a child, and I did not succeed. I have come to the conclusion that I am not going to get over, past, or around that unassailable fact. It is one of the great failures of my life, even if it is one for which I cannot be blamed. Infertility is as much a part of me as the state of my health, the level of my education, and my marital status. Given the power of that experience, its incredible highs and lows, its ability to change, if not create lives, how could it be otherwise?

In addition, like many women, I have enduring issues about my reproductive system as I age and pass out of my "childbearing years." I find it difficult to imagine that menopause will affect me the same way it affects women who have been able to have children. The "change" will happen for me differently because it will mark the end of—what? The period of promise that remained unfilled?

Because I terminated treatment without having a birth, my infertility will never be cured or resolved. I will never conquer it or manage it. It will always be there, as a static if not defining truth. It is not, perhaps, the major truth about me, but it is a piece that is so significant that no one will be able to get close to me who does not know this part of my story and does not, in some measure, empathize with its attendant pain.

When I say that infertility still has an active place in my life, I mean this: coming to understand that my body is unable to produce a child has had a deep psychological effect on me that is largely negative, and it is an enduring challenge to develop a counter, and more healthy, self-image. It is difficult to love a body that functions incorrectly when the longing is so great, that has a defect the causes and the scope of which are unknown.

In addition, I am still struggling with the fact that treatment itself, not just the outcome, profoundly affected me. While I am glad that I had the opportunity to pursue IVF and GIFT, I was unaware of the toll that such treatments would take in all areas of my life, and I underestimated how passive I would become in order to survive them. For a host of reasons, my treatment and its outcomes left me scarred, weary, and fundamentally altered. Perhaps I now know too much about the limits of technology and personal effort. I no longer believe in the power of individual will and goodness to make positive things happen. Will I ever be truly romantic again? And would I want to be? I count myself lucky that my companion in this adventure struggled with me and participated in all the painful choices, so that, in the end, our relationship was not counted among all the other losses.

Today, four years after my last miscarriage, I still recognize my infertility. I feel it in my discomfort with other women's pregnancies (I always anticipate the worst) and in the way I deal with health providers. I know it's there in the funny way I now live in my body, more like a somewhat satisfied renter than a long-term owner. And I know it is in my vigilant, wary parenting, the overwhelming love I feel for my daughter and my deep-seated fear that she is simply too beautiful to be true.

Someday, my daughter will learn that she was "forsaken on the street," abandoned under unknown circumstances, and waves of pain may send her reeling. But I like to think that I will steady her, that we will share our stories of loss and redefinition. I can hold her hand in mine and show her how to face pain with honesty, integrity, and a deep wonder at its unexpected potential to shape our lives. My little girl has no birth date. She lacks one of the essential pieces of information needed in life. And I, a barren woman, have a beautiful daughter. It just might be a match.

# ABOUT THE AUTHOR

*Ellen Sarasohn Glazer* is the author of *The Long-Awaited Stork: A Guide to Parenting After Infertility* (1990, rev. ed. 1998) and has written three books with Susan Cooper: *Choosing Assisted Reproduction: Social, Emotional, and Ethical Considerations* (1998), *Beyond Infertility: New Paths to Parenthood* (1994), and *Without Child: Experiencing and Resolving Infertility* (1988), the forerunner to this book. Glazer has also contributed chapters on infertility and adoption to numerous other books. She is in private practice as a clinical social worker in Newton, Massachusetts, and is on the staff of Act of Love Adoptions, a program of the Massachusetts Society for the Prevention of Cruelty to Children. She is also program counselor at the Boston Regional Center for Reproductive Medicine. She lives in Newton, Massachusetts, with her two daughters, Elizabeth and Mollie.